Celebrating Entrepreneurs

HOW MIT NURTURED PIONEERING ENTREPRENEURS WHO BUILT GREAT COMPANIES

JUSTIN KNIGHT

Celebrating Entrepreneurship on Demo Day, September 2016, in MIT Kresge Auditorium.

ALL AUTHOR PROCEEDS WILL BE DONATED DIRECTLY TO MIT ENDOWMENT FUNDS THAT SUPPORT THE INSTITUTE-WIDE MIT ENTREPRENEURSHIP PROGRAM.

Anyone who wishes to supplement these donations should visit www.CelebratingEntrepreneurs.com to learn how. Thank you.

EDWARD B. ROBERTS
Massachusetts Institute of Technology, USA

Celebrating Entrepreneurs

HOW MIT NURTURED PIONEERING ENTREPRENEURS WHO BUILT GREAT COMPANIES

World Scientific

NEW JERSEY • LONDON • SINGAPORE • BEIJING • SHANGHAI • HONG KONG • TAIPEI • CHENNAI • TOKYO

Published by

World Scientific Publishing Co. Pte. Ltd.
5 Toh Tuck Link, Singapore 596224
USA office: 27 Warren Street, Suite 401-402, Hackensack, NJ 07601
UK office: 57 Shelton Street, Covent Garden, London WC2H 9HE

Library of Congress Control Number: 2022040100

British Library Cataloguing-in-Publication Data
A catalogue record for this book is available from the British Library.

CELEBRATING ENTREPRENEURS
How MIT Nurtured Pioneering Entrepreneurs Who Built Great Companies

ISBN 978-981-126-650-8 (hardcover)

For any available supplementary material, please visit
https://www.worldscientific.com/worldscibooks/10.1142/13147#t=suppl

Desk Editors: Aanand Jayaraman/Sandhya Venkatesh

Typeset by Diacritech Technologies Pvt. Ltd.
Chennai - 600106, India

DEDICATION

Nancy Roberts

IN SEPTEMBER 1953, my first month as a freshman at MIT, I met Nancy Rosenthal. I was not yet 18 and she was not yet 16. We were married in June 1959 and have lived a wonderful life, together with our three children: Valerie, Mitch, and Andrea; their three spouses: Mark, Jill, and Marc; and our nine grandchildren: Noah, Max, Alex, Sabrina, Solomon, Ethan, Alice, Daniel, and Ruby.

Nancy has been the love of my life, my strongest supporter, and my dearest friend. She has lived through all episodes during the more than half-century described in this book, plus much more. Nancy has been a participant in so many of the events mentioned in this book, and has known so many of the people here. We even co-founded a company that pioneered new computer-based approaches to K-12 education.

Not surprisingly, Nancy has tolerated the reading of many drafts and the hearing of my retelling to her of stories I was describing in this volume. She criticized in a caring manner my excesses, and suggested considerations that I might otherwise have missed. Most of all, she has accepted without much complaint the enormous amount of time I have taken away from her to sit at the computer banging away at this volume. ☺

Thank you, Nancy, for our life together.

Nancy, I dedicate this book to you, with deepest love and devotion.

—ED

CONTENTS

INTRODUCTION

As of 2015, the more than 30,000 companies founded by MIT alumni were generating about $2 trillion in global revenues—the equivalent of the GDP of the 10th largest economy in the world.[1] We know that at its founding in 1861, MIT encouraged faculty to supplement their low academic salaries by doing some outside consulting and even starting small firms. But how did this amazing transformation take place—from MIT itself being a startup, to today's continuing flow of so many new entrepreneurial firms being created and growing to have such dramatic impact? And who are the men and women who have emerged from MIT to found and build great companies, indeed pioneering many new industries by their efforts? This book answers both questions in two Parts that relate the case study of entrepreneurship at and from the Massachusetts Institute of Technology.

Part One, Transforming MIT into an Entrepreneurial Juggernaut, presents all those individuals and groups who have dramatically changed MIT by building MIT entrepreneurship education, research, and nurturing. We especially recognize those who have spread our MIT heritage of entrepreneurship throughout the United States and the rest of the world. Part One is a history, documenting all that has gone into the past half-century of turning MIT into an incubator and accelerator of now well over 30,000 living companies formed by alumni of MIT. But Part One also aims at dispelling the myth that this kind of outcome is some form of miracle that has "happened" to MIT and to one or two other unique institutions. Part One shows that the strengths of culture and tradition at MIT are vital backdrops to generating entrepreneurial outcomes. However, culture and tradition alone are not sufficient. They have been coupled with more than 50 years of cumulative efforts and activities to build up to the enormous impact MIT-related people are now having on the world through the process of founding and growing new firms.

Part One is a guidebook! It communicates possible pathways to those universities, communities, and nations that value what entrepreneurial growth and development might achieve in transforming their own economies and societies. The details of starting and building so many parts of the "MIT entrepreneurial ecosystem" may well aid others to consider and adapt what we have done at MIT to their own situations. The roles played by the MIT leadership might encourage other university presidents and deans, and institutional as well as political leaders, to consider comparable shifts toward the attitudes and policies that have contributed so much to MIT. The many steps taken in institution-building within MIT may provide examples for adaptation to other places. Hopefully, the lessons from MIT's experiences will help those groups to attain for themselves, in shorter time periods than MIT needed, their own goals for entrepreneurial achievements.

Part One is also a personal memoir. I was there to begin MIT's formal pursuits to better understand the whys and whats of MIT entrepreneurial spinoffs. And I have been fortunate over more than the past half-century to participate in nearly every organizational development at MIT that has accelerated entrepreneurship growth and prosperity from our community and beyond. So, I have written much of this book in first person form, relating details and personal stories that I hope will help illustrate the brilliance, drive, and imagination of MIT institution-building entrepreneurs. This does mean that my personal biases and views about various events and the contributions of others inevitably creep into my narrative. Fortunately, the large number of interviews and the transcripts of the many presentations at our recent celebration provide details and personal stories from many others as well, with their own experiences and perspectives.

Chapters 1 through 5 present a cluster of histories. The first chapter lays out the bases of MIT's increasing entrepreneurial outcomes, from its founding in 1861 through about 1960. Chapters 2 through 5 relate the dramatic, though long in evolution, transformation of MIT entrepreneurship from the first New Enterprises classes in 1961 until today. More specifically, Chapter 2 presents in depth the sluggish road from 1961 through the 1990 founding of the MIT Entrepreneurship Center.

Chapters 3 through 5 (along with the Appendix) go beyond the beginning of MIT's formal internal programs for entrepreneurs up to 2019. They are filled with identifications of and testimonials from the many key contributors of alumni, faculty, and staff who initiated and developed all of the present organizations that are frequently together called the "MIT entrepreneurial ecosystem". All of the organizational entities presented here have targeted and resulted in the continuing and dramatic increases of participation and impact of MIT student, alumni, faculty and staff entrepreneurs, and the companies they have created. The founders and leaders of all of these internal organizations are the principal sources of testimonials as to the goals they sought, the challenges they faced, and the outcomes they produced. As often as possible, they speak in their own voices as to their experiences.

Chapters 6 and 7 are global in focus. They present the huge array of efforts and programs, undertaken by MIT people but aimed at the rest of the United States and the world, seeking to bring to them the benefits that flow from MIT-style innovation-driven entrepreneurship. Chapter 6 focuses on the impact of the company entrepreneurs as a group, and the efforts to broaden that entrepreneurial base to the millions outside of MIT. It also provides a synopsis of many of the trends we have found from our extensive research projects over the years about MIT entrepreneurs and their firms. Chapter 7 reaches from MIT and the United States to the rest of the world, with all the efforts made to bring entrepreneurial benefits to other countries. Those who have moved these outreaches forward tell their own stories. In retrospect, that so many people and parts of the MIT system have gone outside to extend their reach and influence is remarkable, but consistent with MIT's overall global role and aspirations for impact.

Part Two, Entrepreneurs who Built Innovative Companies that Pioneered New Industries, provides in-depth insights to the MIT alumni and faculty entrepreneurs who have founded and built significant companies that pioneered wholly new industries. Indeed, they represent the tens of thousands of MIT-related men and women who, since MIT's founding, have created enterprises that have served and advanced society. Part Two makes permanent for all its readers the stories told, and the vital entrepreneurial lessons hopefully learned.

Part Two is a very different form of history from that told in Part One—the personal stories from MIT faculty and alumni entrepreneurs who pioneered wholly new industries by forming and building great innovating companies. It begins with identifying the few firms who have thrived over the entire period of the past half-century. As part of my personal tribute to MIT entrepreneurs, I indicate in bold font all of them and their companies when they are first identified in Part Two. My apologies to any I have missed.

Part Two addresses four selected industries, each quite different from the others, in which the minds and hands of MIT people were primarily responsible for industrial growth. Except for constraints of time and space, several other industries might readily have been chosen for comparable examination. Chapters 8 through 11, respectively, cover: Life Sciences and Biotechnology, the Internet, from CAD-CAM to Robotics, and the world of "Modern Finance". The life sci-ences startups clearly come directly from MIT and other university laboratories into further market development and commercialization. The primary actors are initially faculty and their advanced students, joined by others in bringing forward the fruits of the underlying research. The three other industries certainly reflect academic advances, by faculty and their graduate students, but more clearly and more frequently they depend upon advances made in industry by well-educated and trained technologists and their managerial partners.

The stories of the efforts and consequences of these entrepreneurs are not replicated elsewhere. The entrepreneurs themselves relate their personal beginnings, their motivations, the partnerships with other co-founders that were instrumental to their companies, and the challenges they faced and overcame. They also relate their connections to MIT, before, during, and since the successful growth of their companies. Part Two is likely to be of most interest, and usefulness, to current, past, and would-be entrepreneurs.

These four chapters end with my attempts to identify the key lessons that should be learned by current and prospective entrepreneurs. Those lessons stem primarily from the experiences described by those MIT entrepreneurs whom we studied throughout the four industries they pioneered. I add to those experientially-based observations my findings from close to 60 years of my and my colleagues' entrepreneurial research, combined with my own perspectives from a similar period of personal serial entrepreneurship, extensive board service with young and growing firms, and decades of investing in perhaps 150 ground-zero startups. Of course, such synopsized lessons learned might themselves be the subject for a separate book, but not right now ☺.

The final chapter of the book, Chapter 12, relates how all that is described in Parts One and Two is continuing to move forward, growing and always changing. It glimpses at the shifts over the past 50+ years in how MIT has provided encouragement, education, nurturing, and support for its entrepreneurial offspring. It shows the differences in prior knowledge, preparation, and even staffing and strategy between MIT-based companies that were started many years ago versus those of more recent vintage. We also praise those young entrepreneurs who are continuing in the tradition of their MIT predecessors and creating companies all over the world. They reflect a much wider diversity of origins and directions for their entrepreneurial talents and targets. Again, as much as possible, the entrepreneurs speak for themselves about their beginnings and movements forward.

And Chapter 12 describes the creation of new programs at MIT to help nurture entrepreneurial solutions of global issues. Finally, it communicates our views of how MIT's experiences can be transferred in various ways to other institutions, regions, and countries.

A FINAL WORD

If you are an educator or economic developer, MIT's own lessons, documented thoroughly in Part One, may well be applicable to you, in part or whole, modified to better fit your own specific situation. We will be delighted if our experiences help you in any way.

If you are an entrepreneur, please learn from the trials and tribulations of those who have eventually succeeded. Each person's story in Part Two is different, but many elements are in common. And the lessons synopsized at the end of those chapters should provide at least some stimuli for rethinking your own entrepreneurial practices.

And do appreciate what we have been doing for the current and future generations who want to follow your paths. May you, and hopefully especially those interested in becoming entrepreneurs, gain a shared sense of satisfaction, and insights, from the adventures pursued so successfully by those whom we honor and whose stories we tell in Chapters 8 through 12.

I have so enjoyed my years at MIT since becoming a freshman in 1953. Being able to stay here throughout my graduate school years, and then since 1961 as an MIT faculty member, has provided me with an exciting and fulfilling life. In particular, my engagement in starting and leading the buildup of MIT entrepreneurship has been most demanding and totally rewarding.

Thanks to all who have enabled me to devote such a major portion of my past 66 years to this pursuit, and who have been my colleagues and partners in achievement.

REFERENCES AND NOTES

1. Edward B. Roberts, Fiona Murray, & J. Daniel Kim, Entrepreneurship & Innovation at MIT: Continuing Growth and Impact, MIT, December 2015.

(overleaf) top left
Simon Johnson, teaching a class in 2013.

top right
Graduating E&I students in front of the Sloan Building. Faculty members in first row are (from left to right) Simon Johnson, Ken Morse, Alex d'Arbeloff, Ed Roberts, and Russ Olive.

bottom right
The Entrepreneur Walk of Fame in Kendall Square.

bottom left
Michael Cusumano, with panel of our PhD alums.

PART ONE

Transforming MIT into an Entrepreneurial Juggernaut

It is both easy and difficult for a participant and observer who is not a professional historian to write an in-depth history that covers nearly 60 years of an institution's and of many individuals' activities and accomplishments. The easy part is that I was there the entire time and intimately engaged in so much of what happened. In addition, I have a reasonably good memory and large numbers of old folders filled with papers. The hard part is, first, to know what I may have forgotten! The second issue is to try to be objective, especially when deciding which small number of incidents and encounters are perhaps better left omitted.

To overcome these difficulties, I drew up a long list of every MIT organization I could think of that played a key role in establishing and developing the current widespread MIT entrepreneurship activities. I remembered the key people who were active in the early creation of each organization and invited them to engage in a detailed, recorded discussion with an independent professional interviewer. Many of these same leaders participated in our 2016 event to celebrate MIT entrepreneurship, and their remarks, discussions, and responses to audience questions were recorded and transcribed. Part One presents this half-century history of the creation of the "MIT entrepreneurial ecosystem".

1

The Foundations of MIT Entrepreneurship

THE LEGACY OF MIND AND HAND

Entrepreneurship is, at its very core, the ultimate manifestation of MIT's motto **mens et manus,** mind and hand, enunciated by its founder William Barton Rogers in 1861 when he created an institution to "respect the dignity of useful work"—the Massachusetts Institute of Technology. To Rogers and his supporters then, the motto reflected a commitment to moving theory into practice, to going from ideas to their implementation—as it does still now, 160 years later. And entrepreneurship is an ultimate fulfillment of that vision of carrying a concept forward into the world of use by building an enterprise that moves that concept to those who will be its beneficiaries. Two years after MIT's birth, the Massachusetts legislature approved the traditional MIT logo that shows the scholar and the blacksmith standing over the *mens et manus* slogan. For a long time, MIT was virtually alone as a university that embraced rather than shunned linkages to the so-called "real world", including government and industry.

Soon after MIT was founded, MIT faculty and students began to move ideas not just to existing firms, but also to their own startup companies. This was true especially in areas of new technology and industrial change. As examples, early MIT pioneers contributed substantially to creating new firms related to the automotive industry, the aircraft industry, petroleum drilling and processing, electricity generation and use, as well as new materials and manufacturing tools and capabilities.

Several developments during MIT's first 100 years laid a foundation for the far more accelerated entrepreneurship of the past half-century. The underlying culture initiated by Rogers provided a common stimulus and base of support for all of these developments. In this chapter I describe the early growth of entrepreneurship by MIT faculty, which was followed—and eventually dwarfed in scale—by the building of new enterprises by alumni. I then describe how MIT's role during World War II dramatically altered its development as an educational institution. That and the resulting takeoff of postwar scientific research and technological development contributed substantially to the baseline for modern MIT-linked entrepreneurial endeavors. I complete the chapter by observing the pre-1960 shifts in the Greater Cambridge community of investors, lawyers, and supportive infrastructure, as well as the first hints at MIT of entrepreneurial perspectives and content in educational undertakings.

FACULTY ENTREPRENEURSHIP

In the early years, President Rogers's perspectives aligned well with financial needs to supplement low academic salaries. And Rogers encouraged the MIT faculty of technology leaders to undertake outside consulting activities with industry. The earliest MIT-linked entrepreneurship was frequently faculty consulting, carried out first by individuals and later by firms. For example, professors of physics Edward C. Pickering and Charles R. Cross were thus able to help Alexander Graham Bell in the 1870s in research essential to development of the telephone. Professor Samuel Prescott helped Lyman Underwood to produce canning in the 1890s, which would help prevent food spoilage. That led MIT alumnus **JOHN DORRANCE** (1892) to launch **CAMPBELL SOUP COMPANY**.[1]

This uniquely open stance in encouraging faculty members to develop close associations with industry soon began to evolve into formal business partnerships. The traditions of MIT faculty involvement with industry have long been legitimatized in the university's official "Rules and Regulations of the Faculty", developed over many years by faculty members but with encouragement and approval of the MIT administrative leadership. As in the past, today the administration still encourages external service and active consulting by faculty members of about one day per week, and more impressively—especially during MIT's early years—approves part-time efforts by faculty in forming and building their own companies, a practice still discouraged at many universities. This openness to extracurricular entrepreneurial activity on the part of its faculty was rare for a university in the late 1800s, but not out of character at MIT. My recent visit with the Chancellor of a distinguished European university elicited this response: "Heavens! How is it possible to carry on proper teaching and research if one devotes a day a week to consulting? Perhaps a day a month might be feasible!" MIT's academic output and leadership do not seem to have suffered from its more "permissive" policies on external relations of the faculty. MIT has for the past several decades carefully worked to balance the ever-present potential for economic conflicts of interest of faculty entrepreneurs with MIT's fundamental desires to move science and technology to the market, where good can come from them.

"Entrepreneurship" may mean many different things to different people, for example, being an important part of organizational change or helping to set up new educational programs or social endeavors. All of these may have a significant impact upon society. But throughout this book, "entrepreneurship" refers only to those acts of actually creating and then building new for-profit enterprises. An "entrepreneur" in this book is a person who was present at the very founding of the enterprise and accepted by any co-founder(s) as being one of them![2]

Faculty-founded consulting companies during MIT's first 100 years include **ARTHUR D. LITTLE, INC.** (**ADL**, 1909), **EDGERTON GERMESHAUSEN AND GRIER, INC.** (**EG&G**, 1947), **BOLT BERANEK & NEWMAN, INC.** (**BBN**, 1953), and many others. As these examples suggest, these new enterprises consolidated consulting activities among multiple faculty members or between faculty and their former students. They typically started as informal ties, became partnerships as they grew, then later corporations. Only later in some of these cases (EG&G, BBN, and more prominently **BOSE CORPORATION** (1964)) did they extend their domains into the realm of developing their own products for manufacture and/or sale.

Faculty entrepreneurship generally was extended to the research staff as well, who were thereby enabled to "moonlight" while being "full-time" employees of MIT labs and departments. The result over time has been that a large fraction of all MIT spinoff enterprises, including essentially all faculty-initiated companies and many staff-founded firms, were started on a part-time basis, smoothing the way for many entrepreneurs to "test the waters" of innovative technology entrepreneurship before taking the full plunge. These companies are concrete examples of direct movement of laboratory technology into markets not otherwise served by MIT, clear manifestations of *mens et manus.*

By at least the immediate post-WWII period if not sooner, MIT was rare among universities for its willingness to grant licenses to faculty and students for commercial use of the technologies they developed as part of their jobs at MIT. Few faculty founders ever resigned their MIT positions. Well-known academic entrepreneurs including **AMAR BOSE** '51 (founder of **BOSE CORPORATION**), **ROBERT LANGER** '74 (a brilliant biomaterials scientist who has co-founded more than 40 companies), **PHIL SHARP** (a Nobel Prize winner and co-founder of **BIOGEN** in 1978 and **ALNYLAM PHARMACEUTICALS** in 2002), and **ROD BROOKS** (former head of MIT CSAIL and co-founder of **iROBOT** in 1990 and other robotics firms since) all preferred to remain at MIT for years, carrying forward their research and teaching. Perhaps because the Institute had a more encouraging attitude in this area, the entrepreneurial faculty members who remained often created mutually beneficial relationships between the Institute and their businesses. These arrangements also enriched the students, in both their educations and their careers, as many faculty founders who kept their duties at MIT handed over the reins of running their companies to former students and lab colleagues.

This particular pattern is so familiar at MIT that former MIT President **PAUL GRAY** '54 initiated and for many years hosted a quarterly meeting for about 150 entrepreneurial alumni called **THE MIT TECHNOLOGY BREAKFAST**, now led by MIT Chancellor Eric Grimson '80. The event starts with an MIT faculty member discussing her/his research work that had gone on to be commercialized, followed by a former graduate student or research associate who led the early stages of creating a new company based upon the research or technology. Faculty entrepreneurs have in this manner directly facilitated the "entrepreneuring" activities of their students and research staff. Furthermore, and with far greater leverage due to the numbers involved, faculty entrepreneurs have thus become the earliest role models for their many classes of students as to what is both legitimate and desired behavior for someone coming out of the Institute.

GEORGE HATSOPOULOS '49 (founder of **THERMOELECTRON**), **JAY BARGER** '50 (co-founder of **DYNATECH**), **ALAN MICHAELS** '44 (founder of **AMICON**), and **TOM GERRITY** '63 (co-founder of **INDEX SYSTEMS**) are among the few tenured faculty who left MIT to pursue their entrepreneurial endeavors on a full-time basis, with great success achieved in all four cases. And these few individual exceptions to the "rule" of faculty staying at MIT inevitably formed strong continuing ties to MIT.

EARLY ALUMNI ENTREPRENEURSHIP AS WELL AS INDUSTRY CONNECTIONS

Alumni entrepreneurs are discussed in far greater depth in Part Two (Chapters 8 through 11), which starts by giving special tribute to those few MIT-alumni-founded companies that have indeed flourished under founder ownership and leadership and survived over the entire period of the past half-century. Those chapters then honor, in much greater depth, those MIT entrepreneurs who have significantly pioneered four selected industries: Life sciences and biotechnology; the Internet; from CAD-CAM to robotics; and modern finance.

The tradition of MIT alumni making important contributions to the world via their creation of new enterprises, especially at the earliest stages of new industries, began soon after MIT's founding. Early alumni of "Boston Tech" (what MIT was "fondly" called before its move from Boston to Cambridge in 1910) pioneered the new industries that were starting at the turn into the 20th century. Over the following half-century, **DIGITAL EQUIPMENT, HEWLETT-PACKARD, INTEL, KOCH INDUSTRIES, MCDONNELL DOUGLAS, QUALCOMM, RAYTHEON, TEXAS INSTRUMENTS**, and other MIT-alumni-founded companies created models of how to start and build great firms. Alumni-founded enterprises also became far more numerous as more alumni each year moved from MIT into key roles across all industries. All companies formed before 1960 preceded MIT having any formal institutions that provided education, stimulus, or mentoring for entrepreneurship.

Beyond individual enterprise formation and operation by faculty and alumni, MIT encouraged its ties with industry for the application of MIT-generated science and technology. This led to early creation of a unique organization. "MIT was the first university to start a formal and systematic liaison with firms. President Maclaurin first attempted this with his Technology Plan in 1918",[3] and the resulting entity is still the world's largest university-industry collaborative, renamed the MIT Industrial Liaison Program (ILP) in 1948. The ILP has about 200 of the world's leading research- and technology-based companies as its members. For many years MIT has also been number one in the nation in the extent of industrial support it receives for sponsored research (22% of its total research expenditures in 2018), symbolic of the strong two-ways ties between MIT and industry in the development and application of science and technology.

THE HERITAGE OF WORLD WAR II SCIENCE AND TECHNOLOGY

Global pursuit of research, technology, and innovation-based industrial and economic development has mushroomed in the past 75 years. But what started this explosion at MIT in particular and elsewhere?

With the onset of World War II, the U.S. government charged the Institute to apply its expertise to developing tools and technologies for the war effort. In addition to the urgent expansion and redirection of university research, the war made necessary the reorganization of research groups and the formation of new working coalitions among scientists and engineers, between these technologists and government officials, and between the universities and industry. These changes were especially noteworthy at MIT, which during the war became the home of major technological efforts.

These wartime programs extended into the postwar period, broadened both in scope and in university-industry interactions. For example, the MIT Radiation Laboratory, a source of many major developments in wartime radar, evolved into the postwar MIT Research Laboratory for Electronics. The MIT Servomechanisms Lab, which contributed many advances in automatic control systems, started the research and development projects near the end of the war that developed the Whirlwind computer, created numerically controlled milling machines, and provided the intellectual base for the initiation of the MIT Lincoln Laboratory in 1951. Lincoln Lab focused on creating a computer-based air defense system (Semi-Automatic Ground Environment system, called SAGE) to cope with the then-perceived Soviet bomber threat. From that beginning, Lincoln Lab has continued with basic and applied research and technology development in many aspects of electronics, including computing, CAD-CAM, and the Internet. In parallel, the MIT Instrumentation Lab (now the independent non-profit Draper Laboratory) grew from the wartime gun-sight work of Professor Charles Stark Draper '26, its founder and Director throughout his career at MIT, and continued its efforts on the R&D needed to create inertial guidance systems for aircraft, submarines, and missiles. It followed up with significant achievements in the race to the moon with developments of the guidance and stellar navigation systems for the Apollo program, now continuing far beyond those initial space objectives.

These MIT labs were spawned during a period in which little debate existed about a university's appropriate response to perceived national emergencies. While successfully fulfilling their defined missions, these labs also provided a base of advanced technology programs and experts who would contribute to major developments in the post-World War II years. The atomic bomb, inertial guided missiles and submarines, the postwar computer-based defense of North America, and the race to the moon are phenomena that became prominent in the post–World War II years. These initiatives engaged the entire nation—government, business, and society—and specifically MIT, including significant entrepreneurial efforts to meet new needs and opportunities. For MIT, by the end of World War II and its immediate aftermath, the *mens et manus* culture now covered a much-expanded domain of laboratories and people, far broader than the Boston startup institution that was MIT in 1861.

BUILDING UNIVERSITY SCIENCE AND TECHNOLOGY

With the exception of the wartime science-technology buildup at MIT and other universities, government support of university research had been essentially nonexistent. And research activities in the university world were quite small. For example, research expenditures at MIT (essentially all government sponsored) reached their wartime peak in 1945 of about $500 million (as measured in 2015 constant dollars). That dropped by 1948 to a bottom of about $100 million.[4] In November 1944, President Franklin Roosevelt sent a detailed letter to Dr. **VANNEVAR BUSH** '16 (former MIT Vice President and Dean of Engineering and co-founder of what became **RAYTHEON CORPORATION**), Director of the U.S. Office of Scientific Research and Development throughout World War II, requesting a report on how the nation should continue the growth of its science and technology initiatives that played such a key role in the war effort. Dr. Bush's report, "Science: The Endless Frontier",[5] submitted to the following President (Harry Truman) on July 25, 1945, provided an in-depth analysis of the impact and potential benefits arising from scientific research in many fields, and called for dramatically expanded federal programs and funding. The Bush report specifically proposed the creation of a single organization to lead this effort forward, which became the National Science Foundation (NSF), aimed at providing government research funding in a wide array of fields. The NSF had been preceded by the creation of the more narrowly focused National Institutes of Health (NIH) in 1870. But the NSF was a game changer in government sponsorship of basic research, and is still critical to the nation's well-being.

MIT research and development expenditures have grown impressively since 1951, dramatically increasing from time to time to fund major programs necessitated by such things as Sputnik, Project Mac, and the founding of such medical institutes as the Whitehead and the Broad. In 2018, MIT-sponsored research reached close to $1.8 billion (including $1 billion for the government-funded Lincoln Laboratory), about half of MIT's total operating expenditures.[6] The implications of these numbers are multifold: (1) Dramatic changes in the number of related faculty carrying out that research, along with dedicated research staff and funded graduate students; (2) the emergence and development of wholly new fields of study; (3) the accumulation of vast amounts of new knowledge and breakthrough discoveries; and (4) massive transfers to the world of know-how and technology. These impacts certainly have been primary contributors to the foundation of MIT entrepreneurship. The tributes to MIT entrepreneurs in Part Two clearly identify how basic scientific research provided underpinnings for numerous entrepreneurial breakouts in the four industries treated.

CHANGING THE NEIGHBORING INFRASTRUCTURE

The wartime leadership of MIT's distinguished President **KARL TAYLOR COMPTON**, who engaged with the federal government in coordinating and directing national R&D, brought MIT into an intimate relationship with the war effort. In the immediate postwar years, Compton restarted his earlier efforts toward improving the commercial use of university science and technology, as well as of the military developments from the war, leading the efforts to create the first institutionalized venture capital fund, **AMERICAN RESEARCH AND DEVELOPMENT (ARD)**. (This is discussed extensively in Chapter 11, The World of "Modern Finance".)

Several scions of old Boston Brahmin families became personally involved in venture investments. For example, in 1946, William Coolidge helped arrange the financing for **TRACERLAB**, MIT's first nuclear-oriented spinoff company. Coolidge also invested in **NATIONAL RESEARCH CORPORATION (NRC)**, a company founded by MIT alumnus **RICHARD MORSE** '33 to exploit advances in low-temperature physics. (This chapter's final section has more on Morse and his role as the first teacher of entrepreneurship at MIT.)

Boston entrepreneurs also eventually benefited from these private investors as well as from more understanding bankers, each group setting examples to be emulated later in other parts of the country. In the 1950s, the First National Bank of Boston (later becoming BankBoston and now part of Bank of America) had begun to lend money to early-stage firms based on receivables from government R&D contracts, a move seen at the time as extremely risky even though the loans seemed to be entirely secured. Arthur Snyder, then Vice President of commercial lending of the New England Merchants Bank (which became Bank of New England and later part of Citizens Bank), regularly took out full-page ads in *The Boston Globe* that showed him with a model aircraft or missile in his hands, calling upon high-technology entrepreneurs to see him about their financial needs. Snyder even set up a venture capital unit at the bank (one of the first Small Business Investment Corporations (SBICs) in the United States) to make small equity investments in high-tech companies to which he had loaned money. The growing ties between Boston's worlds of academia and finance helped create bridges to the large Eastern family fortunes—the Rockefellers, Whitneys, and Mellons, among others—who also invested in early Boston startups.

Other aspects of the surrounding infrastructure were slow in developing. By and large, Boston lawyers were uninformed about high-tech deals, and general law firms had no specialists in intellectual property (IP). Only two Boston law firms focused on IP issues: Fish & Richardson and Wolf Greenfield, and both dealt primarily with life sciences and materials companies. As late as the early 1980s, few Boston lawyers knew how to set up the complex structure of a venture capital firm. One well-known lawyer in the early Boston high-tech community was Richard Testa, senior partner of Testa, Hurwitz & Thibeault, the firm that became the legal underpinning for numerous startups in which ARD and others invested. After Dick Testa's early death in 2002, his former associates renamed the conference room at the MIT Entrepreneurship Center in his honor.

As the decades passed, MIT's physical surroundings slowly began to change. Long before the 1950s expansion of the Route 128 circumferential highway around Boston facilitated the movement of growing technology-based firms into the suburbs, Memorial Drive in Cambridge (along which MIT rests!!) used to be called "Multi-Million Dollar Research Row". This nickname reflected the uniqueness of having a few early technology firms located next to MIT, including National Research Corporation, Arthur D. Little, Inc., and Electronics Corporation of America (ECA). In fact, the illuminated dome of MIT Building 10 and the flashing rooftop sign of ECA were prominent parts of the Cambridge riverside skyline in the postwar 1940s. But further change finally took place during the first two decades of the 21st century: NRC's former headquarters building (70 Memorial Drive) now houses the primary classrooms of the MIT Sloan School of Management. ADL's headquarters at 30 Memorial Drive are now also part of MIT Sloan. ECA's former site at One Memorial Drive is now Microsoft's regional technology development center, and also includes some innovative high-tech as well as venture capital firms. Only in the late 1960s did startups begin to be located in the area of old and empty factories and warehouses behind MIT. And gradual improvement of those buildings, and of the area in general, attracted increasing numbers of companies coming out of MIT (and elsewhere) to locate around Kendall Square, MIT's backyard. Not until 2001 did the **CAMBRIDGE INNOVATION CENTER (CIC)** begin to attract new firms into small offices at One Broadway, across the street from MIT. (Chapter 5 includes more discussion of CIC's role and impact.)

THREE SMALL BITES OF MIT ENTREPRENEURSHIP EDUCATION

As MIT approached 1960, its founding culture of *mens et manus* was nearing the 100-year mark and was still robust. The scientific and technology community, as well as its knowledge base, were growing apace in and out of MIT. Faculty and many more alumni technology-based startup companies were expanding in numbers as well as in public notice. Supportive external resources such as money, legal advisors, and even accessible real estate were accruing. Yet little was happening inside of MIT with regard to developing or spreading insights about forming and growing new enterprises, except perhaps by word of mouth! Neither formal education nor organized mentoring yet existed within MIT.

As a partial exception, Professor Rupert Maclaurin, son of the eighth President of MIT, Richard Maclaurin, began in the late 1940s to teach The Economics of Invention and Innovation. He built upon the theories of his mentor, economist Joseph Schumpeter, as well as his own studies of the radio industry. Valuing the local presence of young innovative firms, Maclaurin arranged for occasional visits to his class by entrepreneurs such as Edwin Land, the founder of Polaroid Corporation (1937), and **WILLIAM GARTH** '36, the founder of several firms including **COMPUGRAPHIC** (1960). Entrepreneurship was thus correctly pictured as one of the possible outcomes of invention. But the subject did not address the challenges encountered in starting and/or building a new company. Maclaurin died in 1959 and no one continued to teach his subject.

In 1963, MIT alumnus Robert Rines '42—who combined several careers, primarily patent law and extensive inventing—started a new subject in the MIT Department of Electrical Engineering, Patents, Copyrights, and the Laws of Intellectual Property, focusing upon his own experiences as an inventor and lawyer. He was indeed very prolific in both areas, but his subject at that time did not attract very many students. According to some who took his classes, Rines was very suspicious that large companies were likely to attempt to steal ideas from "innocent engineers", and sometimes extended those views to apply to students from the then MIT School of Industrial Management. His subject continued under his teaching until he retired and has been carried on by others since that time, traditionally taught in the EECS Department to small numbers of students.

In 1961, just before Rines got his start, Richard Morse began teaching MIT's first subject that actually focused on entrepreneurship: New Enterprises. Morse, too, had been a successful scientist and inventor, but in 1940 he also became an entrepreneur, creating National Research Corporation to try to translate his

!5.921 New Enterprises (A)
Prereq.: 15.412, 15.501
Year: G (1) 2-0-7

Organization and management of technically based companies. Financing of new enterprises through private, corporate and public capital sources. The role of government and the impact of Federal R and D on corporate growth. Trends in science and technology in terms of business opportunities. Preparation of cases by study of the operations of local companies and detailed development of plans for launching of new business ventures.

(Enrollment limited to 15 students: admission by permission of Instructor.) R.S. Morse

MIT catalog description of New Enterprises

and others' inventions into commercial successes. NRC generated several startup firms, but is best known for its development of frozen orange juice concentrate and its resulting founding of **MINUTE MAID CORPORATION**. Morse became Assistant Secretary of the Army for R&D in 1959, more or less concurrent with the 1960 sale of Minute Maid to Coca-Cola. Upon returning to Cambridge, he offered his services to the MIT School of Industrial Management to develop and teach a course focused on starting new companies. Enrollment in those earliest years seldom was more than 20 students, but the subject persisted over time. It remained as MIT's only class in entrepreneurship for many years, and still exists today, but now as part of a vast array of related subject offerings, with two sections of it offered in both semesters with high enrollment. As indicated in Part III, many MIT entrepreneurs who graduated after 1961 took the New Enterprises subject and remembered key lessons and influences coming from Dick Morse and successor teachers of the subject.

Richard Morse

Thus, by the early 1960s, a broad variety of foundation stones had been put into place for growing entrepreneurship at MIT.

REFERENCES AND NOTES

1. Joost Bonsen, MIT SM thesis, "The Innovative Institute", June 2006, p. 19, contains these examples.
2. On occasion, I do hedge and identify those faculty members who created and initially built the key organizations that constitute the "MIT entrepreneurial ecosystem" as, appropriately, "academic entrepreneurs"!
3. Bonsen, *op. cit.*
4. MIT Office of the Provost, http://web.mit.edu/fnl/volume/292/numbers2.html (accessed on September 23, 2019).
5. National Science Foundation, https://www.nsf.gov/od/lpa/nsf50/vbush1945.htm (accessed on September 23, 2019).
6. MIT Facts, 2019.

2

From "Merely" Culture and Tradition to an Entrepreneurship Center

More than 50 years ago, in the early 1960s, major changes relating to entrepreneurship began within MIT. In addition to MIT-related individuals and teams pursuing entrepreneurial efforts to create new firms, individuals and groups initiated institutional activities at MIT to generate and support entrepreneurship education, research, nurturing, and stimulus. This led to an accompanying dramatic increase in the rate of formation of new enterprises by MIT faculty, staff, students, and alumni.

Chapters 2 through 5 focus on this past half-century of formal development within MIT of its overall entrepreneurship program—of faculty and staff, curricula, numerous organizations with various special support activities, and student clubs. These elements have strongly contributed to the dramatic increases in MIT-related entrepreneurship, and have over time led to closer ties between the internal programs and actual new company formation.

AN UNEXPECTED GIFT DROPS FROM THE SKIES!

In February 1961, President John F. Kennedy appointed James Webb as the second Administrator of the National Aeronautics and Space Administration (NASA).

In May 1961, in a somewhat delayed response to the Soviet "Sputnik Challenge", President Kennedy announced the nation's goal of landing a man on the moon and returning him to Earth within the decade. Soon after the Kennedy speech (or perhaps even before?), Webb contacted MIT President Julius Stratton '23 and told him that NASA wanted to develop a relationship with MIT in the area of organization and management of the space program. President Stratton asked Howard Johnson, then Dean of the MIT School of Industrial Management (and later MIT President), to go to Washington D.C. to confer with Webb on this unexpected and rather unusual request. The result of the Johnson-Webb meeting was that four MIT persons were appointed as a team of Consultants to the Administrator to determine in a summer study if NASA had "researchable management problems" that might be tackled by MIT faculty. (MIT was clearly seeking to carry out research, not to do management consulting!) The team was: John Wynne '56 (Associate Dean of the School of Industrial Management and former MIT Sloan Fellow from the Air Force); MIT Professor Donald Marquis (distinguished psychologist and former department head at University of Michigan and Yale); Bernard Muller-Thym (ex-McKinsey strategy consultant and Senior Lecturer to the MIT Sloan Fellows); and me (then a 25-year-old half-time instructor in Industrial Dynamics computer modelling and PhD student in Economics, working on my dissertation, *The Dynamics of Research & Development*). At that time, despite age and status, I was the only person at MIT who was studying issues related to managing large-scale government-industry research and development.

It was a very exciting summer. In our first meeting in June, Webb pronounced our role: "I charge you with finding new ways to link government, industry, and universities together to meet the great challenges of our society! The space program is merely the first." We sat in front of him, watching as he pounded his desk for emphasis, his body framed by the large picture window, behind which we could see the White House lawn and the White House itself. The four of us spent the summer in meetings with Mr. Webb and senior NASA officials, and in interviews with Werner von Braun and his team at Huntsville and with similar NASA leaders at Cape Canaveral and other NASA field centers.

At summer's end we submitted a proposal to Mr. Webb to create the first research center in the MIT School of Industrial Management. And Dean Howard Johnson informed me, quite unexpectedly, that I was being promoted to Assistant Professor, despite being one year away from completing my PhD in Economics. Our proposal was funded in February 1962, designating us as "NASA Organization Research Center #1", reporting directly to Webb's office. Professor Marquis became Director of the Center, later joined by me as Associate Director.

This book does not focus on the growth, development, research output, and impact of the Center's work on managing R&D and technological innovation over the next half-century. Yet our expanding faculty was the first and for many years only group at a leading business school with such a concentration. Thomas Allen '63, my longest serving and closest colleague, was our first PhD recipient and faculty hire. Soon after the Center's 1962 start, faculty from other MIT Sloan academic groups also became actively involved. In 1973, Don Marquis died of a heart attack and I became head of the group. I soon hired Eric von Hippel '68 and James Utterback '69, followed by many more faculty members who joined us after 1980. The Center has evolved over the 57 years since its founding into today's Technological Innovation, Entrepreneurship, and Strategic Management (TIES) group at MIT Sloan.

STARTING ENTREPRENEURSHIP RESEARCH AT MIT

In 1964, through a fortuitous event, the Center began its research activities on technology-based entrepreneurship. Just one year earlier, NASA had funded the MIT Center for Space Research in the Department of Aeronautics as its Aerospace Research Center #1, giving MIT parallel NASA Centers on organizational research and space research at precisely opposite ends of the campus. In September 1964, Dr. Frank Harrington, the Aerospace Center Director, called Don Marquis with a problem. NASA Headquarters had asked him to produce a report on how NASA-sponsored university research led to economic benefits. Harrington volunteered to fund any Management School faculty member who could do such research. Don invited me to accompany him to meet with Harrington.

After two hours of disappointing efforts to identify any Management School faculty member who might do such research, I hesitantly suggested an analysis of those who left the Aeronautics Department's labs to set up new companies, which might allow the tracing of technology flow from the lab's projects into the market. Harrington enthusiastically approved what became my proposal, "The Transfer of Government-Sponsored Research to the Market Via the Formation and Growth of Technology-Based New Enterprises".

And the **MIT ENTREPRENEURSHIP RESEARCH PROGRAM** was born! It was the first in the world, and started in a typical MIT interdisciplinary manner, with studies of School of Engineering labs, funded by an engineering center, carried out by a School of Management faculty member and his graduate students. Dr. Harrington continued his funding of my expanding line of entrepreneurial research studies for the ensuing seven years.

FORMING AND GROWING THE MIT ENTREPRENEURSHIP RESEARCH PROGRAM

Getting that initial research underway was very difficult, as the field didn't yet exist! The most prominent book on empirical studies of entrepreneurs was *The Entrepreneurial Man,* which examined all of the company founders in the State of Michigan. The average education of those founders was two years of high school. The average duration of their company's existence was two to three years. This was a far cry from what I hoped to learn from research on MIT-spinoff compa-nies. But Professor Marquis encouraged the work, and I moved ahead by hiring a second-year graduate student, **HERBERT WAINER** '65, as my research assistant. Herb eventually became my research associate, working closely with me for several years, before returning home to Cleveland to head Horizons Inc.

Herb Wainer

When we felt ready to move ahead with data collection, I cold-called Professor Charles Stark Draper '26, head of the Aeronautics and Astronautics Department as well as the MIT Instrumentation Laboratory (I-Lab), and told him of my desire to study the people and new companies that had spun off from the I-Lab. Draper's enthusiasm was overwhelming. He burst out, "Entrepreneurs are the most important people in the world. They make things happen! My lab alumni who leave to become VPs of large companies, or professors at other universities, or to start new companies are the great ones. Staying at a place like this forever is only for old geezers like me! . . . When can you get over here?" One week later, Wainer and I showed up for what turned out to be a meeting with Draper and his entire senior staff. Professor Draper already had them work up a starting list of engineers who had left to set up new firms over the entire life of the I-Lab. Draper forcefully instructed his colleagues that he expected the utmost cooperation in this study effort, and provided one of his graduate students, Paul Teplitz '62, to add, as Draper said, "some bodyweight" to the effort. Teplitz later did his master's thesis with me on the I-Lab research results, our first completed study, in which we identified 30 startup companies. Many more companies later resulted from the Instrumentation Lab's pioneering development of the guidance and navigation systems for the Apollo spaceship and the moon lander.

C. Stark Draper in moon-rover mock-up

As we were nearing completion of the I-Lab study, I decided to move ahead quickly to study spinoffs from Lincoln Lab, the other major Defense Department-supported MIT lab. I called the Director of Lincoln, introduced myself and our study topic, and described the support we received from NASA for the MIT Sloan Center and Aerospace Center research. I told him how well the I-Lab study was going, and that we now wanted to replicate our work by studying Lincoln Lab spinoffs. I promised that we would not be disruptive in our work, merely requiring some interviews with senior people and group supervisors to get a start on identifying our hopefully comprehensive sample of companies. He responded immediately: "Entrepreneurs are the biggest pains we have in the Lab. They always want to do their own thing and contribute little to our real objectives. I have no interest in participating in your study!" So not everyone matched Professor Draper in his love of entrepreneurs. Without asking permission (!!!), I cold-called the MIT Vice President of Research, James McCormack '37, a former Air Force general (and later chairman of Communications Satellite Corporation). I told him what had occurred with the I-Lab and about Professor Draper's enthusiasm, and then what happened with Lincoln Lab. I suggested that Jim Webb might be rather unhappy to learn that a major MIT government-funded lab was unwilling to cooperate with his research interests. General McCormack politely responded that he would see what he could do. Three days later I received a telephone call from the Director of Lincoln Lab, telling me that he had been thinking about our conversation and concluded that they could probably find a way to work with our research. We ended up with a very successful identification and study of 50 spinoff firms from Lincoln Laboratory, with Herb Wainer incorporating that work into his master's thesis.

The spinoff studies of I-Lab and Lincoln Lab, the two biggest laboratories at MIT, set the pattern for my successive research on other major MIT labs (Electronic Systems Lab and Research Lab for Electronics), followed by studies of companies formed by faculty and staff of several MIT academic departments. After the Lincoln Lab work was done, we received very good cooperation from everyone else we approached. We followed careful procedures that enabled us to identify (nearly) all of the companies formed by previous or current full-time employees of each organization, and to contact and conduct face-to-face interviews with their founders. We then compared these MIT findings with our next studies of spinoffs from a nearby major government research center, a related large non-profit corporation, and two technology-based firms in the Greater Boston area (all four organizations being left unidentified to preserve their anonymity), and drew conclusions rather similar to what we had found at MIT.

The research program then examined new company formation (not limited to founders from MIT) in a wide variety of technical industries, including biomedical, energy, computer hardware, software, and several others. The data by then covered over 800 companies, all gathered from in-depth, face-to-face, extensively structured interviews with the company founders. My research assistants and I, along with thesis students, carried out other studies of personal characteristics of entrepreneurs (including psychological), financing decision-making by venture capital firms, product development challenges of young firms, and many other aspects of technology-based entrepreneurship. We studied the engineers who remained at the Instrumentation and Lincoln Labs to compare them with those who left those same labs to start new firms, determining significant differences between the two populations. After this prolonged burst of studies, I became increasingly involved in MIT-wide efforts on healthcare management and biotechnology. As a result, I began in 1980 a series of studies on biomedical entrepreneurship, focusing on their greater base in science rather than engineering, the impact of government regulations, longer lead times for development, and typically higher capital requirements.

One of our studies of spinoffs from a large company illustrated for me the potential for larger firms to benefit from stimulating more entrepreneurial behavior within their own organizations. The personnel staff of the firm we studied, after their careful analysis of its departures, cautioned us at the outset that they expected we would be disappointed, as they could only identify three possible new companies formed by ex-employees. Pitifully, the company was unaware of the losses of many more talented employees who preferred to self-direct their careers. We ended up identifying and interviewing 38 company founders who broke away from that organization, their total sales volume being twice that of the "parent" organization. The company VP of R&D later told me that no one could hold back such entrepreneurial people. Our data and his response encouraged me to broaden my research to include so-called "intrapreneurship" studies as well.

INTRAPRENEURSHIP refers to entrepreneurship-like actions internal to an existing organization.

Thus, in parallel with research on new firms, I soon began to study attempts by large corporations to become more entrepreneurial. Again, with research assistants and thesis students, we researched internal venture efforts in various companies, studied corporate programs of venture capital investment in early stage firms, and looked into large firm alliances with small and young companies aimed at gaining more rapid access to new technologies. My publications of this intrapreneurship research stream started in 1972 and supplemented our research on new enterprises. As a result, R&D and business development executives of large companies gradually began to pay more attention to the studies of startup entrepreneurship, finally seeing the complementarity. (Much later, these large company entrepreneurial ventures efforts became far more popular, and I then participated in leading a major government-sponsored study of all U.S. corporate venture capital activities to understand better their motivations for investing in startups, as well as their impact.[1]) These studies formed the basis for my new subject, Corporate Entrepreneurship, one of the earliest in our MIT entrepreneurship curriculum, which I taught for many years to mixed classes of MIT Sloan Fellows and Management and Engineering School graduate students.

From my perspective then and now, it was unfortunate that I was essentially alone in carrying out all of this work, pioneering a broad new field of academic research over the 27-year period through 1990, partnering only with my graduate research assistants and with graduate thesis students from across the Institute. While many of MIT's leaders, especially the engineers, were themselves company founders, they had little thought that their actions and those of others in creating new firms could be subjects of rigorous research. In the 1980s I was joined by other MIT colleagues in carrying out comparative studies of entrepreneurship in two other countries, as described in Chapter 7. The rest of these entrepreneurship studies (deliberately omitting corporate venturing research in order to focus only on new company formation and growth) and their conclusions, with many examples, are aggregated and presented in my book *Entrepreneurs in High Technology: Lessons from MIT and Beyond,* Oxford University Press, 1991. The book was my attempt to demonstrate that academic study could provide meaningful knowledge to supplement the experience of the entrepreneurial practitioners who were forming and building new companies.[2] It was the first comprehensive book on innovation-driven entrepreneurship based on empirical

Edward Roberts

research, and received the Association of American Publishers Award for "Outstanding Book of 1991 in Management and Business".

I made early presentations on the individual studies to academic audiences, in MIT classes and seminars, and to alumni groups and professional technical organizations (mostly in Greater Boston, but also throughout the United States and abroad). In January and February 1967, I did an invited speaking tour of eight universities throughout England and Scotland, and gave a special session for British industry leaders at the United States Embassy in London to help them understand the entrepreneurial creation of new companies in the United States. Many articles about the studies and their findings appeared in MIT journals and in the trade press, in addition to the numerous academic journal articles that my collaborators and I authored. These talks and write-ups accelerated following the publication of my book. Cumulatively, these many communications reached an increasingly sizable audience, which for the first time had concepts and data to form their own opinions on how new enterprises are created, developed, and succeed or fail. Of course, what I learned from those studies strongly influenced my ideas as to what should be emphasized in developing additional entrepreneurship subjects and programs, more specifically identified in the discussions of the **MIT ENTREPRENEURSHIP CENTER** later in this chapter.

After I started the MIT Entrepreneurship Center in 1991, additional faculty who were oriented towards entrepreneurship became part of the expanding teaching and research programs, bringing their own diverse foci and ideas into developing MIT's entrepreneurship endeavors. They are all discussed in Chapter 3, Building the Entrepreneurship Faculty, Curricula, and Research, and its Appendix: MIT Entrepreneurship Faculty.

ALUMNI ENTREPRENEURSHIP SEMINARS

In February 1967, I presented an overview of the research on MIT entrepreneurs to the MIT Alumni Council. It took two years, with the research studies then five years along, before the MIT Alumni Association (MITAA) appointed a small group of reasonably well-informed local MIT alumni to discuss what, if anything, the MITAA should do about the perceived growing interests in starting new businesses. During our group's second meeting, **MARTIN SCHRAGE** '63 came up with the idea of trying to attract at least 30 alumni to a weekend session at MIT on "How to Start and Operate a Small Business". "If the workshop succeeds", Schrage argued, "it would show that an Alumni Association 'entrepreneurship interest group' should be established."[3] Two MITAA staff pushed the proposal and managed to overcome the doubt and resistance of others. The Alumni Association had not been effective in launching programs that attracted young alumni and were not very sympathetic to the notion that entrepreneurship was a good way to go. I saw this resistance as symptomatic of the general

Martin Schrage

lack of belief that entrepreneurship was an important phenomenon, and indeed a major driving force of our economy. The proposal finally got the go-ahead and Schrage chaired the team of ten alumni to organize and carry out a trial **MIT ENTREPRENEURSHIP SEMINAR FOR YOUNG ALUMNI**.

The underlying concept was that this was a new way of "MIT alumni helping MIT alumni". **KEN OLSEN** '50, co-founder-CEO of **DIGITAL EQUIPMENT CORPORATION**, was the dinner speaker and **AMAR BOSE** '51, founder-CEO of **BOSE CORPORATION**, led one of the sessions. Much to everyone's astonishment, 330 alumni attended the inaugural event on October 4–5, 1969, in MIT's Kresge Auditorium, with enrollment being cut off one month ahead of the sessions. Martin Schrage remembers with pride, "This was a wake-up call for the Alumni Association leadership as well as for many others that change was in the air."

The committee immediately announced a repeat session at MIT to be held a few months later, and began planning a nationwide rollout. I was the "kickoff" speaker at the very first workshop held at Kresge (and at all of the multi-year follow-up sessions hosted at MIT and elsewhere across the county), reporting on my studies of MIT alumni entrepreneurs, their personal characteristics, the numbers of entrepreneurial firms from various MIT labs and departments, the company survival rates, and other findings coming from the studies. Over the next three years, similar seminars were conducted in eight cities across the United States, with local MIT alumni running the programs and guiding the various sessions on financing, legal, marketing, product development, and production. Some of these were organized in collaboration with local alumni clubs from other universities, who later developed similar programs.

As an adjunct to each year's programs, the new National Alumni Entrepreneurship Coordinating Committee published a bound book entitled *The MIT Entrepreneurship Register* to facilitate continuing contact among those participants who voluntarily registered their names, background information, and interests. Over 3,000 MIT alumni attended these seminars, the largest attendance ever generated by the MIT Alumni Association for any program before or since. (It would be wonderful to know how many of these alumni later started their own firms!) As these alumni entrepreneurship workshops continued, they were also expanded to cover more subject matters.

SESSIONS WERE held in 1970 and 1971 at MIT, Chicago, Cleveland, New York, San Francisco, and Washington D.C. on "How to Start and Operate a Small Business" and then again on "Managing a New Enterprise in Today's Economy". More seminars were held at MIT, Washington D.C., and Anaheim in 1972, plus several special short entrepreneurship courses for alumni at MIT. My early research program synopsis, Edward Roberts, "How to Succeed in a New Technology Enterprise", *Technology Review*, December 1970, was distributed at all sessions in 1971-72.

William Putt '59 edited the book *How to Start Your Own Business,* based upon cases presented in the various workshops, contributing to the growing consciousness of alumni and others about entrepreneurial opportunities.[4]

Cover page of original brochure (designed by Susan Schur '60)

THE MIT ENTERPRISE FORUM

The Alumni Entrepreneurship Seminars stimulated a variety of responses by attending individuals and by several MIT alumni clubs, including their organization of follow-on entrepreneurship workshops of their own. Numerous MIT alumni later testified that the seminars pushed them to move ahead with their earlier thoughts about starting new companies. Part Two mentions unsought testimonials of this effect from Neil Pappalardo (co-founder of Meditech), Bob Metcalfe (co-founder of 3Com), and Harry Lee (co-founder of Applicon). In their responses to the **MIT ALUMNI ENTREPRENEURSHIP SURVEY** published in 2009, many other alumni mentioned these seminars as influencing them.[5]

As a direct result of the 1971 Alumni Entrepreneurship Workshop in New York, John Jenkins '43 led the start of the New York Venture Clinic that same year. The Clinic featured monthly presentations by MIT alumni entrepreneurs about their business plans, where they could present any issues to alumni review panels and to large audiences of alumni. The New York group also organized many other programs to inform attendees and to stimulate entrepreneurship. In 1978, prodded by Jenkins during his several visits to Boston, eight Greater Boston alumni and friends followed his urgings and created the **MIT ENTERPRISE FORUM (MITEF) OF CAMBRIDGE**, which quickly flourished and continues to this day. One important difference is that the MITEF opened its membership to non-MIT alumni as well, insisting only that the executive committee of the club maintain a majority of MIT alumni. The Cambridge sessions were held monthly, usually under the Dome in MIT 10-250, a familiar home for MIT undergraduate alumni, with an attendance of up to 250 members and guests.

In 1982, **AARON KLEINER** '69 (co-founder with his roommate **RAY KURZWEIL** '70 of multiple companies) led one early innovation within MITEF Cambridge, the **STARTUP CLINIC**. It provided less threatening small-group sessions to hear and counsel ground-zero startups in a dinner session in the MIT Faculty Club. That encouraged young entrepreneurs who had more hesitations about their ideas to come forward. For example, **BILL WARNER** '80 presented his ideas for

AVID TECHNOLOGY, a fully digital nonlinear video editing system, to the dinner session. He received important feedback and encouragement that led to his first round of funding for Avid, which repeatedly disrupted the video industry with new innovations. In 1984, MITEF Cambridge added a four-day educational program at MIT during the January Independent Activities Period (IAP) that attracted large numbers of students from across MIT. This offering was followed by the creation of IAP's day-long "**BITS AND BITES FOR STARTING NEW COMPANIES**" by **JOSEPH HADZIMA** '73, involving many alumni and faculty presenters over the years up to the present. Following the example set by Bill Putt for the Alumni Entrepreneurship Seminars, Stanley Rich and David Gumpert authored a book based on MITEF cases, *Business Plans That Win $$$,* that drew increasing membership to MITEF activities.[6]

In 1983, the New York and Cambridge activities led to the beginning of a nationwide (and later global) expansion of MITEF chapters, totaling 19 in 2019, half in other countries. The Cambridge office for **MITEF, INC.**, formed in 1987, also started a program of sessions conducted for large audiences, usually at MIT Kresge Auditorium. Starting in 1996, these sessions were video-recorded for simultaneous telecast via satellite and for later downloading to numerous MITEF chapters and MIT alumni clubs worldwide. They provided increased entrepreneurship education and stimulus to the widening audience of MIT alumni and others. The MIT Enterprise Forum has inevitably helped stimulate thousands of new company formations and growth all over the world.

Another short-lived effort by MITEF Cambridge was also aimed at attracting larger numbers to its sessions. Its officers approached me in the late 1990s for permission to establish the Edward Roberts Award for Distinguished Young Entrepreneurial Leadership, believing that prominent entrepreneur recipients (who had achieved success prior to age 35!) would help increase audience size. They deliberated carefully and selected Michael Dell as the first to be honored. Indeed, Dell's resulting award and speaking event did generate large numbers at MIT's Kresge Auditorium. Incidentally, Dell Computer became the most successful recruiter from MIT that year! In the next year, the committee informed me that it was having trouble identifying a suitable candidate for the award who might become as successful as Dell. They told me that they had considered two young people in California who had founded a young firm called "Google". But the committee was hesitant to invite them because Google's future was so uncertain! ☺ That same hesitation caused the committee to shut down its award efforts after two more years of avoiding potential embarrassment of Michael Dell!

A REVITALIZED MIT TECHNOLOGY LICENSING ORGANIZATION

The only institutional change related to entrepreneurship that occurred within MIT during the decade of the 1980s was an overt shift in MIT's policies and organization for technology licensing. That function had been created early in MIT history, with activities in 1932 devoted to licensing technologies coming from MIT faculty and staff research. In 1945, MIT formed the Patent, Copyright, and Licensing Office. Similar to all other universities, its primary clientele were large corporations that paid MIT licensing fees, either fixed in dollar amount at the outset or based upon the revenues generated over time by the products that used the MIT technology. As in most other universities, lawyers who negotiated and executed the contracts with businesses dominated the organization.

MIT renamed the organization the **TECHNOLOGY LICENSING OFFICE (TLO)** in 1985 and hired a new Director, John Preston, and a new Associate Director, **LITA NELSEN** '64, to implement new policies. The TLO's goals were to become more proactive in moving MIT science and technology into commercialization, and to place greater emphasis on the role of new companies in accomplishing that. These goals reflected the TLO's recognition that large corporations are more often interested in technologies that are ready for the market. In contrast, most MIT discoveries and developments are usually in need of further (often significant) R&D before they are ready for commercialization. While the TLO continues actively to license both large and medium sized firms, the new companies that seek licenses are most often being started by MIT faculty and/or their students or staff. These folks have a better understanding of the actual stage of development of the licensed technologies and are usually prepared to invest considerably more time and energies into developing them further.

As part of its new policies, MIT agreed to accept on occasion a small equity ownership in startup firms in lieu of a cash payment, which new companies frequently lack. In addition, MIT decided that, when appropriate, it would be willing to grant exclusive licenses to new companies, as technology exclusivity provides firms with at least one potential source of competitive advantage over existing large firms that have much greater technical, market, and financial resources. Regarded by many other universities as radical and undesirable, MIT leadership believed it was a vital step in aiding entrepreneurial *mens et manus.*

The new TLO policies and leadership made a significant impact, and soon MIT became the top university in the world in the number of startup companies licensed by the university itself. Recent data indicate that around 35 new firms are founded each year based on licensed MIT technology. Lita Nelsen, who took over as director of the TLO in 1992, and was its dominant force until her retirement in 2017, explains that the long-term successes that the TLO has helped to foster go beyond these policies:

> We didn't just act as a filer of patents and negotiator of license agreements. We were sort of coaches and guides to everyone as to where they could find help. I hired people with strong technology basic education, but who had also spent 15 or 20 years in industry, not just at the bench. Many of them had been involved in startups at some point

in their careers. In addition to doing the evaluation of hundreds of invention disclosures a year [now over 800] coming into the TLO, the staff were also able to provide a lot of advice on how to get started, pointing faculty and students in directions where they might get money. This was especially needed before the coming of such things as the MIT Entrepreneurship Center, the Deshpande Center, and the Venture Mentoring Service. Sometimes the TLO help was by saying, "Look, this won't work because . . .". All this wasn't adequate, but it was better than nothing.

Lita Nelsen

Over the years, we made a reasonable amount of money for MIT, but the emphasis was never "How do I get the most out of this deal?" Instead, we stressed "How do we get investment into the technology, get it moving as a company, and hope that it will become real?" . . . I made up a little motto: "Impact is not primarily income." This focus on impact is something the upper administration of MIT has consistently supported. This is very different from most tech transfer offices in the world. In making friends with both the investment and the entrepreneurship communities, you've got to make a fair deal, not necessarily the best deal. Get it done and go onto the next one. I say, rather than trying to pick winners, the technology is usually so early and unripe that you can't tell the cherries from the pits. So, get lots of things going, and some of them will turn out wonderfully.[7]

Over most of her 25 years at the TLO, Lita's right-hand person was **JACK TURNER**, the Office's Senior Associate Director, who retired in August 2019. Jack had been highly visible in all of MIT's entrepreneurial endeavors and very available to help students and me personally in my efforts to build MIT entrepreneurship. Lita's successor as TLO Director is Leslie Millar-Nicholson.

MIT OFFICIALLY RECOGNIZES THE IMPORTANCE OF ITS ALUMNI ENTREPRENEURS

In December 1984, I proposed to Abraham Siegel, Dean of the MIT Sloan School, the creation of an honor society for MIT entrepreneurs. As with any honor society, we would need to develop clear criteria for admission, such as tangible measures that might include a mix of a firm's number of employees, revenues, assets, and capital valuation, as well as less tangible metrics such as its overall benefits to society. Dean Siegel concluded that he should bring a slightly modified proposal to Gerry Wilson '61, Dean of the School of Engineering, who quickly shared his enthusiasm for the likely benefit to MIT of closer entrepreneur involvement in classes and school activities. The two deans brought the proposal to MIT President Paul Gray '54, who found it an interesting concept.

President Gray appointed a very senior committee to examine the proposal, headed by Professor Michael Dertouzos '64, Director of the MIT Laboratory for Computer Science, and including five additional professors from across the Institute and three senior MIT officials. By early December 1985, our committee concurred on specific suggestions, which President Gray enthusiastically endorsed in a meeting with us. However, his presentation of that proposal to a later MIT Academic Council meeting was rejected, the then Provost arguing that no group of MIT alumni should be treated differently from the rest of the alumni body.

Toward the end of the 1980s, however, MIT overall was being impacted by the increasingly positive publicity that MIT entrepreneurs were receiving for their creation of significant firms across the United States and in many other countries. In addition, alumni were initiating nationwide seminars and alumni activities in the growing number of MIT Enterprise Forum chapters. With President Gray in the lead, in 1989, MIT moved beyond mere speeches to officially praise alumni entrepreneurship achievements. On March 3, 1989, the MIT Corporation resolved to recognize alumni who had created important companies in Massachusetts, and established April 29, 1989, as a day to honor them. The special program was called "**EVENT 128**", coinciding fortuitously with the 128th anniversary of MIT and alluding to what was then known as the "Route 128 phenomenon", in which technology firms, predominantly from MIT, populated that area surrounding Boston. During that extraordinary evening, President Gray extolled "the energy, confidence, and vision of 99 members of the MIT family who had the courage to take risks, the knowledge to solve problems, and the creativity to dream dreams".[8] President Gray also stated that the Bank of Boston estimated that a total of 600 firms started by MIT alumni were in the Greater Boston area, which provided a significant revenue and employment impact. Those selected 99 entrepreneurs were the honored guests of the MIT Corporation, each receiving a silver bowl in recognition and having a page dedicated to her or him and their related enterprises in a photo album distributed to all. (Other universities might consider doing similar honoring of their entrepreneurial alumni.)

Event 128 gained such a supportive response that MIT organized a similar event in Silicon Valley one year later. Chase Manhattan Corporation produced a brochure for that evening titled *MIT Entrepreneurship in Silicon Valley.* It identified and listed information on 176 MIT-alumni-founded companies with branches in northern California, employing 90,000 people. Nineteen of those firms were headquartered there.

LAUNCHING THE MIT ENTREPRENEURSHIP CENTER

By 1990, I was encountering increasing numbers of MIT Sloan and other MIT students, both undergraduate and graduate, who were expressing interest in obtaining more entrepreneurship education and training activities. Their only options at the time were the New Enterprises subject and thesis work primarily with me. A group of students was already trying to organize a business plan competition to gain some practical experience. In 1990, that was tried as a $1K prize experiment.

Based on student demand, and taking advantage of the increased MIT-wide acknowledgement of the importance of entrepreneurship, including the special honoring events of previous years, I submitted an ambitious proposal to MIT Sloan Dean Lester Thurow for the School to form an MIT-wide entrepreneurship program, led by a new **MIT ENTREPRENEURSHIP CENTER** to be housed within the Sloan School. The Center's goal would be "to educate and develop those who will create, build, and lead tomorrow's successful high-tech ventures". My proposal called for a dramatic increase in, and central coordination and integration of, MIT-wide entrepreneurship classes and student activities. More tenure-track faculty and experienced practitioners would be needed to develop and implement the teaching and counseling activities. The relevant functional areas of the Sloan School (e.g., the Organization Behavior, Marketing, and Finance groups) and the Management of Technological Innovation group (MTI, which I had chaired since Donald Marquis's death in 1973) would jointly appoint most of the new tenure-track faculty. Funds obviously had to be raised to provide an endowment, as well as increased operational support. At Dean Thurow's direction, I met with a number of MIT Sloan faculty from different areas of the School. Within a couple of months, the faculty leaders of all the functional groups in the Sloan School signed their approval for moving forward with this unique initiative, and Dean Thurow then approved the proposal. I remember the end of that meeting with particular relish:

> **DEAN THUROW:** Okay Ed. So what are you going to do now?
>
> **ED:** I'm going to organize an advisory board of alumni from across MIT who founded and are running important companies. People like Amar Bose (Bose Corp.), **ALEX D'ARBELOFF (TERADYNE)**, **KEN GERMESHAUSEN (EG&G)**, **BERNIE GOLDHIRSCH (INC.** magazine), George Hatsopoulos (Thermoelectron), **PAT MCGOVERN (INTERNATIONAL DATA GROUP)**, Ken Olsen (Digital Equipment), and maybe others.
>
> **DEAN THUROW:** How in the world do you think you're going to get those guys?
>
> **ED:** Lester, that's what you don't understand about entrepreneurs. I know all of them. I'll call each one and each will immediately, enthusiastically agree to serve. They will be delighted with the idea of creating an MIT Entrepreneurship Center. Entrepreneurs love entrepreneurs!
>
> **DEAN THUROW:** Ed, if you can really do that then I will agree to become chairman of your advisory board!!!

Lester Thurow and Ed Roberts at the announcement of the MIT Entrepreneurship Center

ED: Lester, is that the kind of gift one cannot refuse?

DEAN THUROW: *(Still laughing.)* Absolutely.

ED: In that case I am thrilled to have you as chair of the advisory board!

Dean Thurow expressed concern that our main problem would be to identify and recruit qualified faculty to do teaching and research in this new field of technology-based entrepreneurship. He also agreed to provide help with fundraising for the E-Center.

I have chaired the Center from its start up to the present. It has since been renamed the **MARTIN TRUST CENTER FOR MIT ENTREPRENEURSHIP**, in honor of Marty's timely philanthropy. I also served during most of this time as the Center's Faculty Director, with great help from the increasing numbers of faculty, staff, and dedicated students.

I emphasized four stated operating goals in the proposal discussions, heavily influenced by the findings of my own research studies:

(1) Engagement across the entire MIT campus. Although based in the Sloan School of Management, the initial and continuing vision for the MIT Entrepreneurship Center was that it would work to establish cross-campus collaboration with the four other schools of MIT. I thought it essential to connect our business-oriented students with the science and technology students who would likely have far more advanced technical skills and ideas. This collaboration/integration would be vital for generating student teams to work together on real technological developments proposed by the MIT faculty. No doubt I was influenced in that view by having spent my life since age 17 at MIT, earning degrees from three different MIT schools!

(2) "Dual-track" education based on integrating entrepreneurship academics with successful entrepreneurship practitioners. All other university entrepreneurship programs at that time rested primarily on experience-sharing by entrepreneurs and investors. Our proposed Entrepreneurship Center would uniquely follow the MIT tradition of *mens et manus*. The E-Center faculty would have to connect the rigorous, scholarly pursuit of knowledge underlying entrepreneurial success with the effective transfer of that knowledge into practice. The proposal envisioned a "dual-track faculty", consisting of "tenure-track" academics along with adjunct practitioners, linking entrepreneurial researchers with successful entrepreneurs and venture capitalists. We would build an ambitious teaching program accompanied by direct coaching and mentoring of student would-be entrepreneurs. Students would be offered classes that focused on academic understandings of entrepreneurship, as well as on strategic and operational experiences. Whenever possible, our goal would be to combine both kinds of teachers in the same classroom. Over the past 29 years, almost all other leading business schools have adopted this dual-track model as a goal for organizing and managing their entrepreneurship programs.

(3) Heavy emphasis on real-world "action-learning", mixing management students with science-technology students to work on real emerging technology opportunities. To effect the *manus* objective as much as possible, MIT's entrepreneurship program would pay heavy attention to creating classes in which students engaged with real problem-solving situations in young entrepreneurial firms. Furthermore, to encourage more technology-based company foundings, linkages would be fostered between all the students and emerging technology developments from MIT science and technology faculty. MIT Sloan now labels these kinds of efforts as "action learning".

(4) Focus on teams rather than individuals as the primary vehicle for com-pany founding and development. Based on my research going back to 1964, teams rather than individuals would be the base for as much project work and class activity as possible. This reflects the consistent findings that solo founders are far less frequently successful in building growing and profitable firms than teams of co-founders.

Throughout the past quarter-century of growth, development, and impact, those four founding principles of the MIT Entrepreneurship Center have been critical success factors.

REFERENCES AND NOTES

1. Edward Roberts, I. MacMillan, V. Livada & A. Wang, "Corporate Venture Capital (CVC): Seeking Innovation and Strategic Growth", *National Institute of Standards & Technology Special Report GCR 08-916,* June 2008.
2. All of the 40 individual studies and their contributors discussed in *Entrepreneurs in High Technology* are identified in that book's Appendix, "A Quarter-Century of Research", 359–375. The primary findings from the research are presented in the book's final chapter, "Technological Entrepreneurship: Birth, Growth, and Success", 339–358.
3. Interview by Michelle Choate on February 17, 2017.
4. William Putt, editor, *How to Start Your Own Business,* MIT Press, 1974.
5. Edward Roberts and Charles Eesley, *Entrepreneurial Impact: The Role of MIT,* Kauffman Foundation, 2009.
6. Stanley Rich and David Gumpert, *Business Plans That Win $$$: Lessons from the MIT Enterprise Forum,* Harper & Row, 1985.
7. Interview by Michelle Choate on May 6, 2016. Some of Lita's comments here are from her presentation at our celebration of MIT entrepreneurship on November 12, 2016.
8. *Event 128: A Salute to Founders,* MIT, April 29, 1989.

3

Building the Entrepreneurship Faculty, Curricula, and Research

Dean Lester Thurow was correct when he stated that the key stumbling block to building the MIT Entrepreneurship Center was the overall lack of entrepreneurship scholars and the non-existence of "feeder" university PhD programs that might produce them. The faculty, the curricula they create and sustain, their related research, and their support for student activities and for student advising are instrumental to our (and to any) university entrepreneurship program. Fortunately, some of the faculty who had previously been recruited into the Management of Technological Innovation (MTI) Group to focus upon technological innovation, not entrepreneurship, were willing and able to do some "filling in", as I indicate below.

This chapter and the Appendix provide an overview of the detailed bringing-on-board and gradual development of the MIT entrepreneurship faculty, of the courses they developed and taught, and of the new research areas they explored. I hope that many readers do seek better understanding of how a successful university entrepreneurship program was built, in some ways stone by stone. But certainly, some readers are not especially interested in the specific people of MIT and the important roles they have played in building MIT entrepreneurship and its impact. To avoid possibly difficult reading, I have placed much of the details in the Appendix: MIT Entrepreneurship Faculty.

GROWING THE ACADEMIC FACULTY, THEIR RESEARCH AND TEACHING INTERESTS, AND A BROAD ENTREPRENEURSHIP CURRICULUM

In the past 30 years, the number of faculty and the curriculum in entrepreneurship have grown enormously, from one part-time practitioner and a fraction of one academic faculty member into a huge number of MIT faculty, research efforts, and subjects offered across the Institute. I thank all of those who were here at MIT when we started in 1990, and all who have arrived since then and contributed to our growth, development, and success. The adjacent sidebar lists, in order of their dates of arrival, MIT academic faculty who have taught and/or carried out research in the area of technological entrepreneurship. The Sloan School of Management faculty are first, as most began their entrepreneurship-linked activities soon after their arrival. The dates indicate that many who eventually became engaged in entrepreneurship, up through Professor Steve Eppinger, were already at MIT at the time the MIT Entrepreneurship Center was approved in 1990. But none had taught MIT entrepreneurship subjects, and I was the only one who had done entrepreneurial research. So, these "early birds" became important contributors to building the academic program, before new entrepreneurship-targeted faculty were recruited.

Entrepreneurship-Related MIT Faculty

Management – Edward Roberts 1961-; Thomas Allen 1966-2017; Eric von Hippel 1973-; James Utterback 1974-2017; Dorothy Leonard (Barton) 1979-83; Mel Horwitch 1980-88, 1993-94; Charles Fine 1983-; Michael Cusumano 1986-; Richard Locke 1988-2013; Steven Eppinger 1988-; Scott Stern 1995-2001, 2009-; Scott Shane 1996-99; Simon Johnson 1997-; Fiona Murray 1999-; Diane Burton 2000-06; Antoinette Schoar 2000-; Yasheng Huang 2003-; Catherine Tucker 2005-; Pierre Azoulay 2006-; Alexandra Kacperczyk 2009-16; Matthew Marx 2009-17; Christian Catalini 2013-; Jacob Cohen 2013-; Benjamin Roin 2014-19; Catherine Turco 2017-.

Engineering – Anthony Sinskey 1968-; Charles Cooney 1970-; Martha Gray 1986-; Alex Pentland (Media Lab) 1987-; Douglas Hart 1993-; Eugene Fitzgerald 1994-; Martin Culpepper 2000-.

The Engineering faculty are listed next in the sidebar in order of their arrival at MIT, as all of them focused for many years solely on their technology research and teaching before later becoming involved in MIT's entrepreneurship programs. Due to rapid recent growth of entrepreneur-oriented classes, especially in several departments in the MIT School of Engineering, I have inevitably but unintentionally omitted some Engineering faculty members.

To enable more elaborate discussion of the many contributions made by each person, I have placed all of the detailed information about these Academic Faculty members and their contributions in the Appendix: MIT Entrepreneurship Faculty.

GROWING THE PRACTITIONER FACULTY

Since its beginning in 1990 (and as listed in the adjacent sidebar), the MIT entrepreneurship program has been blessed with the part-time contributions of many

LECTURERS, Senior Lecturers, and other part-time practitioner educators, in alphabetical order, probably incomplete:

Noubar Afeyan, John Akula, Howard Anderson, Kirk Arnold, William Aulet, Gordon Baty, James Baum, Joost Bonsen, Phillip Budden, Barbara Bund, Georgina Campbell Flatter, Elaine Chen, Zen Chu, Elliott Cohen, Patricia Cotter, Todd Dagres, Alex d'Arbeloff (Professor of the Practice), James Dougherty, Paul English, Jonathan Fleming, Josh Forman, Joseph Hadzima, Brian Halligan, Dennis Hoffman, Tod Hynes, Peter Kurzina, Donna Levin, Peter Levine, Valentin Livada, Shari Loessberg, Alan McCormack, Ken Morse, Rajesh Nair, Russ Olive, Rory O'Shea (Visiting Faculty), Francis O'Sullivan, Luis Perez-Breva, John Preston, Imran Sayeed, Louis Shipley, Andrew Wolk, Andrey Zarur, Ken Zolot, and many more.

practitioner entrepreneurs and venture capitalists who have brought their years of experience into the MIT classrooms. In fact, the first new subject we offered after the start of the MIT Entrepreneurship Center was Entrepreneurship Lab (E-Lab), taught initially by **JOHN PRESTON**, then Director of the MIT Technology Licensing Office and later a part-time E-Center Senior Lecturer. E-Lab's simple but wonderful concept has lasted in our curriculum to the present time. Teams of four or five students work on projects for a full semester in a nearby young entrepreneurial firm. We explain E-Lab's goal as to have the teams "help resolve problems that keep the CEO up late at night"! It was clearly intended as a shared learning experience for the teams of students to better understand entrepreneurial firms and their issues. My arguments about the need to build mixed teams of technical and management students finally persuaded the MIT Sloan School to hold back 20% of the seats in New Enterprises for engineering students. Thus, every E-Lab company project had at least one engineer as part of its team.

Many of the practitioners developed their own subjects, often in collaboration with others. They have carried the titles of MIT Lecturer or Senior Lecturer, but our students regard their classroom offerings as being just as professorial as those presented by our academic faculty from Management or Engineering. The practitioners have taught New Enterprises, E-Lab, and various venture classes, usually with others, sometimes with academic faculty sharing the same classrooms for the benefit of the students. The initial goals of the MIT Entrepreneurship Center emphasized the blending of academic and practitioner faculty, which is best done in the same classroom whenever possible!

All of these experienced practitioners have also frequently made themselves available for guest lectures in classes not their own and, even more importantly, for counseling and mentoring individual students and startup teams. The first ones to follow **RICHARD MORSE** in teaching New Enterprises were **RUSSELL OLIVE** '52, who started even before the MIT Entrepreneurship Center was underway, and **BARBARA BUND**, who also introduced a new subject, Entrepreneurial Marketing.

Russ Olive

And then over time came many experienced and interesting practitioners, recruited often by our Managing Directors **KEN MORSE** and then **BILL AULET**, and sometimes by me. Some of their efforts and results are described in Chapter 4, frequently reflecting the initiatives of the two Managing Directors, who are the focus of that chapter. I thank all these Lecturers and Senior Lecturers for their valuable assistance, without which the MIT entrepreneurship program could not have developed and thrived so well.

To enable more detailed coverage that focuses primarily on those practitioner faculty who created and ran their own specialties and/or exercised primary roles in other classes, I have placed that information in the Appendix, along with the rest of the MIT entrepreneurship faculty members.

Barbara Bund

MANAGEMENT OF TECHNOLOGY (MOT) PROGRAM

In the late 1970s, Professor **HERBERT HOLLOMON**, of the School of Engineering, and I conceived of a new one-year executive education degree program to attract and educate young technologists into a management development program that would help them achieve technology-management excellence first, on their way toward bridging into general management leadership roles. We organized a joint faculty task force from the Engineering and Management Schools to work on the concept and to develop a detailed design to gain joint Schools and then MIT approvals. That was achieved and adopted in 1980 as the **MIT JOINT PROGRAM ON THE MANAGEMENT OF TECHNOLOGY**, a 12-months full-time program that would award the MIT Master of Science degree in MOT, with the individ-ual choosing whether the degree would be awarded by an individual Engineering Department or by the MIT Sloan School. It was the first degree program ever oper-ated by two MIT Schools, and had the added distinction that admissions and the degree were available from both.

Faculty were recruited from both Schools, and I became the founding Faculty Director, leading the program through 1999, when other faculty succeeded me as Chairman. It was the only MIT executive program that identified both com-pany-sponsored candidates as well as self-sponsored entrepreneurial candidates for admission. That resulted in an increasing flow of individuals who had strong entrepreneurial aspirations, as well as some who already had entrepreneurial experience. They in turn focused numerous of their required SM theses upon entrepreneurial topics, implicitly recruiting interests from many faculty thesis supervisors across the Institute, and especially within the Sloan School.

We still had only one MIT subject focused upon new companies, New Enterprises, and I created a new subject, Corporate Entrepreneurship, that treated internal ventures in existing firms, corporate venture capital, and strategic alliances between large firms and younger technology-based companies. I enrolled mixed classes of students from the MOT and Sloan Fellows exec ed degree programs, as well as grad students from Engineering and MIT Sloan. I taught that subject until the founding of the Entrepreneurship & Innovation Track (next topic) overloaded my teaching schedule, so I then turned the subject over to part-time lecturers. In Chapter 7, **NOUBAR AFEYAN** '87, founder and CEO of **FLAGSHIP PIONEERING**, identifies that subject as his one exposure to entrepreneuring education while an MIT student, and the beginning of our long-time friendship. In Chapter 12, **DHARMESH SHAH**, co-founder and CTO of **HUBSPOT**, says he came to MIT for graduate study explicitly to benefit from the MOT Program, and claims to have been its final degree recipient in 2006. MOT was merged with the Sloan Fellows Program in 2005 to become today's MIT Sloan Fellows Innovation and Global Leadership Program.

ENTREPRENEURSHIP & INNOVATION (E&I) TRACK

In the summer of 2006, the **ENTREPRENEURSHIP & INNOVATION (E&I) TRACK** was initiated for selected applicants in the entering MBA class of 2008. This was a dramatic change for MIT entrepreneurship. MBA applicants now could specify their desire to focus on entrepreneurial studies and activities and potentially enter a track that would help to fulfill their goals. I have had the great pleasure of chairing E&I from the outset, focusing the program on teaching committed graduate students how to launch and develop "innovation-driven companies". And given that we are at MIT, the obvious thrust of the E&I Track is toward emerging technology enterprises, but not limited to technology. The E&I Track attempts to build a lifetime cohort of collaborating entrepreneurial MBA classmates, and leads to an MIT Sloan Certificate in Entrepreneurship & Innovation in addition to an MBA degree. Wholly consistent with the goals expressed for the MIT Entrepreneurship Center at its founding, the E&I curriculum that we developed heavily emphasizes team practice linked to real-world entrepreneurial projects. It balances theoretical and practitioner education, and provides a thorough exposure to the many building blocks of an entrepreneurial career. Due to limitations of classroom size, about 30% of the entering MIT Sloan MBA students are able to enter this entrepreneurship concentration, with more on the wait list. (In 2018, 128 were admitted with 25 more on the Wait List!) Over half of the students admitted to MIT Sloan indicate that they applied to the school primarily because of its entrepreneurship program and opportunities. In 2011, and again in 2019, half of the entering MBA students applied for admission to the E&I Track. But the E&I Track has been capped at about 120 students per year from 2006 to the present. Two additional tracks, the Practice of Finance and Enterprise Management (targeted at students who want to enter strategic consulting or work for large companies), together account for about one-third of the class, and the remaining third are "untracked" (i.e., able to spread their electives over all areas of the school without concentration).

The E&I Track students enroll during their first term in Introduction to Technological Entrepreneurship, which I teach, in addition to other required first-term MBA subjects. In the spring term, E&I students are required to take New Enterprises, Entrepreneurial Strategy, and the Silicon Valley Study Tour, all mentioned previously or in the Appendix, along with other electives. During their two years at MIT, E&I students must also take at least one elective that is a firm-focused entrepreneurial "internship", E-Lab or G-Lab or something similar. E&I students also must enroll in an entrepreneurial elective that is focused on developing a product or service, such as the so-called "venture courses" (iTeams being the most popular) and others such as Product Design and Development. Almost every one of these required and elective E&I subjects features mixed teams from the Sloan School and the School of Engineering or another MIT school, and engages the students in real-world projects. The E&I students must take several other elective entrepreneurial subjects, and finally must be part of a team that enters the final phase of the $100K or Clean Energy Prize Competitions or do something equivalent to an attempted company development. While this is a heavy load for the typical MBA student, I find that aspiring entrepreneurs are not typical. Most are used to—and want to carry out—hard work efforts, especially if they see the promise of a startup arising from those efforts. More and more of our E&I students are launching firms prior to their graduation! It has also been rewarding to see how many of the E&I students manage their course loads while also moving into leadership positions of many student activities, perhaps to be expected of these uniquely entrepreneurial students.

In recent years we have observed that many in the E&I Track enter without clear commitments to starting a firm. Some identify from the start that they want initially to be "Joiners", i.e., to seek and join an early-stage firm upon graduation, but not as a co-founder. Chapter 6 reveals how this category has been a vital career path for so many MIT alumni from across the Institute, a large fraction of whom later formed their own companies and performed well. A few of our E&I entrants, perhaps gradually increasing in numbers, want to become an entrepreneurially-behaving employee of a large firm, and we label them as desiring roles as "Corporate Entrepreneurs". Other E&Is think they'd like to work in venture capital partnerships, and still other students are merely curious to better understand what entrepreneurship is all about, and whether it fits into their own future career plans! We try to serve all of these personas as best we can, while still focusing as much as possible on educating those who truly want to form and build new innovation-based companies.

SUMMING UP: FACULTY AND CURRICULA

The pace of growth and change in academic and practitioner entrepreneurship faculty—and of the many subjects they teach—is impressive, and is now clearly no longer under one person's control! By 2001, we had about 10 subjects underway with close to 1,500 "student seats" taken in those classes. We made good progress in our first decade. But look at where we are now. The sections above, and the Appendix, list and describe aspects of 32 academic and 18 practitioner current faculty members. I also identify some 48 unique MIT subjects. And the Trust Center website (http://entrepreneurship.mit.edu/classes/) lists even more subjects in entrepreneurship across the Institute.[1] This scene has been changing rapidly, especially through new additions by other MIT departments that previously had offered few if any subjects in entrepreneurship. I apologize to those who may have been omitted from one or another of these accountings!

SOME BRIEF COMMENTS ON MIT ENTREPRENEURSHIP RESEARCH

As I reviewed the growth of the MIT Sloan academic entrepreneurship faculty in the first section of this chapter and its accompanying Appendix, I indicated for each person some of her or his research interests and achievements over the years. It is important to observe that we were the first academic research program in entrepreneurship, beginning back in the early 1960s. Also note that at MIT, every faculty member in every field is expected primarily to be advancing the state of research and knowledge creation. *Mens et manus* requires "*mens*" for its beginnings! That is as true for the MIT Sloan School of Management as it is for the School of Science and the School of Engineering.

In many ways, the development of a scholarly PhD program accompanies, and is frequently the root of, faculty research. At the outset of the MIT Entrepreneurship Center in the 1960s, neither we nor any other academic institution had a related PhD program. We depended on master's degree thesis students from across the Institute to aid in carrying out field studies, interviews, and data analyses to advance the study of entrepreneurship. But as our faculty interests and involvements began to grow, so too did our entrepreneurship research. This growth began in the 1980s and accelerated rapidly in the 1990s, as new faculty were hired who focused on entrepreneurship as their primary emphasis. Gradually PhD students whose interests were in entrepreneurial studies were accepted into MIT Sloan, which led to the evolution of a full-fledged PhD program in Entrepreneurship and Innovation. Over the years, more than 30 academic faculty members, some of whom are still at MIT, have carried out entrepreneurship-related research and have nurtured and graduated over 60 PhD students with similar research and teaching interests. Both our faculty and PhD student alumni (almost all of whom are faculty members at institutions across the United States and around the world) have continued to develop research findings that influence their academic colleagues as well as practitioners and policy-makers. Each of them is a "carrier" of the impact of MIT entrepreneurship. Many of them have created comparable entrepreneurship programs at their own institutions, often the first in their countries.

Today, we are fortunately part of a worldwide community of academic scholars who advance the understandings of entrepreneurship in every way. Some focus on the people involved and their characteristics and origins. Others examine the founding and/or growing processes of new enterprises, and/or the development of teams, strategies, and financing. Still other academic scholars examine and try to improve governmental policies that affect entrepreneurship in their communities and countries. The academic disciplines of the faculty researchers range widely, from human and organizational studies, to economics and finance, to strategy and policy. Some universities are primarily single-discipline in their entrepreneurship research orientation. MIT Sloan's entrepreneurship research has from the outset tended toward multi-disciplinary work, in fact, often among interdisciplinary colleagues and co-authors. A natural outgrowth of our MIT surroundings, MIT entrepreneurship faculty members (and our PhD students, too) have frequently had prior engineering or science experience in study and/or work. This has provided a sound foundation for better understanding the people and the phenomena of technology- and innovation-based entrepreneurship.

This book is not attempting to review the scholarly achievements over the past half century of our MIT academic research in entrepreneurship. That is an appropriate goal, but not for this volume. However, I do want to communicate what has developed here that makes our MIT entrepreneurship research have a flavor of its own, somewhat different from the rest of our field. For that purpose I turn to remarks made by my colleague, Professor Scott Stern:

> Over the past 50 years, MIT has succeeded in turning entrepreneurship from an area of interest and practice into a discipline, albeit with far more yet to learn than we already know! I highlight three reasons for why MIT arguably continues to play an important role in developing the field of entrepreneurship research. The first is MIT's very motto of "*mens et manus*", with the emphasis on "*et*", i.e., "and"! That became an organizing insight that Ed Roberts pushed along with the development of our Entrepreneurship Center. We take seriously that there's a necessary interplay between theory and practice, between academic research study and real-world practical application. Our entrepreneurship research is grounded heavily in close contacts with practice, so that we can better understand and hopefully improve it.
>
> Second reason, not unrelated, is that MIT much more than most other places has been totally comfortable that there's no single privileged discipline nor methodological approach that will uniquely illuminate what we need to know about entrepreneurship.... At MIT, we have always welcomed the diversity of modes of thought and approach to finding new insights. When I arrived at MIT as a junior faculty member, Ed Roberts, Tom Allen, Eric von Hippel, and Jim Utterback were already here, each very different in his thought processes and consequently in

> his research foci and methods used. Not only was that rather unique to me, but it was stimulating to my own idea generation and work.
>
> The final reason is in fact how we currently describe the Sloan School – our branding is "Ideas that are made to matter". MIT is a place that takes people and their ideas seriously.... Very smart, ambitious people often say things that are novel, which were not obvious before but are often obvious once said. That is also true in our research. A senior faculty member once told me that the big difference between MIT and most other places is that at MIT we evaluate the contribution of faculty more by their students than necessarily by the latest paper they published. That paper does matter, but also what matters are the people we develop and their impact. This involves being in an environment where you encourage people to explore new ideas, where you invest in people in a way that allows them to nurture those ideas to really come to fruition. The after-the-fact measure of them, and you, is: Of what consequence is your work? On whom and on what did you have impact?[2]

I agree wholly with Scott's words, and take pride in the achievements of our entrepreneurship faculty, in the impact that their research, teaching, and mentoring have had on our graduates at all levels, and in what those graduates have accomplished, whether in industry or government or academia.

REFERENCES AND NOTES

1. Accessed on September 9, 2019.
2. From transcripts of Scott Stern's talk at our MIT entrepreneurship celebration on November 12, 2016, with some liberties taken in my editing.

4

Leading the E-Center and Creating New Programs

THE MANAGING DIRECTORS

When we started the MIT Entrepreneurship Center, it was physically just my office! In the ensuing decades, we moved into a small space, then a larger space. In 2011, the E-Center was renamed the Martin Trust Center for MIT Entrepreneurship, in honor of a gift from Martin and Dina Trust, and moved into accommodations far larger and more suitable for our mission. No matter where we have been located, we have had the good fortune of having two superb Managing Directors, serving a total of more than 23 years thus far: **KENNETH MORSE** and **WILLIAM AULET**. I am indebted to them both for their enormous contributions to the growth and success of our MIT entrepreneurship program.

Kenneth Morse

In 1996, Ken Morse '68 became the first full-time Managing Director of the MIT Entrepreneurship Center. As a Senior Lecturer, Ken co-taught New Enterprises and E-Lab, which were offered in both terms in order to meet growing student demand. Ken was instrumental in getting several new initiatives off the ground, and was very important in raising major funds for the E-Center. In the time before his departure from MIT in 2009, the MIT entrepreneurship program grew significantly, with student annual enrollments in entrepreneurship classes going from about 220 to an estimated 1,600 "student seats".

When Ken arrived at MIT, he joined John Preston to become co-teacher of E-Lab. I then pushed the Dean's office to adjust our "electives bidding process" to set aside about one quarter of the seats in the class for engineering students. This allowed for the mixed teams we preferred. Ken approached local law firms and venture capital firms to recommend companies for this "mini-internship", and we rapidly began to grow the number of applicant companies as well as students. We also included some Harvard Business School (HBS) cross-registrants in the teams, as HBS had essentially no entrepreneurship activity, and many of those cross-enrollees were MIT undergrad alumni. In the best scenario, each student team would spend one day a week at its "client" company, working on its problems. The single most frequent issue they tackled was the potential market launch of a new product. Every spring term we held a cocktail party celebration to honor the CEOs of E-Lab companies, inviting all of the earlier years' CEOs to attend as well, along with key members of the Greater Boston legal and VC community. This quickly built up our reputation and network relationships with the outside world linked to entrepreneurship. When new MIT organizations were created, such as the **VENTURE MENTORING SERVICE**, **DESHPANDE CENTER**, **LEGATUM CENTER**, and the **MEDIA LAB**'s entrepreneurship classes (more recently adding the **SANDBOX FUND** and program), we also invited their leaders to join our party, and organized periodic meetings with them to cooperate across campus. This welcoming behavior, strengthened through coordinating and collaborative meetings, were the root for building an "MIT entrepreneurial ecosystem" that indeed functions as a true operating system!

MIT Entrepreneurship Center Shareholders Group (2000)
Front row, from left to right: Damodar Ratha, David Morgenthaler, Ronald Kurtz, Alex d'Arbeloff, Bill Porter, Allan Will. Back row: Ron Thomann, Mary Shaefer, Ken Morse, Charles Head, Dean Richard Schmalensee, Lissa Morgenthaler (David's daughter), Ed Roberts, Leon Liebman, Laura Morse (Ken's wife), Simon Johnson, Matt Utterback.

Ken became very active in fundraising from successful alumni entrepreneurs, as well as from companies interested in our development of young entrepreneurs. He formed the **MIT E-CENTER SHAREHOLDERS GROUP**, an assemblage of generous MIT alumni who met periodically to provide advice on directions and priorities of the Center. They also enjoyed learning about and contributing to what we were building and engaging in active conversation, as well as socializing with one another.

Ken's key initiatives included the 1999 launch of the **ENTREPRENEURSHIP DEVELOPMENT PROGRAM (EDP)**, a one-week executive education program aimed at a combination of startup entrepreneurs, academics, and economic development officials from across the globe who wanted to build their own regional or national entrepreneurial economies. The EDP became an essential but informal part of many of the global programs launched by MIT to aid other countries in becoming more innovative, such as the **CAMBRIDGE-MIT INITIATIVE (CMI)** in the U.K., more fully described in Chapter 7. Numerous countries, such as Australia and Scotland, tested the early years of the program and then began creating their own country recruitment, selection, and sponsorship activities. This effort has been continued very effectively by Ken's successor, Bill Aulet. Now we observe annual country-level commitments to sending multiple entrepreneurial candidates to EDP that range from the likes of Scotland, Wales, and Northern Ireland to the United Arab Emirates and Saudi Arabia. Several of these countries have sent upwards of 100 participants to the MIT EDP effort over the years. A typical class includes 120 students, in MIT Sloan's largest classroom, with lecture and workshop participation by many of the MIT entrepreneurship faculty. Recently, the Scottish Development Authority studied the effectiveness of its investment in the EDP and found a 12 to 1 return, one of the highest of any economic development efforts it has supported.

Ken also acted in support of our efforts to recruit new academic faculty for MIT entrepreneurship, at times flying across the country to assure the spouse of a prospective faculty member that additional job opportunities for him or her would be accessible, or that good schools would welcome their young children. Once the additional faculty members began to generate new MIT subjects, Ken and I worked together to avoid scheduling conflicts among the increasing number of educational offerings, and helped communicate to the rest of the MIT student body the new insights into starting businesses that the MIT Sloan School was providing. Organizationally, this was relatively easy at that time, as nearly all of the faculty were members of my academic group, or staff and volunteers of the E-Center, which I led. But as we grew, and as more faculty from other MIT Sloan groups and MIT departments became involved, this process became more complicated.

When the E-Center was offered larger facilities across the street in building E40, Ken surprisingly seemed rather saddened by the prospect of moving. He explained that the little office he would be moving out of had belonged to his father, Richard Morse, founder-CEO of National Research Corporation, which had constructed the original building at 70 Memorial Drive. Ken had even placed his desk in the same spot that his father had occupied!

The new offices, located in MIT E40, right across from the Sloan Building and the Tang Center, quickly filled with cubicles, desks, and filing cabinets. The offices were in a building that contained some MIT interdisciplinary labs, making us seem more hospitable to students walking down from the main campus. The space provided a wonderful home for housing and nurturing a wide array of new entrepreneurship-related clubs and activities. And Ken was helpful in providing them with experienced coaching and guidance. It soon became a tradition for all those student clubs to have their homes in the MIT Entrepreneurship Center. The logistics support gradually advanced into more mentoring for individual students and their teams who were engaging in startup endeavors. Key staff members such as **AUDREY DOBEK-BELL** and **PATRICIA FULIGNI**, and later Assistant Directors such as **MATT UTTERBACK** and **JOSE PACHECO** '94 became increasingly important to E-Center operations.

In 2006, Dean Richard Schmalensee '65 approved the creation of the **ENTREPRENEURSHIP & INNOVATION TRACK (E&I)**, as mentioned in Chapter 3. Suddenly, in addition to our "regular" students with some interest in entrepreneurship, we now had a very different workload of 100–120 new MIT Sloan grad students each year, many of whom were in a dedicated search for personal progress in getting new companies underway. E&I required that we rapidly escalate our course offerings, and devote more direct attention to coaching and mentoring along with formal teaching. And traffic dramatically increased in the E-Center itself. Ken was very encouraging of all of these developments, and designed and led the annual (and continuing) one-week **SILICON VALLEY STUDY TOUR** for the E&I students. Supportive MIT alumni in Silicon Valley VC firms addressed our annual E&I group, and in many cases opened up their investment portfolios—including those still in "stealth mode"—so our visiting students could gain better insights into what was happening in West Coast entrepreneurship.

Bill Aulet

BILL AULET '94 joined the Center in 2006 as an Entrepreneur-in-Residence, having just completed the sale of his third company since graduating from the MIT Sloan Fellows Program. He asked, "Would it be okay if I just hang around and help when I can?" That help was quick in coming. MIT President Susan Hockfield had recently announced the MIT Energy Initiative, spurring new research and teaching across the Institute. Bill proposed creating an Energy Ventures subject that would follow the lines of iTeams, but Bill would identify and recruit faculty energy-research projects from all around MIT as the bases for commercialization assessment. As he began working on that, he realized that in addition to providing the students with more entrepreneurial opportunities, we needed to give them a basic understanding of energy policies and markets. Bill approached Professor **DONALD LESSARD**, an energy guru within the MIT Sloan School, to create the Energy Policy and Management subject, in collaboration with Senior Lecturer **HENRY WEIL** '64, who still teaches a variant of that course today. In implementing those new subjects, Bill undertook several more actions to assure their success. He persuaded Professor **CHARLES COONEY** '67 from the Department of Chemical Engineering to co-sponsor the two subjects, and to cross-list them as ChemE offerings to get more attention from engineering students. Bill and Charlie then arranged for those two classes to be held back-to-back in the same School of Engineering Department classroom. (With this experience as a model, we adopted those practices for many more subjects to enhance the recruitment of mixed classes from Management and the rest of MIT.) A student could, if she wished, sit in the same seat for three hours, twice a week, to get the whole picture of energy venturing opportunities, from concept to practice. Bill also recruited grad students from the Harvard Kennedy School of Government to provide more policy and regulatory inputs to the energy-focused teams.

Not finished with his task, Bill worked with several MIT graduate students to create the Energy Track of the **MIT $100K BUSINESS PLAN COMPETITION**, and then to spin it off as the separate **MIT CLEAN ENERGY PRIZE** competition, raising significant prize funds from both the Massachusetts state government and major utilities. The competition then went nation-wide, receiving U.S. Congress funding for six centers across the United States, ending with a final competition that is still held annually at MIT. Bill co-taught Energy Ventures alongside Senior Lecturers **TOD HYNES** '02, an early alum of the class and now an energy-sector entrepreneur, and **FRANCIS O'SULLIVAN** '04, Director of Research of the MIT Energy Initiative.

In 2009, Bill became Senior Lecturer and the Managing Director of the E-Center, which made him responsible for coordinating our large and increasing array of educational and student "business development" endeavors. The physical center became very overcrowded, with student teams using it as their workspace (with ready access to mentor advice) or just to hang around with kindred folk. But despite constraints, Bill had limitless ideas for launching new subjects, new projects, and new approaches to helping the students. Bill was especially interested in advancing the capabilities of the Center beyond guiding individuals and teams through the introductory phase of entrepreneurship. He did this in several ways. First, he started adding new subjects, for which he brought in high-performance entrepreneurs as co-teachers. Examples listed in the Appendix include Building the Entrepreneurial Firm: Advanced Tools and Techniques, Scaling Entrepreneurial Ventures, and Entrepreneurial Sales. Then he produced programming to intensify the student's year of entrepreneurship projects, starting with **t = 0**, held the very first weekend of the fall semester. He encouraged the addition of various **"HACKATHONS"** (medicine, the arts, MIT!)

that engaged students in quickly formed groups on different challenges, and converted the January Independent Activities Period for potential entrepreneurs into **MIT FUSE**, a three-and-a-half-week set of "hard work, not home work" sessions to engage students in a micro-accelerator.

Then Bill developed a summer-long real accelerator to encourage, teach, and coach carefully selected MIT student teams through the pre-launch stage of their startup ideas. Bill started the MIT accelerator in a pilot mode during 2010 and 2011, then fully initiated it in the summer of 2012 as the **FOUNDERS' SKILLS ACCELERATOR (FSA)**. Over 100 teams applied from across the Institute, even though there was only space available for eight. At the last minute, Senior Deputy Dean **S.P. KOTHARI** provided additional space for over 40 teams who had not been accepted into the FSA, who then organized themselves into the **BEEHIVE COOPERATIVE** in an empty floor of the Sloan School's Building E52 while the building was undergoing gut renovation. Bill provided periodic visits and visitors to the BeeHive group, sometimes in joint sessions with the FSA teams. In 2013, the MIT accelerator became **GLOBAL FSA**, with support from the MIT-Skolkovo program and with the addition of a couple of Russian student teams. Beginning in 2014, Jack Goss and the Anne Goss Foundation became the primary sponsors of this MIT summer accelerator. In 2016, the program was renamed **DELTA V**, and included 17 teams, a doubling from its formal beginning four years earlier.

With constant improvement over the years, the underlying model has remained the same. Participant teams receive entrepreneurship training and direct advising from coaches and mentors, including mock board reviews. Each team can "earn" up to $20,000 in equity-free milestone payments as venture funding, plus office space and access to prototyping tools and lab space as needed. The MIT

delta v teams on Demo Day, September 2019

Massachusetts Governor Charlie Baker, speaking at Demo Day 2016

students in those teams (some non-MIT team members are permitted) also received a $2,000 monthly fellowship for three months from the Goss Foundation (now from general Trust Center funds after the end of that grant). At "Demo Day" during the first week of September, the teams "show their wares" at a big function in MIT's Kresge Auditorium, with a very large student attendance from across MIT, as well as many entrepreneur and venture capital guests. In 2016, the Demo Day teams then for the first time traveled to New York and San Francisco to present to alumni and other groups, now an annual part of delta v "graduation" events. **TRISH COTTER**, the Center's Executive Director, is now responsible for the delta v program, including its Demo Day.

Our accelerator program has provided special opportunities for faculty from across the Institute to engage with the entrepreneurial activities of some of their best students. Many School of Engineering faculty, and recently increasing numbers of School of Science faculty, come by to check in on their current or former students, who often serve as primary mechanisms for bringing faculty research to the market. Bill Aulet has devoted significant time and attention to nurturing these contacts and relationships as part of our dedication to making the E-Center available and effective across the MIT campus.

The latest addition to our accelerator programming is the **MIT NYC SUMMER STARTUP STUDIO**, which in 2017 admitted seven MIT student-led teams for three months. It focused on four industries that are particularly strong in New York City: Media, creative arts, real estate, and "FinTech". Many New York City-area alumni and friends were recruited as mentors for the teams in this pilot activity. This additional accelerator program contributed to graduating a total of 27 delta v teams in September 2019, the largest number to date.

As mentioned above, Bill continues to successfully run the **ENTREPRENEURSHIP DEVELOPMENT PROGRAM**, and has played a key role in the creation and continuing operation of **REAP**, which is discussed in Chapter 7.

In 2014, Bill and I also came up with a new program idea to spread entrepreneurship education and practice into multiple areas of MIT. Called the **PRACTICE LEADERS PROGRAM**, it was funded for its first three years through a partnership with the **CELIA LIPTON FARRIS AND VICTOR W. FARRIS FOUNDATION**. Graduate student research assistant "practice leaders" are recruited from across MIT to assist in organizing exposure and stimulus programs in multiple sectors of potential entrepreneurial practice. They bring in speakers, help create hackathons, and assist faculty in developing new subjects related to the creative arts, healthcare, energy and water, financial technology, and educational technology. These efforts have had great success in engaging students and faculty who were previously untouched by entrepreneurship, and in making permanent additions to MIT's scope of entrepreneurship.

The most recent addition to our programming has been the addition of the **SUMMER ENTREPRENEURSHIP INTERNSHIP PROGRAM**, generously funded by

BOB POZEN, MIT Sloan Senior Lecturer. It provides summer stipends for MIT students wanting to work at a startup firm for the summer, helping those startups to employ talented young people and providing the students with work experience in new firms. Our 2015 research data (see Chapter 6) show that early employment at a startup significantly increases the likelihood of later entrepreneurship by MIT students.

Certainly, Bill has had lots of help to do all of this, and has received major contributions from numerous MIT Sloan faculty and their new counterparts from the School of Engineering and the Media Lab. Bill recruited a series of Entrepreneurs-in-Residence (EIRs), who Bill over-modestly says "have raised the bar from the standards that I met when I arrived in 2006"! That key crop of experienced EIRs includes **ELAINE CHEN**, **TRISH COTTER** (now also Executive Director of the Trust Center), **KIT HICKEY**, **NICK MEYER**, and **WILL SANCHEZ**, all of whom are mentioned in Chapter 3's Appendix, as well as **SORIN GRAMA**, who works with the MIT Legatum Center, which is discussed in Chapter 5. Earlier, **DONNA LEVIN** was an EIR, who became a Senior Lecturer and ran the E&I Track during my sabbatical leave in 2017. All have added to the teaching resources, done heavy lifting in counseling students, and taken on different managerial responsibilities within the Center. To handle the growing programmatic responsibilities and far more students, Bill has added some key staff, who include **TOMMY LONG** (Operations) and **GREG WYMER** (Marketing and Communications). Bill also brought in the **BOSTON UNIVERSITY LAW CLINIC** to provide both general and targeted legal input for the entrepreneurial students, completely free of charge. Every one of these additions has dramatically enhanced the teaching, coaching and operational capacities of the Trust Center.

But Bill has made another very substantial contribution to entrepreneurial education and practice, by writing the book *Disciplined Entrepreneurship,* and its recent companion *Disciplined Entrepreneurship Workbook.* They have sold like hotcakes into the entrepreneurship programs of many universities that would consider themselves as our competitors. And they have now been translated into two dozen languages to aid the global market's thirst for building innovation-driven economies. And Bill, in cooperation with other faculty and staff, has created a large series of videos on entrepreneurship, distributed for free to the world by edX and MITx, MIT's

Bill's E-Center logo

two different online video education endeavors. The audience for these educational videos, including those reached by the **MIT GLOBAL ENTREPRENEURSHIP BOOTCAMP**, has grown toward 1,000,000 as of September 2019.

Shortly after becoming the Managing Director of the E-Center, Bill introduced a new logo for the Center. It was a pirate ship, with a quote from Steve Jobs underneath: "I'd rather be a pirate than join the British Navy!" Bill explains how he interprets that logo:

> Some say, "Entrepreneurs just need to be like pirates!" I say, "No, no! It's not at all about *being* a pirate, but rather *having the spirit* of one. And at the same time, *having the discipline* of Navy Seal Team 6!" An entrepreneur is doing something new. But the process has been done before. And that process is where the discipline comes in. We can certainly teach the disciplined process, and the students can learn from it.

In recognition of all he has contributed to MIT entrepreneurship and his continuing outstanding leadership, Bill Aulet was promoted to **PROFESSOR OF THE PRACTICE** in 2017.

THE MARTIN TRUST CENTER FOR MIT ENTREPRENEURSHIP

In 2011, thanks to a gift from MIT Sloan alum **MARTIN TRUST** '58 and his wife **DINA**, the E-Center was extensively expanded and renovated, and re-dedicated as the Martin Trust Center for MIT Entrepreneurship, with even stronger enrichment of its cross-campus mission and offering vital steps forward for MIT entrepreneurship. **DAVID SCHMITTLEIN**, the John C Head III Dean of MIT Sloan, called the new Trust Center "the heart and home of entrepreneurship" at the Institute.

Martin and Dina Trust (middle), framed by Dean David Schmittlein and MIT President Susan Hockfield

Martin Trust provides excellent perspectives on why MIT entrepreneurship became the target of his and his wife Dina's philanthropy:

> The MIT Sloan experience taught me what was possible and got my entrepreneurial spirit going. It was all about never closing myself off to an opportunity for knowledge or growth. And I learned that at MIT. I carried with me an awareness of the power of new technologies and the importance of taking advantage of them in a well thought out, strategic way. Around 1970, I started a small company of my own, which supplied garment companies in the United States with material I imported from my network in the Far East. The rest, as they say, is history.
>
> One of the many reasons I became a benefactor of the Trust Center for MIT Entrepreneurship is the impressive quality of the young people who come to the Center to learn how to start companies. I like the increased variety of the students we are attracting, some even from art schools who are coming up with business ideas related to the art world. Also, more students are approaching entrepreneurship from a philanthropic point of view. They see a need for something in the world and want to create a product and company to address that need.[1]

Bill Aulet worked closely with design and construction teams from MIT to "create an ideal physical location for students to explore and advance their entrepreneurship capabilities. . . . The goal was to provide 'distinct neighborhoods' for students to do different types of work and enable the conversations, teamwork, debate, and creative exchanges necessary for entrepreneurial innovation." The new Trust Center has a total area of 7,200 square feet, includes ten conference rooms, and can accommodate the 1,000 people who show up on a typical weekday (and easily handles the 300 who come on weekends)!

The Center's expanded space has enabled the addition of **PROTOWORKS**, our own maker space, which is part of MIT's *Project Manus*, headed by Professor **MARTIN CULPEPPER** '97 of Mechanical Engineering, who now co-teaches Introduction to Making at MIT with Bill Aulet.

Program expansion and new program creation continue apace, limited only by the primary constraints of funding and space. But the engaged student and faculty population in MIT entrepreneurship remarkably grows rapidly.

REFERENCES AND NOTES

1. Interview by Michelle Choate on May 6, 2016.

5

Growing the "MIT Entrepreneurial Ecosystem"

What has been called the "MIT entrepreneurial ecosystem" is the subject of esteem—and replication efforts—the world over. It's not uncommon for representatives from countries around the globe to visit the campus and consult with the Institute's entrepreneurial brain trust to ascertain the secrets behind this *ne plus ultra* of innovation, collaboration, and commercialization. For a decade after the founding of the Entrepreneurship Center, this ecosystem was rather lean. The **MIT ENTREPRENEURSHIP CENTER** was being supplemented by just the **MIT ENTERPRISE FORUM** and the **TECHNOLOGY LICENSING OFFICE** in aiding and abetting student and alumni entrepreneurial efforts. These were joined at the outset in 1990 by the **MIT $10K BUSINESS PLAN COMPETITION**. Beginning in 1996, the ecosystem began to change as discussions started about new organizations dedicated to encouraging entrepreneurs. But these new MIT organizations did not come into being until the year 2000, when a flurry of activity was underway.

The newer MIT entrepreneur-focused organizations are introduced below, in order of their founding. Some student clubs were started at or soon after the beginning of the E-Center, and I discuss them and their roles later in this chapter.

THE VENTURE MENTORING SERVICE

David Staelin

Before the **VENTURE MENTORING SERVICE (VMS)** came into being in the year 2000, the concept had been in active discussion from at least November 1996, pushed primarily by Electrical Engineering professor **DAVID STAELIN** '60, the true "academic entrepreneur" behind VMS. (My E-Center files contain a one-inch thick folder of notes, memos, and meeting reports, all prior to the 2000 launch of the VMS, from which I have assembled this background.) Staelin talked to many key players at MIT and set up several small group meetings, getting tacit approval for establishing VMS from **CHARLES VEST** (MIT president), **JOEL MOSES** '67 (Provost), and others in Engineering and Sloan. **KEN MORSE**, the E-Center Managing Director, and **EDWARD CRAWLEY** '76, a professor of Aero-Astro, were asked to develop the proposal further. In Staelin's memo of February 6, 1997, he laid out very clear principles that have also guided the MIT Entrepreneurship Center and its successor, the Martin Trust Center for MIT Entrepreneurship:

> I believe that . . . MIT can promote more successful spinoff ventures through increased offers of competent financially-disinterested mentoring . . . [and] that the only form of MIT investment in new startups should be our traditional transfer of technology rights through the MIT Technology Licensing Office. Four of the more important concerns [if MIT provided financial support] are: (1) The unhappy unfunded MIT entrepreneur; (2) the unhappy MIT competitor to a funded entrepreneur; (3) investment quality assurance; and (4) the business-versus-education nature of the activity.

Professor Staelin also expressed concerns about the need to avoid conflicts of interest by mentor investment in or compensation by the startups they were helping. Later memos were co-authored by Staelin, Crawley, and Morse in 1998 to try to move things along.

The recommended structure for VMS that came from detailed discussions and further meetings was that it would be physically located within the E-Center, with an independent Director. Both the Director and VMS itself would report to the Provost, who would provide or help raise the needed operating funds. By spring 1999, the initial funding was provided by substantial gifts from Professor Staelin and alumnus **ALEXANDER DINGEE** '52, both of whom were successful serial entrepreneurs. (**RAYMOND** '57 and **MARIA STATA** later provided significant funds for VMS, with further gifts from many others including **ROMAN LUBYNSKY** '89.) Dingee was designated to become the initial Director of VMS. As these discussions continued, I became concerned that the mentoring process would frequently get mentors and their primarily student "clients" into funding discussions with outside angel investors and venture capital firms. I worried that

AUTHOR'S NOTE

I don't know if Staelin's views were affected by MIT's short-lived experiment, the MIT Development Foundation (MDF). MDF accepted corporate donations for its capital base in 1972 and made only two failed investments in startups associated with MIT faculty members. In a quirk of fate, the residual funds were eventually turned into a small endowment fund for the MIT Entrepreneurship Center.

Alexander Dingee

Sherwin Greenblatt

the operation of VMS within the E-Center would bring us too close to "the money flow", and lead us away from our dedicated educational and conflicts-free role. So, Ken and I decided that we would prefer that VMS be physically separate from us, and eventually the Provost provided space in the main MIT buildings.

Dingee ran VMS during its first three years, successfully launching coaching for MIT students, staff, and local alumni. He also began the difficult process of building a cadre of mentors, most of them alumni, but many without entrepreneurial experience. In 2002, **SHERWIN GREENBLATT** '62 joined VMS as a mentor, and a year later became its Director. Sherwin had been Amar Bose's grad student, with whom Amar started Bose Corporation. After several years at Bose, Sherwin became President of that exceptional firm. Aside from a leave of absence for Sherwin to serve as the temporary MIT Executive Vice President, he has led the growth and development of VMS up to the present. Sherwin comments, "VMS will assist any of its prospective clientele who come in with an idea, a passionate desire to build it into a company, and whose idea does not violate the laws of physics or of the United States!" (And he adds that numerous initial ideas have violated one or the other.)

Further clarifying how VMS acts, Sherwin explains:

> The idea is that an entrepreneur and a mentor meet as long as is needed and as often as seems to help. It doesn't take the place of classes or anything else, but those things are offered elsewhere at MIT. ... As we developed our model, one of the important changes we made is that we now mentor in teams of two or even three mentors for a single entrepreneur, with or without her or his teammates.... And now we have close to 250 active "cases" and around 160 mentors serving them. So, we've become a key part of the so-called MIT entrepreneurial ecosystem.[1]

In 2007, the MIT Entrepreneurship Center awarded the **ADOLF F. MONOSSON AWARD FOR VENTURE MENTORING** to David Staelin, Sherwin Greenblatt, Alex Dingee, and the entire operating staff of VMS to honor their distinguished support of MIT entrepreneurs.

THE MEDIA LAB VENTURES PROGRAM

Professor **ALEXANDER "SANDY" PENTLAND** '82 started his Development Ventures subject in 2000, the first of what eventually became a substantial series of entrepreneurship offerings covering "media technology". About six years later, Sandy created his second subject, Media Lab Ventures. His newest venture classes are Imaging Ventures and Revolutionary Ventures, for which additional MIT faculty members also co-teach. Sandy points out:

> People who present in these classes provide inputs from broad areas of technology. And the other persons who present are former students who were in those seats a couple of years ago.
>
> We don't have a syllabus for any of my entrepreneurship classes, and we don't teach, full stop. We give people opportunities to learn and to network, to find opportunities and to practice pitching and developing their idea. It's a jump-in-and-learn type of thing. Instead of helping my students to turn an idea into a plan, I encourage them to find a general direction they want to take, get inspired about something, and network around with their classmates and anyone else to find the people they want to work with.[2]

Both Professor Pentland and his "right-hand man" of years, **JOOST BONSEN** '90, are described in the Appendix section on Engineering faculty.

THE BIOMEDICAL ENTERPRISE PROGRAM (BEP)

In 2001, a number of MIT biomedical faculty began working with several MIT Sloan faculty to solve what they jointly perceived as a vital need and opportunity: How might bio-scientists increase the commercialization of the numerous life-saving and life-enhancing ideas coming from their labs? Professors **MARTHA GRAY** '81 and **ANTHONY SINSKEY** '67 and several bio colleagues teamed up with Professors **TOM ALLEN** '63 and **JIM UTTERBACK** '69 and others from MIT Sloan, aided by MIT senior research scientist **STAN FINKELSTEIN** '71, an MD who had also served in the Sloan School, to propose the **MIT-HARVARD HEALTH SCIENCES & TECHNOLOGY (HST) BIOMEDICAL ENTERPRISE PROGRAM**. The two-year joint degree program required working towards two accelerated master's degrees, one through the **MIT MANAGEMENT OF TECHNOLOGY PROGRAM (MOT)** and the other through a planned new accelerated biotechnology program. Several classes were admitted and graduated, and some of the core subjects are still taught, but BEP itself died, struggling against the very different cultures that were dominant at MIT in contrast to the Harvard Medical School.

THE DESHPANDE CENTER

MIT President Charles Vest announced the formation of the **DESHPANDE CENTER FOR TECHNOLOGICAL INNOVATION** in 2002. It was funded by the magnanimous gift of $20 million from **JAISHREE** and **GURARAJ "DESH" DESHPANDE**, who have been giving back to society from the benefits they have accrued from successful entrepreneuring. Their donation provides internal funds for MIT faculty whose research proposals have been evaluated as having a high potential for commercialization. (Over the years since the founding of the Deshpande Center, many others have added their financial support, including **BRIT D'ARBELOFF** '61 and **MARK GORENBERG** '76.)

Jaishree and Guraraj "Desh" Deshpande

ALEX D'ARBELOFF '49, Chairman of the MIT Corporation and co-founder/CEO of **TERADYNE CORPORATION**, was instrumental in evolving this concept in partnership with Desh Deshpande, a successful serial entrepreneur, and his wife Jaishree. D'Arbeloff and Deshpande were in every sense the entrepreneurial co-founders of the Deshpande Center. Professor **CHARLES COONEY** '67, the initial Faculty Director, adds perspective on the Deshpande Center mission: "Reducing the disconnect between academia and the marketplace is an exciting opportunity that promises to accelerate the rate that technological innovation reaches communities well beyond the boundaries of MIT".

In fact, six weeks prior to President Vest's announcement, d'Arbeloff, at that time also Professor of the Practice at MIT Sloan, arranged for Professor Cooney and I to meet to discuss how the E-Center might collaborate to assist in the Deshpande Center's mission. Professor Cooney and I hit it off well, and we came up with the idea for what became the iTeams (Innovation Teams) subject. It would pull together student teams from Engineering and Sloan to work on commercialization assessment of real MIT research projects that would be progressing under Deshpande Center support. Each final team report would include a course of action recommended by the students for the project they were working on. The alternatives would be a startup proposal, licensing to industry via the TLO, further research in the lab, or cancellation, as well as key next technical, market, and commercial milestones. The iTeams classes are actually taught in the heart of the MIT campus in the Stata Center. By making the class physically accessible to students in science and engineering as well as to MIT Sloan students, we end up with a very balanced class. And that balance forces a very different conversation. It allows technical students to learn about management, but also allows management students to learn to respect but not be afraid of technology. Cooney comments further: "After a decade plus, we have had over 600 students taking this course, and it has been very successful for the Deshpande Center and for the students." (The E-Center's Energy Ventures, Healthcare Ventures, Linked-Data Ventures, and similar subjects have followed the iTeams approach.) The cooperation of the E-Center with the Deshpande

Center was included in the formal MIT press release on the Deshpande Center's initiation.

Professor Cooney observes:

> Although I reported to the Dean of Engineering, and Ed's Entrepreneurship Center reported to the Dean of Sloan, both of us were pan-Institute in our attitudes and aspirations for our organizations. We also shared enthusiasm for fostering ever more entrepreneurship at MIT, something that was not typical among our colleagues. I remember a dinner meeting in the early '80s among seven of us, all of whom had started several companies – Dave Staelin, Phil Sharp, Bob Langer, Yossi Sheffie from Civil Engineering, and a couple of others. We discussed that most faculty usually kept to themselves this fact of starting firms. Academic entrepreneurship wasn't celebrated at MIT or elsewhere; it was not socially acceptable. We realized that we needed to do things that would broadly acknowledge and stimulate this kind of behavior. Creating the Deshpande Center was a great step forward in the direction begun by the founding of the MIT Entrepreneurship Center.

Much more information on the entrepreneurial activities of Professors Cooney, Langer, and Sharp is featured in Chapter 8, Life Sciences and Biotechnology.

Cooney continues:

> At the outset of the Center, we decided upon two types of faculty grants, so-called "Ignition Grants" of $50,000 to explore a concept, and the somewhat more generous "Innovation Grants", later on of $250,000, to support research that was judged to be translational in moving the concept into more of a developmental stage. Our grants were short-term and targeted at de-risking a later outside investment that might be the beginning of a new firm. We hoped to bring a faculty research project to a stage that made it interesting to outside venture investors. We did not fund companies, nor could I get involved in any of those resulting companies.... We supplemented our usual MIT faculty research evaluators with friendly entrepreneurs and venture capitalists to help judge the commercial potential. And they also helped as needed in coaching faculty about directions of their research that might enhance the chances of success.[3]

LEON SANDLER, who later became Executive Director of the Deshpande Center, makes a strong point about the second mission of the center, which is to educate faculty and students on the process of how to commercialize technologies: "That education happens by getting them actively engaged in doing that commercialization", Leon explains.

> We do active mentoring throughout every project, frequently working with the Venture Mentoring Service and the Trust Center in providing that help.... I call what we do advancing the research through "proof of product", not just "proof of concept". During our one-to-three-year period of funding, a piece of what we are doing is connecting the academic researchers to the marketplace, to potential customers, to experts who understand the real market requirements. Every market you look at has existing products or solutions. You have to basically come up with something that is much better....
>
> Our job is to actually get the project to the point that it leaves MIT! When one of these projects spins out, it is the PhD, postdoc, or group of them who become the employees of the company. The professor may stay engaged, spending a day a week as private staff, consulting with the company. It is very unusual for the professor to leave MIT to go and do this full time.[4]

In recent years, Leon has worked closely with me to create and implement "student hackathon" class sessions. In each year he has recruited a dozen willing faculty members to provide briefs on ideas they had that might attract student attention. And then mixed student teams from across the Institute organized around each of those ideas to "hack" around the issues and business opportunities that they thought might be worth pursuing. This made our mini-hackathons into effective short-term extensions of the iTeams approach.

Leon Sandler

Desh Deshpande has gone on from this initial entity at MIT to create comparable entrepreneurship-based non-profit economic development organizations and programs in his native India and then in Lawrence, Massachusetts, the city with the lowest economic status in the state.

THE LEGATUM CENTER

Since its founding in 2007, the **LEGATUM CENTER FOR DEVELOPMENT AND ENTREPRENEURSHIP** has encouraged MIT students to found companies in low-income countries, with the ultimate goal of alleviating poverty and accelerating economic development. The Legatum Center was started and initially developed by **IQBAL QADIR**, and funded primarily by the **LEGATUM FOUNDATION**, the development arm of the Legatum Group, which "allocates capital to projects, people, and ideas that create sustainable prosperity". Qadir later added Mastercard Foundation and others as major donors.

The Legatum Center is now led by Professor **FIONA MURRAY** as Faculty Director, with **GEORGINA CAMPBELL FLATTER** '11 serving as its Executive Director for several years. The two brought about significant shifts in the Legatum Center's activities. Georgina briefly describes them[5]:

> The Legatum Center really is about extending MIT entrepreneurship into emerging and frontier markets. Our customers are MIT students, but in particular those looking to explore developing country markets with the specialized resources, funding, community, and education that they'll need to navigate the more complex and unique challenges of operating in these countries.
>
> Our capstone program at the Legatum Center is our fellowship. Through the fellowship we build a cohort of around 20 students a year and provide them with tuition and a stipend of up to $50,000 a year, in addition to $10,000 of travel and prototyping funds, to build and scale their businesses. More recently, the Legatum Center has been working closely with the Trust Center to broaden our portfolio of programs and to serve students who are currently building businesses in the developing world.

Georgina Campbell Flatter

Georgina has a great phrase that captures the essence of the Legatum Center's mission: "A global hub for entrepreneurial leaders to move ideas to impact in the developing world". She has recently returned home to the U.K.

INITIATIVES OF MIT PRESIDENT SUSAN HOCKFIELD

Nearing the end of her MIT Presidency (2004–2012), **SUSAN HOCKFIELD** became actively engaged in communicating the impact of MIT entrepreneurship upon the world. But she also knew that even more could be done to accelerate the entrepreneurial output of MIT. President Hockfield led a series of small group meetings with faculty to better identify what actions she might encourage for MIT, and perhaps for comparable science-and-technology-based universities around the world. One outcome was that the MIT Entrepreneurship Center and Professor **CLAUDE CANIZARES**, MIT Vice President of Research, co-sponsored the **MIT FACULTY SEMINAR SERIES "FROM IDEAS TO IMPACT: LESSONS FOR COMMERCIALIZATION"**, which was intended to broaden the base of the MIT entrepreneurial ecosystem. Professor Fiona Murray and I organized and led the eight weekly sessions, held from March through May of 2011. The topics announced in President Hockfield's invitation to all ~1,100 MIT faculty members covered the gamut of key issues of potential interest to them. The session speakers included the program leaders of key MIT ecosystem entities as well as highly respected MIT faculty entrepreneurs. Despite all of this, the largest audience at any of the sessions was only 30 faculty members, a disappointing response to the organizers, even though the attendees gave very positive feedback on all the sessions they attended. No further program targeted at faculty members has yet been undertaken.

In late 2011, President Hockfield appointed an MIT faculty committee on the subject of entrepreneurship, the first ever in MIT's history. I interpret this as a continuation of President Hockfield's efforts regarding the importance of entrepreneurship to MIT. The **COMMITTEE ON INNOVATION AND ENTREPRENEURSHIP** had very senior membership from across the MIT faculty, and reported jointly to the Deans of Engineering and Management. Its charge was to report on all aspects of the innovation and entrepreneurship ecosystem, internal and external to MIT, and to recommend proposals to strengthen it in many different specified areas. I headed its subcommittee on education, surveying all MIT faculty teaching any subjects that seemed to be part of entrepreneurship and innovation (E&I) and gathering data on enrollments across the Institute, among other tasks. A number of MIT alumni entrepreneurs and other relevant outsiders were invited to address committee sessions. The committee also gathered data that demonstrated the amazing financial impact that MIT alumni entrepreneurs had on MIT annual fundraising and capital campaigns—the donors clearly were giving back in appreciation of MIT's role in their own experiences and success. Some of the final committee recommendations included establishing an undergraduate minor in Entrepreneurship, and increasing student access to lab and prototype spaces to advance their entrepreneurial projects. It took years for both of these recommendations to eventually be implemented.

In early 2012, President Hockfield appointed a second group, reporting to the Dean of the MIT Graduate School. The **COMMITTEE ON STUDENT ENTREPRENEURSHIP** included nine faculty members and two student representatives, and was concerned largely with policy issues affecting faculty conflict of interest as well as student-faculty relationships in regard to commercialization of MIT technology.

My service on both committees led me to believe that this was a signal turning point in MIT recognition of the importance of E&I to its overall mission. By the time this set of all-encompassing discussions and recommendations took place, it had been 50 years since the first New Enterprises class was taught at MIT!

OTHER INSTITUTIONAL ADDITIONS TO THE ECOSYSTEM

Following the beginning of the MIT Entrepreneurship Center in 1990, other programs have developed throughout MIT that relate in different ways to MIT entrepreneurship. Earliest among these was **THE LEMELSON-MIT PROGRAM**, started in 1994. Its first Chairman was Lester Thurow, then Dean of the MIT Sloan School; the MIT School of Engineering now administers this program.

> The Lemelson-MIT Program promotes the work of individual inventors through annual awards and competitions. It awards an annual $500,000 Lemelson-MIT Prize and a series of graduate and undergraduate Lemelson-MIT National Collegiate Student Prizes in the amounts of $10,000 and $15,000. It also sponsors Lemelson-MIT InvenTeams, which supports high school teams of young inventors, culminating in a EurekaFest competition for "best invention" awards among many high-school teams. The program also funds MIT faculty and students to work on inventions for the developing world.[6]

But the Lemelson Program stops short of encouraging entrepreneurship per se. Jerome Lemelson was a lawyer who focused his attentions on inventions throughout his career, and his Foundation has continued that orientation throughout the world.

Other programs have evolved from their initial foci to increasingly include entrepreneurship as a primary means to achieve their organizational goals. One example is **MIT D-LAB**, started by Lecturer **AMY SMITH** '84 in the Department of Mechanical Engineering to apply engineering talents to solve problems of underdeveloped countries. In recent years, D-Lab students have sought to create entrepreneurial startups that might implement the ideas generated in their classes and project work. One such firm recently won the MIT $100K competition. D-Lab has been aided by many government and foundation grants, plus numerous donors, and especially by **MOHAMMED JAMEEL** '78. Under the leadership of Professor Daniel Frey '97, D-Lab has become a major action-focus for its aspirations that are shared with the Legatum Center as well as the Trust Center.

The **MIT INDUSTRIAL LIAISON PROGRAM (ILP)** has created the **MIT STARTUP EXCHANGE (STEX)** to foster connections between firms started by MIT alumni or faculty, or firms using licensed MIT technology, and the 200 member companies of the ILP. The ILP conducts seminars in different fields of possible common interest, and makes one-on-one introductions between the companies. Numerous ILP member companies have already become customers of, investors in, or alliance-partners with these MIT spinoffs.

In 2012, a magnificent gift from the **TATA FOUNDATION** initiated the **MIT TATA CENTER FOR TECHNOLOGY AND DESIGN**, headed by Professor **CHARLIE FINE** and **ROB STONER**. The program funds about 60 graduate students per year from across MIT to work on technology and entrepreneurial ventures intended to help people in emerging economies. Some projects are by social entrepreneurs interested in starting non-profit organizations, while others are by those looking to start for-profit enterprises. Professor Fine taught the first section of his new

Operations for Entrepreneurs class in Hyderabad, India in 2013 and at MIT the next year.

In 2015, alumnus **SAMUEL TAK LEE** '62 established the **MIT REAL ESTATE ENTREPRENEURSHIP LAB** with a generous donation. Its mission is "to create a new generation of socially responsible entrepreneurs and academics in the fields of architecture, planning, and real estate". In collaboration, the Trust Center has recently added real estate as an interest area to its programming, especially in its recent annual NYC Summer Startup Studio within its delta v efforts.

In 2016, while serving as Dean of the School of Engineering, Professor **IAN WAITZ** initiated the **MIT SANDBOX INNOVATION FUND PROGRAM**, for which he currently serves as Faculty Director. The Fund provides $5,000 in summer seed money to essentially any MIT student who can identify a compelling idea that he or she hopes someday to turn into a company. Up to $25,000 in seed funds can be awarded to those who are selected by a screening board comprised of entrepreneurial, venture capital, and corporate sponsors of the Fund, some of whom also serve as mentors to the students. The Executive Director is **JINANE ABOUNADI** '90, who works closely with the Trust Center as well as VMS in helping Sandbox Fund recipients.

Dean Ian Waitz

Jinane Abounadi

Anantha Chandrakasan, now MIT Dean of Engineering

Professor **ANANTHA CHANDRAKASAN**, previously the department head of Electrical Engineering & Computer Science (EECS) and now Dean of the School of Engineering, began working in 2014 with Bill Aulet and others of the Martin Trust Center to design and pilot **SMART6**. This Bootcamp for Course 6 (EECS) students took place during MIT's month-long January Independent Activities Period (IAP), focused on how to start a new firm. The program is now called **SMARTMIT**, and is available for all MIT students during IAP, a mini-accelerator for those interested in entrepreneurship. Since 2017, SmartMIT has featured guest sessions with numerous MIT faculty and alumni entrepreneurs. Participating students visit several local MIT-alumni young firms, in addition to their regular "input" sessions from MIT entrepreneurship faculty. A special panel session with several women entrepreneurs works on encouraging female participation. In late 2017, 25 SmartMIT undergraduate students traveled to Silicon Valley to broaden their exposure to entrepreneurship by visiting several firms and meeting with founders/CEOs, beginning an annual undergraduate entrepreneurial trek to the West Coast. The program is now co-sponsored by the Schools of Engineering and Management, and the MIT Sandbox Innovation Fund.

Inevitably, as has been done in the School of Architecture & Planning and in EECS, other parts of MIT are beginning to create programs to stimulate entrepreneurship in their fields and for their students. As those new programs grow, in one way or another they become part of the overall MIT entrepreneurial ecosystem.

THE MIT INNOVATION INITIATIVE (MITII)

Vladimer Bulović (above) and Fiona Murray, Co-Directors of MITII

In 2015, President **RAFAEL REIF** announced the **MIT INNOVATION INITIATIVE (MITII)**. At the outset, this MIT-wide program was co-directed by Professors **VLADIMIR BULOVIĆ** and **FIONA MURRAY**, who also were appointed Associate Deans for Innovation in the School of Engineering and the MIT Sloan School of Management, respectively. This elevation of innovation and entrepreneurship programming to the office of the MIT President, and concurrently to the offices of the Deans of the two major MIT Schools, is symbolic of a new level of attention and importance to MIT's mission. MITII is steadily increasing the number of its activities, including the development of a new **LABORATORY FOR INNOVATION SCIENCE AND POLICY**. Direction of **REAP (REGIONAL ENTREPRENEURSHIP ACCELERATION PROGRAM)** was transferred from its initial home in the Martin Trust Center to MITII. (REAP and MITII's other global endeavors are discussed in Chapter 7.)

MITII's most important activity, in my opinion, is to oversee the newly approved **MIT UNDERGRADUATE MINOR IN ENTREPRENEURSHIP AND INNOVATION**, available to all MIT undergrads. In December 2011, Professors Fiona Murray and Scott Stern joined with me in proposing that an undergraduate minor in entrepreneurship be established. We presented an initial integrated educational design, and requested that a working group of faculty from across the Institute be established to advance that design. Five years after that initial proposal, MIT faculty finally approved the E&I minor. Aimed at juniors and seniors, the minor began during 2016 with two required foundational subjects: Innovation: Moving Ideas to Impact and Venture Engineering. **LUIS PEREZ-BREVA** '07 and I, working with Professor **DOUGLAS HART** '85, developed the prototype for Ideas to Impact as part of the MIT-Skolkovo Institute program, discussed further in Chapter 7. Professors Stern and **EUGENE FITZGERALD** '85, in collaboration with Professor of the Practice Bill Aulet, taught the first version of Venture Engineering. Professor **MICHAEL CIMA** has now replaced Professor Bulović, MIT's new "czar" of nanotechnology, as the School of Engineering co-head of MITII.

Prior to this, occasional entrepreneurship seminars and short courses had been offered to undergraduates, although MIT undergraduate students who meet prerequisite requirements have always been able to take graduate subjects. But now a full-blown and highly visible means has been created to aid undergraduates who wish to learn more about entrepreneurship while continuing their major fields of study.

BEING PART OF THE MIT ENTREPRENEURIAL ECOSYSTEM

As the formal organizational parts of the MIT entrepreneurial ecosystem have evolved, we all have devoted more time to coordination. The several leaders meet frequently to discuss common issues and to enhance understanding of the similarities and differences among their programs. One example is that we have, with some exceptions, unified our policies towards avoidance of conflicts of interest by our staffs and by those in advisory and mentoring roles. But collaboration goes beyond coordination, as we frequently engage in cross-referrals and in calling on each other without hesitation to assist in projects or with specific students and/or teams.

An important lesson we all have learned is how much the entrepreneurs emerging from MIT today are in a real sense our "joint product". It clearly would be unreasonable for any single part of this extraordinary system to claim sole credit for any firm that is formed by MIT faculty, staff, or students. Indeed, some entrepreneurs may have participated in delta v or the E&I Track or in another program of the Trust Center, or learned vital lessons from one or more of our myriad classes. Some have received great help from the advisers in the Venture Mentoring Service. Many firms may be based on ideas that were partially funded and helped along by the Deshpande Center or the iTeams classes, or by TLO actions and guidance. Some startups were certainly notably strengthened by the several stages of the MIT $100K, and may even have received prize money from it or from the Clean Energy Prize Competition, both discussed below.

But the strength of the MIT system is that it contains so many parts, with such an intertwining of roles and contributions, that it becomes naïve for any single entity to lay claim on the products of the whole—our MIT entrepreneurs and their new enterprises.

STUDENT CLUBS HAVE CONTRIBUTED ENORMOUSLY TO GROWING MIT ENTREPRENEURSHIP

Over the years, the increasing number and activities of the MIT student clubs linked to entrepreneurship have become key aspects of the MIT entrepreneurship system. A very important aspect of the connections is that all of the major ones that are specific to entrepreneurship are housed and hosted in the Trust Center. This provides them with a common and friendly home, nearby Entrepreneurs-in-Residence (EIRs), experienced staff to answer their many questions, and rooms for meetings and work. Many of the student leaders "hang out" in the Center, creating connections among one another, and not only with the members of individual clubs.

All of the now vibrant club activities started with the **MIT $1K**, a pilot business plan competition that took place in 1989, just before the beginning of the

MIT Entrepreneurship Center. One year later, that competition became the **MIT $10K**, with 54 student teams competing in its first year. This was the "granddaddy" of university business plan competitions, and its model has been followed in academic settings all over the world, as well as in sponsorships by all kinds of private and governmental organizations. In the years after the $10K became a student club, with continuous student leadership, team entries have grown by the hundreds. The first-prize award money has grown as well, first to **$50K** and then in 2006 to **$100K**, when the organization became the **MIT $100K ENTREPRENEURSHIP COMPETITION**. The knowledge and visibility gained by the competitors over the past three decades have helped many of them launch companies, with many successes and of course many more failures! For several years the first prize was the **DAVID** '40 and **LINDSAY MORGENTHALER** $10K award. That was succeeded by a substantial gift by the wife and family of the late **ROBERT GOLDBERG** '65 to raise the first prize at that time to the $50K level, and then to becoming the Grand Prize of $100,000.

AUTHOR'S NOTE

Deliberately omitted from this chapter is a discussion of the "MIT Engine", the first MIT top-down organizational commitment to seeing entrepreneurship as a critical element in solving the world's major problems. That effort was announced at the end of 2016 and launched a few months later with initial fundraising and staffing. I leave that discussion to Chapter 12, which focuses on directions of future growth and development of MIT entrepreneurship.

Over the years, the precise "tracks" within the overall competition, and its several stages, have changed from time to time. In 2017, the three stages became "Pitch", "Accelerate", and "Launch", with different judges and awards at each stage. The cross-MIT participation has grown quickly, and in 2005 the co-heads of the $50K were for the first time one each from Sloan and Engineering. That collaborative leadership has continued since then. The judges at each stage, typically venture capitalists and successful entrepreneurs, have always been generous with their time, advice, and encouragement for the student teams. The general quality of those judges, from even the earliest days, is suggested by list of judges in 1998: **BILL PORTER (E*TRADE), MITCH KAPOR (LOTUS DEVELOPMENT), BILL PODUSKA (PRIME COMPUTER** and **APOLLO COMPUTER)**, and **DAVID MORGENTHALER (MORGENTHALER VENTURES)**. In total, over $300,000 was awarded in the 2017 $100K competitions, with comparable amounts since then. It is important to note that the $100K, similar to all the other MIT entrepreneurship-linked clubs, is entirely student run, without faculty or staff supervision. We have justified faith in the capability of our students to carry forward these activities responsibly and successfully.

The impact of the $100K (and the $1K, $10K, and $50K before that) has been enormous. We do not like to credit any single MIT entity as "birthing" a specific new enterprise, but especially in the early years, when little else existed to attract and help new MIT student-based startups, this "business plan competition" motivated many MIT students (with some non-MIT co-founder add-ons) to bring together their ideas and teams to form the beginnings of a real firm. **BRAD FELD** '87, distinguished entrepreneur, venture capitalist, co-founder of Techstars, and entrepreneurship author, comments:

> The number of ultimately successful companies that went through the $100K just when I was a judge [1993-1997] was remarkable. I ended

> up making later angel investments in a bunch of finalists, including NetGenesis (my first angel investment), abuzz, Thinkfish, and Harmonix. I stopped judging the year Direct Hit and Akamai were finalists (oops!). . . . While I don't know the dollar value generated by $100K companies over the years, my guess is it's greater than $25 billion. . . . Pretty amazng for a business plan competition.[7]

And remember all these were startups by students, not yet even alumni!

A major spinoff of the $100K organization has been the **MIT GLOBAL STARTUP WORKSHOP**, founded in 1998 by students who wanted to teach others about starting and running similar competitions. I discuss this further in Chapter 7, as it is focused on bringing MIT-style entrepreneurship to everyone else worldwide.

The **CLEAN ENERGY PRIZE COMPETITION** is similar in style to the $100K, and was initiated by a few students and Bill Aulet when he was an entrepreneur-in-residence at the E-Center, as mentioned in Chapter 4. The competition started as a track within the $100K, but then became an independent student-run organization. It now has a large campus-wide student club supporting its operations, while engaging students in related clean-energy activities. The competition has received both government and major energy company funding, and quickly became a nationwide competition aided by the U.S. Department of Energy, with

The 2019 Robert P. Goldberg Grand Prize winners of the $100K, with $100K leaders and friends

the finals of the resulting **NATIONAL CLEAN ENERGY PRIZE COMPETITION** held every year at MIT. The total of its nationwide awards is more than $1 million.

The most recent track to spin off from the $100K is the **MIT FINTECH BUSINESS PLAN COMPETITION**, which became an independent competition in 2015.

Within MIT, a number of comparably focused entrepreneurship competitions have been created over the years, offering smaller prize money awards but similar mentoring and judging processes. One example is the **MIT INSTITUTE FOR SOLDIER NANOTECHNOLOGIES "SOLDIER DESIGN COMPETITION"**, launched in 2003, which features a $10,000 first prize. In 2019, the U.S. Air Force initiated a similar program at MIT, including an "accelerator" effort for startup teams focused upon artificial intelligence!

THE MIT VENTURE CAPITAL AND PRIVATE EQUITY CLUB was initially limited to the venture capital interests of students, but expanded its scope over time. It hosts a speaker series throughout the year; arranges student visits to venture capital (VC) and private equity (PE) firms in Boston, New York, and San Francisco; and runs two nationally known and highly regarded major conferences each year, the VC one in the fall and the PE conference in the spring.

Sometimes students move in advance of any club to initiate new areas of entrepreneurial interest. **CATHERINE HALABY** and **KATHLEEN STETSON**, both then second-year MBAs in the class of 2014, worked hard to organize and conduct **HACKING ARTS**. A weekend-long set of events, it attracted more than 200 arts-interested students from MIT and other Boston-area universities to hear arts leaders and startup entrepreneurs in various areas of the arts. The students then grouped themselves into teams to come up with ideas and tentative plans for starting arts-oriented enterprises. The effort led the $100K to add a Creative Arts track to its 2015 competition. Students, related staff, and supportive alumni raised funds to make Hacking Arts an ongoing student-led activity, and Bill Aulet designated a graduate student Practice Leader to work on nurturing creative arts entrepreneurship. That student initiative also led to a creative arts team winning the $100K for the first time! In 2017, Kathleen Stetson, now an alumna, brought Hacking Arts across the country to create Hack Music LA for the Los Angeles Philharmonic Orchestra.

Student entrepreneurship-linked clubs now include many topical areas of interest (e.g., international development, food and agriculture, FinTech, E&I). One club has a very extensive program that focuses on students from China studying at MIT, and even conducts its own business plan competition: **MIT-CHIEF**, the China Innovation and Entrepreneurship Forum! A more complete list of clubs that are connected to the MIT entrepreneurial ecosystem, all serving critical roles, is on page 29 of the 2017 *Annual Report of the Martin Trust Center for MIT Entrepreneurship.*

The direct engagement of students—in the classroom, the labs, student activities, and their own startups—is the underpinning of MIT entrepreneurial success, and the true source of integration of the "MIT entrepreneurial ecosystem".

The best illustration of the ecosystem at work to foster and nurture entrepreneurship is the annual very first class session of the MIT E&I Track's introductory subject. That class is conducted the first week of September in MIT Sloan's Wong Auditorium, permitting all of the admitted E&Is, those still on its Wait List, and other interested MBA students to attend. Of course, I begin with a brief welcoming discussion of the goals, process, and requirements of the E&I Track and its introductory course. But the feature of the session is the next sequence of brief remarks by each of the leaders of all key MIT entrepreneurial ecosystem organizations—the Trust Center, VMS, Deshpande Center, the Media Lab venturing curriculum, Legatum Center, the Sandbox Fund Program—as well as the heads of key student clubs—the $100K, the Clean Energy Prize, the E&I Club. Following Q&A, everyone moves to the large foyer adjacent to the auditorium, where all of the speakers are at their own signed tables to meet and greet interested students, while all are enjoying a sumptuous reception of food and drink. That every ecosystem leader comes together annually for this event with our most entrepreneurially-focused students is strong evidence of what years of strong collaboration and shared goals have produced at MIT.

THE NEIGHBORHOOD: INTERACTIONS AND INTEGRATION

I would be very near-sighted to not observe the ways that MIT's surroundings have changed as the MIT entrepreneurial ecosystem has evolved, and how those changes accelerated the ecosystem's development. As mentioned briefly in Chapter 1, in 2001, startups began to move into the **CAMBRIDGE INNOVATION CENTER (CIC)**, a private shared-space environment located at One Broadway, on the backside of Kendall Square, across from MIT Sloan. The CIC's pioneering entrepreneur and CEO was **TIM ROWE** (MIT Sloan '95), who began by offering small offices on one floor of the MIT-owned building, with rents based on the number of people using the spaces. Over time, Tim began to expand the simple services provided, including adding access to conference rooms when needed, making Wi-Fi available, opening up a small room with a refrigerator for storing brown bag lunches, and soon adding free small goodies like fruit. Tim gradually enhanced the attractiveness of the space, adding a café open in the evenings and hosting periodic social get-togethers with occasional guest speakers. Gradually, lawyers, venture capitalists, and other service providers realized that they would do well to rent space where their clients and prospects were located. The CIC became a magnet for startups and then even for venture-oriented offices of larger firms like Amazon, Facebook, Google, Microsoft, and even pharma giants such as Novartis and Pfizer.

Tim Rowe

Following the observation by MIT Professor Tom Allen that physical closeness generates far more frequent communications, entrepreneurs in the building bumped into each other in the elevators or in the café in the evenings, and built synergistic ties. Entrepreneurial students at MIT could work on their companies at One Broadway and walk over to classes as needed. Venture capitalists based there found it easier to find their way into MIT seminars and to convenient lunch dates in the neighborhood. So the CIC became a key node in the ecosystem feedback network that was rapidly growing at MIT and in its surroundings. The CIC has housed more than 1,000 companies in its original site and nearby buildings.

Similarly, the growing density of entrepreneurs of all types attracted much larger companies to the area, and not just in small offices at One Broadway and nearby. Major IT and pharmaceutical firms settled into Kendall Square, building upward as well as outward, making the area grow into the most intensive entrepreneurial square mile in the world, all integrating into the MIT entrepreneurial ecosystem. And clearly, exemplifying the strong positive feedback that has been underway for a few decades, the MIT entrepreneurial ecosystem was, with MIT itself, the primary sources of magnet strength that has drawn these firms to locate and grow within the Kendall Square surrounds.

WRAPPING UP A HALF-CENTURY OF DEVELOPING ENTREPRENEURSHIP WITHIN MIT

MIT's current entrepreneurship-intensive environment was not a miracle that happened in Cambridge. It started more than 150 years ago with a vision and a set of attitudes that made ideas matter by linking the world of scholarship to the world of work. But it is only during the past 50+ years, and primarily the past 25, that this institution of great research, education, and commitment to idea utilization has built an infrastructure in total support of new enterprise formation and growth. Now its faculty, as well as its students at all levels, both during and after their time spent at MIT, engage in entrepreneurial efforts to a dramatic and visible extent.

Part One of this book has thus far documented:

- the beginnings of MIT entrepreneurship research;
- the activities of early alumni to help others to start new firms;
- the creation of multiple centers to nurture and support student entrepreneurial activities;
- the slow but steady growth of a comprehensive education program to communicate relevant knowledge, both academic and practitioner-based, to all levels of MIT students;
- the diffusion of that supportive environment to large numbers of students to effectively pursue their entrepreneurial aspirations; and
- the accompanying growth of the neighborhood to bring startups, growing firms, and even giant innovation-based corporations into the "MIT entrepreneurial ecosystem".

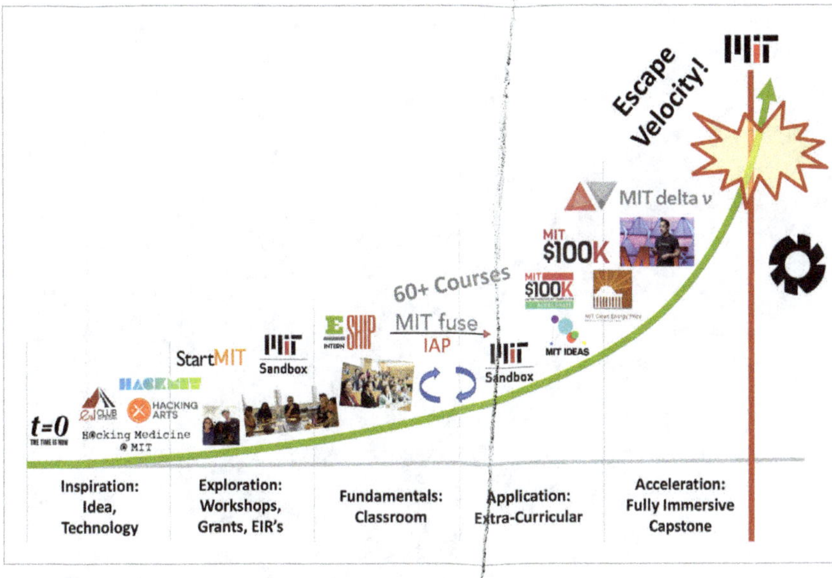

The Martin Trust Center for MIT Entrepreneurship Entrepreneurial Ramp

Note that these achievements would not have been possible without the significant growth of the faculty and staff dedicated to making all of this happen via their own research, their translation of that research into action, and their mentorship of students looking to follow their examples and intent. Nor was this possible without the very significant philanthropic support of the many donors identified primarily in the Acknowledgments at the end of this volume.

In Chapters 6 and 7, I go on to show how MIT organizations, students, and faculty have over time carried their enthusiasm for building entrepreneurial cultures and results outside of MIT. This has created a massive impact on the economy of the United States and the rest of the world, and has given the MIT love of innovation-driven entrepreneurship a global status.

REFERENCES AND NOTES

1. Interview by Michelle Choate on May 2, 2016.
2. Interview by Michelle Choate on May 6, 2016, with some liberties taken in communicating Professor Pentland's message.
3. Interview by Michelle Choate on May 9, 2016.
4. Interview by Michelle Choate on May 6, 2016.
5. From her remarks during the November 12, 2016 "Celebrating a Half-Century of MIT Entrepreneurship".
6. "Lemelson Foundation", *Wikipedia*, accessed on February 21, 2018.
7. Personal communication, November 10, 2017.

Chapters 1 through 5 presented in depth the work done and the organizational outcomes created over the past half-century within MIT. Now, Chapter 6 shows the direct impact that MIT entrepreneurs have had on the United States and the world through their formation and development of new companies. Then I discuss how MIT entrepreneurial people and organizations have moved actively in an amazing number of outreach efforts to broaden their impact on others, throughout the United States (in the latter part of Chapter 6) and the rest of the world (Chapter 7).

6

The Impact of MIT Entrepreneurs

Prior to 2001, primarily anecdotal arguments provided the evidence of how MIT faculty and alumni entrepreneurs had pioneered new industries, built great companies, and generated noteworthy new goods and services, jobs, and economic benefits. My own studies of MIT laboratories and departments were part of these data, which were carefully gathered and analyzed, but always limited to the populations who had worked in those labs and the other organizations we studied.

The Economics Department of BankBoston (now part of Bank of America) published two reports, one in 1989 and the second in 1996, on what it called "MIT-related companies".[1] BankBoston indicated that both of those reports were based on lists of companies provided by MIT. But the definition of "MIT-related" founders was broad: "Founders included an MIT graduate, or a member of its faculty or staff . . . or a spinoff from a major MIT lab . . . or companies based on a licensed MIT technology."[2] And if the companies were still active, then those formed by both living and dead founders were included. Despite this generous inclusiveness, the 1996 BankBoston report was based on only 3,998 then-active identified firms, with a total of 1.1 million employees and annual worldwide sales of $232 billion. Two hundred twenty of those companies were foreign-based, and employed a total of 28,000 people. The report did not provide any information as to how the original MIT listings had been compiled. As I will show below, those numbers were far out of line and dramatically underestimated the impact of MIT entrepreneurs.

OUR FIRST STUDY OF MIT ENTREPRENEURIAL IMPACT

Every 10 years, the MIT Alumni Association surveys all alumni to update its information on addresses and employment. In 2001, it included the question "Have you ever founded a new company?" and received several thousand positive responses, with 23.5% of those surveyed providing answers. By 2003, MIT had decided to move forward with a rigorous in-depth survey of all of those respondents, and I was invited to assist in the development of the survey instrument. My spring term and summer post-doc was **DAVID HSU** '01, who was soon to become an entrepreneurship faculty member at the University of Pennsylvania's Wharton School in September. David is now a tenured full professor of entrepreneurship at Wharton. We were able to strongly influence the MIT questionnaire, but we were not in control of its contents. As the results began coming in, **CHARLES EESLEY** '09, then an incoming entrepreneurship PhD student, joined our team in carrying out the data analyses. Chuck is now a tenured Associate Professor of entrepreneurship at Stanford University. We conservatively included in our study only active companies for which at least one MIT alumnus founder was still alive. We omitted all active companies founded by MIT alumni who were then dead, such as **GENENTECH**, **GILLETTE**, **HEWLETT-PACKARD**, **INTEL**, **RAYTHEON**, and many others. We omitted MIT alumni-founded companies, such as **DIGITAL EQUIPMENT CORPORATION (DEC)**, that had previously been acquired by another firm, even though Ken Olsen was still living. We did not include so-called "MIT-related companies" started by faculty, staff, spinoffs, or licensees if they were not also MIT alumni.

The employment and revenue data submitted by the survey respondents were from 2002 or 2003. We verified and updated them to 2006 numbers by use of Compustat for public companies and Dun & Bradstreet for private firms. Despite all of our explicit omissions, our resulting estimates were strikingly different from the BankBoston numbers.

We estimated that as of 2006, about 25,800 currently active companies had been founded by then-living MIT alumni, employing about 3.3 million people, and generating annual world revenues of nearly $2 trillion, the equivalent of the 11th-largest economy in the world.[3] In addition to the enormous economic impact revealed, the report contained many previously undocumented trends. Those included the rapid increase in the number of "first firms" being formed by alumni over the prior half-century, the steadily declining median age of first-time founders, the significantly increasing percentage of founders who created more than one firm during their lifetime

PROFESSOR EESLEY also continued the comparable research that we started at MIT with Tsinghua University in Beijing on its alumni spinoffs, and has since done similar research in Chile and with several U.S. universities. While at Stanford, Chuck did many analyses of the MIT database, writing numerous papers about entrepreneurial foundings as well as success factors. One satisfying finding was that 42% of all MIT alumni entrepreneurs identified one or more faculty as instrumental in their decisions to become an entrepreneur.

(so-called "serial entrepreneurs"), and many other findings. This was the first-ever comprehensive study of all the entrepreneurial alumni of any university and their economic impact. (I thank William Bonvilian, MIT's Washington D.C. representative, for asking me to carry out these economic analyses to assist MIT President Susan Hockfield, and for putting me in contact with the Kauffman Foundation.) Our study report was published by the Kauffman Foundation, the so-called "Foundation of Entrepreneurship", and it quickly became its highest volume publication, generating a number of follow-up efforts by other universities. The best and quickest follow-up study was done by Charles Eesley soon after he became a faculty member of Stanford University.[4]

OUR MORE RECENT STUDY

The long time lag from the initial 2001 survey identification of MIT alumni entrepreneurs to the final publication of our results in 2009 persuaded us of the need to repeat the MIT study to gain more up-to-date information. In 2014, Professor **FIONA MURRAY** and I, aided by PhD student **DANIEL KIM** '16 (now an Assistant Professor at the Wharton School of UPenn) redesigned and initiated the new study, being even more thorough in our data gathering and analysis, and including backup telephone surveys of non-respondents to the online questionnaire. We published the results promptly the very next year.[5]

The key economic impact results are our estimates that as of 2014, about 30,200 currently active companies have been founded by living MIT alumni (this does not include those founded by non-alumni MIT faculty, staff, lab spinoffs, or technology licensees!), which employ 4.6 million individuals and generate annual global revenues of $1.9 trillion, roughly equivalent in that year to the GDP of the world's 10th-largest economy.

Figure 6-1 (from our report) shows the growth of the number of new companies being formed by MIT alumni over the past 60 years, with a 50% per-decade growth over the past 40 years, including the expected full-decade growth for the 2010s (which had an even higher growth rate for its first four years!).[6] The graph shows that an average of 1,200 new companies per year were started by MIT alumni during the 2000s. This exponential growth is in stark contrast with the continuing decline in the overall U.S. rate of new company formation. And in contrast with most of the MIT alumni companies, most of the nationwide companies are not innovative, growth-oriented firms, but rather what Antoinette Schoar calls "subsistence entrepreneurship".[7]

We found much more evidence of the dramatic rise of MIT entrepreneurism. For example, in the decade of the 1960s, 6.0 per 100 alumni started companies. In the 2010s, that number now appears to have tripled, to 18.0 per 100 alumni becoming entrepreneurs. Overall, 25% of the online survey respondents have been founders or co-founders of their own for-profit firms. A much higher

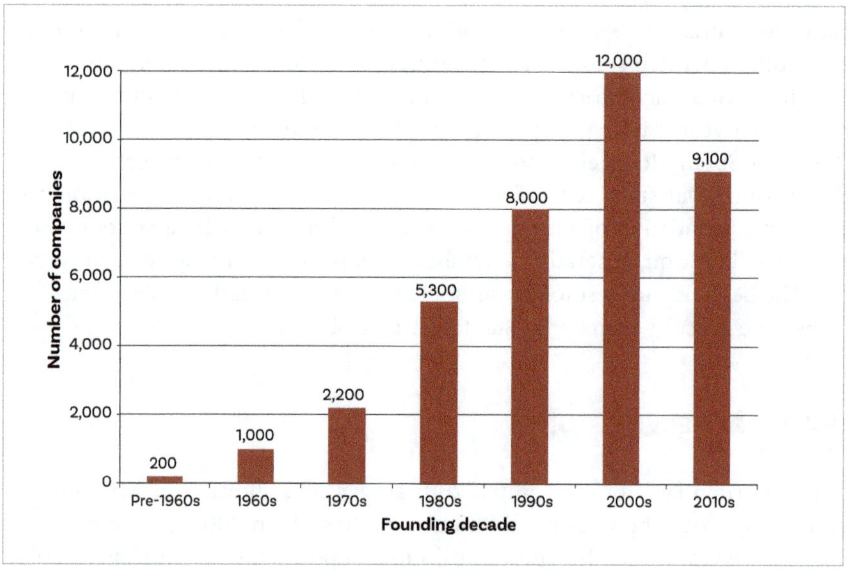

Figure 6-1. **Estimated number of MIT-alumni-founded companies, by founding decade**

NOTE: Data for the 2010 decade are only through April 2014 , when we collected the data.

percentage of the male alumni become entrepreneurs. The telephone backup survey of non-respondents, undertaken to assure that our estimates were reasonable, in fact produced the figure of 35% who had been founders. This is yet another indication that our measures of MIT entrepreneurial impact are likely to be conservative, as all of our estimates are based on the considerably lower online responses.

We do not know for 2019 what might be the resulting numbers of existing companies founded by living MIT alumni, nor of their global employment and revenues. But we do observe the rapidly growing formation rate of first companies and the steady increase of the percentage of earlier MIT entrepreneurs who are creating serial foundings.

Economists might see the exponential rise of MIT-based entrepreneurs as being heavily influenced by the decreased costs associated with forming a technology-oriented company. Rapid prototyping tools, access to low manufacturing costs in China, proliferation of software platforms that simplify development of applications, increased availability of shared office and even lab space—all suggest that a team of entrepreneurs may be able to get underway with less capital. And indeed, investment capital, especially for innovation-driven startups, is also increasingly available. All that is true, but I believe that the primary drivers are the increased prominence of successful entrepreneurs, the increased desire of MIT students to do something on their own, the improved entrepreneurship education available at our and other universities and through online video education, and the increased access to mentoring and encouragement, as we have been providing at MIT.

Our single disappointment arising from our data is the continuing large gap between male and female alumni in their rate of forming new firms, and in the significant average size difference between the firms they have founded. Female entrepreneurship from MIT is growing, but we continue to seek ways of lessening this gender gap.

MIT-alumni founded companies are located all over the world, 23% in foreign countries. While only 8% of MIT undergraduates were from Massachusetts, 31% of the alumni-founded firms are headquartered here, with Cambridge itself boasting 8% of the MIT-alumni entrepreneurship total. California is the second most popular location, hosting 21% of MIT alumni-founded firms. Of course, many MIT alumni are also graduates of other universities, no doubt many of them in California.

Charlie Baker, Governor of the Commonwealth of Massachusetts, extols MIT's contributions:

> Massachusetts, with all the wonderful people and the great organizations we have, is extremely blessed to have MIT as part of our community and our ecosystem. The people who work at MIT, those who do research there, the people who partner with folks in the private sector, are among the most creative and innovative people we have in the Commonwealth. The capacity of MIT and its people year over year to deliver just amazing new things to serve this country and the world is truly remarkable.[8]

The governor went on to mention as examples a number of current Massachusetts companies founded by MIT alumni, including **AKAMAI**, **HUBSPOT**, **MEDITECH**, and **PILLPACK**.

Entrepreneurs are starting at ever-decreasing ages, as shown in Figure 6-2, taken directly from our 2015 report.[9] In the 1960s, the median age of first-time founders from MIT was 38. That has fallen to only 27 during the current decade, in part reflecting what we call "right-side statistical bias", in that most of this decade's graduates who eventually become founders will be older by the time they start their first firms. But on the flip side, we are only counting alumni, and these days many current students, both graduate and undergraduate, who are much younger than the median age shown, are starting firms while still at MIT. They don't yet show up in a roster of MIT alumni. The potential negative side of this is that younger entrepreneurial founders have had far less professional experience on which to build their companies. We do not yet have adequate data to know whether lessened experience is a negative influence on eventual success. (Or does it free up the entrepreneurial mind to be even more creative and daring?)

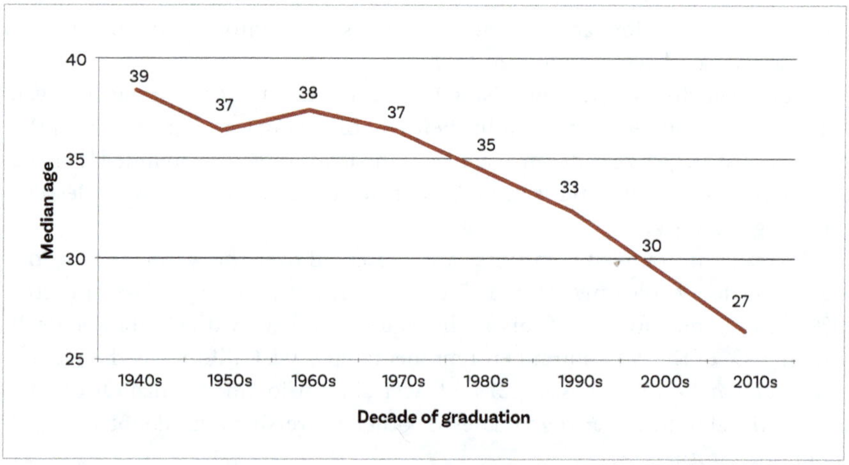

Figure 6-2. Median age of first-time MIT alumni company founders, by decade of graduation, 1940s through April 2014*

*These figures may reflect "right-censoring bias", i.e., an underestimation of the ultimate median age among recent graduates.

The younger median age demonstrates an earlier conviction to start and run an independent organization, but it also indicates that a first-time entrepreneur will have many more years to start second, third, and more companies. That is already confirmed by our data on "serial entrepreneurs". Roughly 40% of the MIT-alumni entrepreneurs in the online survey (and 49% of those in the backup telephone survey) have already launched two or more companies. In this case, the right-side bias leads to an underestimation of how many will eventually become serial founders. The trend data on companies formed as a function of years after earning a degree at MIT suggest to me that about 60% of recent first-time entrepreneurs will eventually become repeat founders. The economic impact of this change is very important, as each entrepreneur becomes more likely to engage in multiple opportunities to generate jobs and revenue outcomes, with far greater cumulative per-person effect. By the way, our company survival data shows that MIT alumni firms last considerably longer than the national average of new companies in the United States.

REMINDER

Our entrepreneurship data exclude MIT alumni-founded firms that have been acquired or closed. Nor do the data include the many vibrant firms founded by MIT alumni who have since died. And they completely omit non-alumni MIT faculty or staff who have started companies, as well as the non-alumni who have left MIT's major laboratories to start companies. Finally, the data do not include the non-alumni entrepreneurs who have licensed technologies from the MIT Technology Licensing Office. Thus, the true impact of entrepreneurial firms arising from MIT is enormous, and still relatively undocumented.

Many more findings from our research amplify the forms of impact arising from MIT entrepreneurship. One of the most fascinating is that 22% of all responding alumni have worked as non-founder employees of early-stage ventures (which we rather strictly defined as less than two years old and with fewer than ten employees!), and this number has grown even more markedly over recent decades. Thirty-eight percent of those "joiners" have already gone on to start their own companies. That percentage is much higher than the startup rate of those who had never worked for an early-stage company. This augurs well for the likelihood of further future increases in founding rates. Perhaps the "quality" experience of working in a startup counters the effect of fewer years of total work. Based on Chuck Eesley's follow-on to our work with his analysis of Stanford alumni, I am sure that a few other great institutions with strong underpinnings of science and technology are making comparable entrepreneurship-based contributions to the world.

In addition to entrepreneurship, this study documents dramatic additional contributions to innovation and company growth: 31% of the responding alumni have been granted patents, and more than half have indicated that they were responsible for product development in firms they had not founded. And none of these survey results even considered the overall contributions of MIT scientists and engineers, at or after MIT, to the advances in their respective fields and to the resulting economic and social contributions worldwide.

MIT BEGINS OUTREACH TO OTHER ENTREPRENEURIAL PROSPECTS

All of us involved in the two MIT studies wrote papers, gave talks, and in general promoted the achievements of MIT alumni in starting companies and affecting regional and national growth and development. The 2009 report was initially released in Washington D.C. sessions arranged by the Kauffman Foundation. My morning presentation was to a National Science Foundation (NSF) task force on strengthening the commercialization of university R&D, followed in the afternoon by a large conclave in a congressional hearing room for all congressional aides in areas related to science and technology. Kauffman was aggressively lobbying for increased attention to and support for entrepreneurship as a driving force for the economy. Susan Hockfield, MIT President at the time of that initial report, addressed public meetings as well as groups of her academic leadership colleagues from other universities, citing the MIT data as examples of how research-and-technology-based universities might broaden their contributions to society. A few years later, when Nobel Prize-winning MIT Professor Phillip Sharp was the outgoing President of the American Association for the Advancement of Science, he used the reported data as part of his presidential address to urge his large audience of academic leaders to broaden the traditional university triumvirate of research, education, and public service to include commercialization of invention and innovation. So, much of MIT and its friends were "talking the talk" of greater emphasis on entrepreneurship.

The MIT Enterprise Forum Initiates the Outreach

In fact, the earliest of MIT entrepreneurship organizations had long been "walking the walk"! In forming the **MIT ENTERPRISE FORUM** in Cambridge and New York in 1978, the charter rules specified that non-MIT alumni were to be welcome members of the local chapters. MIT alumni clubs across the United States followed that pattern, as they too created MIT Enterprise Forum chapters. Each chapter was a nurturing organization, encouraging young founders to present themselves and their ideas and challenges to like-minded MIT and non-MIT individuals to seek criticism and help. By 1985, this led to the nationwide and then global **MIT ENTERPRISE FORUM, INC.**, growing to 28 chapters by 2011, including ten in other countries, with a national coordinating center at MIT to provide guidance. It seemed natural for those enthusiastic about their own entrepreneurial interests to also be enthusiastic about encouraging others, whether from MIT or not.

Vincent Fulmer

Verne Harnish

In 1990, **VINCENT FULMER** '53, then recently retired as MIT Vice President and Secretary of the MIT Corporation, called me with an urgent request. Vince had been one of the strongest supporters of entrepreneurship in the MIT administration, and had co-founded the MIT Enterprise Forum. He asked that I meet immediately with him and **VERNE HARNISH**. Verne had years before founded the Association of Collegiate Entrepreneurs, which had its first conference at MIT in 1984. Now he was proposing a joint venture between MIT, **INC. MAGAZINE** (founded and led by MIT alum **BERNIE GOLDHIRSCH** '61), and Verne's newly formed Young Entrepreneurs Organization (YEO, now renamed EO). **"BIRTHING OF GIANTS"** would be YEO's executive education launchpad for founder-CEOs who were under 30 years old. We agreed and quickly moved forward. The very next year was its first annual program, held at MIT's Endicott House conference center in Dedham, Massachusetts, and co-sponsored by the MIT Enterprise Forum of Cambridge, *Inc. Magazine*, and YEO, with several MIT faculty serving as academic educators, a number of successful entrepreneurs and venture capitalists as practitioner faculty, and me as faculty sponsor. Vince Fulmer participated in all of the sessions for many years, and Verne Harnish was its overall program director and leader for the first 15 years.

In the first year (and in most of the next several), I followed Verne in kicking off the program. MIT faculty, including Professors Edgar Schein, John Van Maanen, Michael Cusumano, Deborah Ancona, and Jack Rockart, among others, conducted many sessions over the years. For that first year, close to 800 entrepreneurs applied and 48 were selected, the housing capacity of Endicott House. That first class, an exemplar of the years that followed, turned out some quite distinguished graduates, albeit at the time they all were young in age and in their entrepreneurial histories. They included **BRAD FELD** '87 (later founder of **TECHSTARS** among others), Alan Trefler (Pegasystems), Ted Leonsis (who became Vice Chair of AOL), and many other later great successes. **PAT MCGOVERN** '59, founder-CEO of **INTERNATIONAL DATA GROUP**, was one of the practitioner speakers.

Verne observes in appreciation:

> In hindsight, I'm convinced that this could only have happened at MIT, because of the overall support and culture and entrepreneurial spirit that permeates everything at the university. MIT took us on when YEO had only 156 members, without concern for risking its reputation, to help nurture young entrepreneurs. Now we have over 14,000 members, and "Birthing of Giants" has been a key building component, with now over 2,000 program graduates.

"Birthing of Giants" was created nine years before the MIT Entrepreneurship Center launched in 1999 its own one-week executive education program, **MIT ENTREPRENEURSHIP DEVELOPMENT PROGRAM (EDP)**, described in Chapter 4. EDP was an early outreach by MIT to the rest of the world, but MIT objectives included helping other universities, regions, and countries to advance their entrepreneurial growth, in addition to aiding individual entrepreneurs and would-be entrepreneurs. Australia and Scotland are among the many countries for which the MIT EDP is an integral part of their overall development strategies. And with larger classroom capacity, MIT EDP has had close to 120 participants every year. To avoid potential conflicts, I and the other MIT faculty members dropped our participation in "Birthing of Giants" when EDP started, but the MIT Enterprise Forum of Cambridge continues its joint sponsorship of the program, which is still held at MIT Endicott House. The YEO and MIT entrepreneurship executive education programs have co-existed since 1999, with little apparent confusion between the two. In 2016, I joined Verne and Vince in celebrating the 25th anniversary of "Birthing of Giants" at MIT. Brad Feld and Alan Trefler, who were Endicott House roommates at the first "Birthing of Giants" session in 1991, also attended the anniversary event.

CREATING INCUBATORS AND ACCELERATORS TO BROADEN AND IMPROVE ENTREPRENEURSHIP

Within MIT, the growing system of classes, clubs, the E-Center, and the evolving ecosystem was providing a strong base to encourage and help young entrepreneurs. But most of the entrepreneurial launches were slow in growing, needed more help in scaling, and had a high failure rate. Early improvement was accomplished internally in part by more attention to mentoring throughout MIT, as well as by offering more advanced coursework. But with the exception of a few other comparable university-based programs, such as at Stanford, these aids were lacking throughout the United States and abroad.

A number of so-called "incubators" did exist, especially during the Internet bubble, but they primarily provided shared office space for multiple startups and occasional mature coaching. The early private incubators sometimes supplied small amounts of initial capital, at what I felt were in exchange for generally outrageous percentages of equity in the firms! My harsh view then was that most of the early stage private incubators were exploiting relatively naïve entrepreneurs. And the public ones that were sponsored by governments at various levels were just generally ineffective. Very selectively, I became an unpaid advisor to two different incubators during the early Internet days to try to help startups, and rejected several others, generally feeling that they were accomplishing little for the startups.

After incubators came "accelerators". Note the difference in terminology. If you are acting to accelerate something, you are trying to speed it up, such as by helping a startup firm develop and grow. Clearly, an accelerator needs at least a systematic training process, and most now have adopted a three-month cycle "per class" of new and/or young firms. I describe here in some depth four accelerators, each different in focus and form from the others, but each one created and led by MIT alumni. As accelerators have been developing rapidly as a tool for building companies, I assume that numerous other ones of which I am not aware have been founded by MIT alumni, especially as adjuncts to venture investing activities.

Bill Aulet and MIT's "delta v" accelerator.[10] If accelerators really can move along early stage entrepreneurial teams, then they ought to have an important role in universities that strive to grow entrepreneurs. In Chapter 4, I described Bill Aulet's creation of what has become MIT's latest effort to cope with the problems of achieving more effective entrepreneurial scale-up. Bill named our internal accelerator "Founders' Skills Accelerator", which then became "Global Founders' Skills Accelerator", until the hip MIT students in the summer 2016 cohort renamed it "**delta v**", in proper MIT fashion. In designing the MIT program, Bill had surveyed already-existing accelerators around the country, both privately and publicly organized. As a result, we developed our own set of policies. We do not take any equity in the teams and companies selected for the three-month summer effort. Instead, all MIT student members of the chosen teams are provided modest stipends from contributed funds to keep them afloat during the summer. In addition, each team is given the possibility of "earning" up to $20,000 in milestone payments for achieving targeted goals in five areas of predefined objectives (set by each team and its multiple coaches, who act as a pseudo-board of directors). A carefully defined program of education is followed with weekly

> **WHY DELTA V?**
> d/dt (velocity) = acceleration, or more simply delta v = a

learning sessions for the entire cohort, as well as weekly practitioner visits. Ten to 12 student teams from across the Institute were selected in the early years from well over 100 team applicants each year, limited by our financial and staff resources. That number increased to about 17 in 2016, thanks to generous funds provided by the Goss Foundation. During the summer of 2017, as mentioned in Chapter 4, an additional seven teams, whose foci were especially relevant to New York City, were invited to participate in the **MIT NYC SUMMER STARTUP STUDIO**. With the growth of delta v, as well as all other Trust Center programs, leadership of our accelerator was turned over to Trish Cotter, MIT Sloan Senior Lecturer and Executive Director of the Trust Center. In the summer of 2019, the total number grew further to twenty at MIT and seven more in New York. All of these teams communicate and celebrate their learnings in a "Demo Day" at the filled Kresge Auditorium in the first week of the new school year. This year they also presented in New York and San Francisco during the early weeks of September

As an educational institution, our focus is more on teaching each of the students how to build successful firms, rather than on the outcomes of their specific companies that are being accelerated. But delta v is not an outreach beyond MIT. We examine next how a number of MIT alumni are moving entrepreneurship to broader outside constituencies, producing important external leveraging.

Brad Feld and Techstars. **BRAD FELD** '87 (mentioned above, as well as in Chapter 11) was a pioneer in identifying the problems of slow new enterprise growth and high failure rate and in trying to solve them. Brad had been an MIT undergrad and then grad student, who combined computer science and manage-ment, focusing heavily on software. He has since become a serial entrepreneur, an active angel investor, a leader of venture capital firms, and a major author of many books on entrepreneurship. Brad's first angel investment was in 1994 in **NETGENESIS**, started by four MIT undergrads. His fourth was in **HARMONIX**, started by two MIT alumni. He did all of this before he entered the field of "accelerating"!

Brad remembers the beginnings of this movement:

> The first real accelerator was Y Combinator, the pioneer in 2005, started down the block from MIT in Kendall Square. It is now very well known in tech entrepreneurship and centered in Silicon Valley. My co-founders and I started the second accelerator, Techstars, one year later in Boulder, Colorado. We ran our first program in 2007, just as an experiment. We had no clue as to whether it was a good idea or not, and our worst-case scenario was we'd make some new friends. We had 10 companies that included 25 co-founders, and about 50 mentors who were mostly entrepreneurs in the Boulder community. Surprisingly, that worked really well, so we decided to do it again.

By the way, we did this with essentially no overhead, so the total cost of doing our first accelerator was $230,000, including the $20,000 investment we made in each company. Now we give the companies $120,000 each. We did exactly the same thing the second year in Boulder, even though lots of places around the country suddenly said, "Hey, we want to do something like that too."

Brad Feld

We now have helped grow companies all over the U.S., but we've started to expand internationally—London, Berlin, Cape Town, Tel Aviv. Also, in places in the U.S., we are helping build the next generation of startup communities, like in Detroit, Chicago, and Austin, versus just being invested in Boston, New York, and the Bay Area. That's both very interesting and motivating to me. We have now funded over 1,200 companies, with a combined asset value of over $10 billion, so we proudly have had a wonderful impact on other entrepreneurs and on society.[11]

As of 2019, the techstars.com website indicated its growth to 10,000 mentors, 300,000 program alumni, and operations in more than 150 countries. Its venture capital fund had $265 million under management that co-invests in the most innovative of Techstars' alumni companies.

John Harthorne and MassChallenge.[12] **JOHN HARTHORNE** '07 was also an accelerator pioneer, but in his case he invented "scale" and created the largest, now global, accelerator, first in Massachusetts, and then he replicated his model in numerous countries. John entered MIT Sloan not sure as to whether he was going to become a consultant or an entrepreneur. Early on, he joined the **MIT GLOBAL STARTUP WORKSHOP** (to be discussed in Chapter 7). In his second year, he headed its efforts to help the rest of the world create effective business plan competitions. John also joined with several engineers in a team that competed and won the MIT $100K. So John was all set to try the entrepreneurial route, except for one major problem: He had $150,000 in educational debt, and because he was married and had a child, he felt a real need to take down that debt before he could proceed responsibly with his life. (The same story is shared by many other entrepreneurial graduates.) John joined a prestigious consulting firm at what became the worst possible time financially—just before the economic crash of 2008. After much suffering with a job he wasn't enjoying, and with a second child on the way, John and another MIT Sloan alum consulting colleague quit together, intending to start a new company, albeit not knowing what it might be!

John Harthorne

Long efforts to come up with an idea finally led to John's recognition that from his MIT experiences, he understood how to attract the best and the brightest into a business plan competition like the MIT $100K, and he also knew how to move ideas like that globally. He and his co-founder networked with countless potential advisors, finding early and excellent guidance from **DESH DESHPANDE**, already engaged in encouraging faculty entrepreneurship via the MIT Deshpande Center. The resulting **MASSCHALLENGE** is a non-profit organization that raises and gives away $1 million in annual cash prizes (and millions in related services) to multiple winners drawn from young firms, with no restrictions in terms of state or country of origin, industry, or even whether it is for-profit or not. MassChallenge takes no equity in any of the companies that it accepts into its four-month accelerator program in Boston's Seaport District. They integrated what they learned from other accelerators into their development process, and expose the selected startups to large numbers of advisors and potential investors. The judging process is by various experts from the Greater Boston entrepreneurial ecosystem. The former governor of Massachusetts, Deval Patrick, became an enthusiastic supporter, and the state provided $100,000 of early grant funds to the organization, as did numerous wealthy individuals, charitable foundations, and major corporations.

DANIEL FEHDER '16 studied MassChallenge for his MIT Sloan doctoral dissertation and found it has had very favorable effects on the performance of its participating firms.

The first program in Boston was run in 2010, and continued there while similar international programs were rolled out, such as **MASSCHALLENGE U.K.** Bringing us up to date, John reports:

> We're now in Boston, London, Israel, Switzerland, and Mexico [in every region operating at a significant scale, with roughly 100 companies annually and a comparable amount of prizes to the winners]. By the end of 2016, we'll have graduated over 1,200 startups. A thousand of them we just surveyed have raised over $1.8 billion of outside capital, generated over $700 million of revenue, and created over 60,000 jobs. We're going to keep growing and adding locations around the world. By 2020, we're committed to be on every populated continent and create these global hubs so that anybody can access free acceleration and support.... We need to create 10,000 companies to assure our desired impact.... I don't care if they make money or are good investments, just as long as they are solving problems for the world."[13]

MASSCHALLENGE has added in the past few years bridging programs toward future full-scale efforts in other countries, full programs in Rhode Island and Texas, and sector programs in HealthTech and FinTech. In early 2019, John Harthorne announced that he was moving on to his next set of challenges, doing direct funding and nurturing to take young firms to even higher growth targets.

Jean Hammond

Jean Hammond and LearnLaunch. While Harthorne has sought to achieve scale of impact, without regard to field, others are highly motivated by the issues faced in specific areas of social need. **JEAN HAMMOND** '86 has focused for years on creating dramatic improvements in education at all levels, from kindergarten to senior citizens, and especially when technology is an enabler. As a serial entrepreneur and long-time angel investor, Jean co-founded **LEARNLAUNCH** to identify and then accelerate the development and growth of promising young firms in educational technology. She has also served as a repeat mentor for Techstars, MassChallenge, and now the MIT delta v accelerator. So, she has experienced the pain and suffering of a large number of early-stage firms, and has learned much that she is now trying to share. LearnLaunch covers multiple phases of company growth.

Jean explains the more complex model of LearnLaunch company development:

> We have two key programs. Like Techstars, a bunch of startups come to us for a boost, which is about three and a half months, and we inject a small amount of equity on entry. As part of that, we've added a target-based milestone for extra funding of additional convertible notes at the three-month and six-month periods after graduation from our initial program.
>
> The human capital it takes to run an accelerator is just extreme, so we do very small numbers. We have about seven firms in the cohort at any time, and we're putting tons of instruction and mentoring resources into those companies. Frankly, I don't think that any company gets very far in three months. If you're going to really grow companies, you're going to get involved with them, connect them to people, stay with them longer, and maybe your accelerator entity itself needs to stick with them longer.
>
> We therefore also created a "breakthrough program" for our later stage ed-tech companies that, instead of working on product-market fit issues, are accelerating their own scale-ups by trying to find distribution partners. And we have become a funding source for our companies that already have substantial revenue, but are having trouble getting to that magical stage of having substantial capital.

Jean pointedly observes:

> Our job in the accelerator side of our operation is to make companies able to obtain funding in the future. We are actually doing a different

Emily Reichert

service in the industry, helping venture capitalists figure out in whom to invest, because some smart people have done hard work on the companies ahead of time. About 30% of the firms that got VC money last year had been to an accelerator at some prior time. That accelerator experience at least provides the selection bias for the venture community to say, "Look here. This one might be more interesting!"[14]

Emily Reichert and Greentown Labs. Jean Hammond's area of concern is education. Dr. **EMILY REICHERT** '12 is worried about the environment and trying to do something about it entrepreneurially. In 2011, MIT alumni founders of four different environmentally-oriented firms came together with the concept of creating a common space for themselves and others like them, creating **GREENTOWN LABS**. Dr. Reichert is the CEO (since 2013) of what she insists is an incubator, indeed the largest Cleantech incubator in North America, but not an accelerator. In my view it is an exciting merger of the two concepts, focused on Cleantech.

Dr. Reichert defends her position:

> We provide a space, resources, and other types of support that Cleantech hardware entrepreneurs need in a warehouse-like setting in Somerville, Massachusetts, adjacent to Cambridge. Companies typically come to us from places like MIT, often having completed accelerator programs like MassChallenge and Techstars. When they join us, they usually have seed funding and are ready to build prototypes and move towards a needed Series A investment round of $5 to $15 million. Especially because we admit companies that are hardware-based, there's not much they can accomplish in three months. They generally stay with us for about two years, and while with us they are growing their team and their company, and figuring out how to turn that bench-scale hardware prototype into a product that can be tested in a real-world environment. We select companies that are not competitive with each other, that fit our culture of collaboration, and that appear to our board to have good potential for success as Cleantech firms. That is our mission. We do not invest funds in them, take no equity, and require only their payment of rents that are rather below nearby alternatives.[15]

"In addition, Greentown now provides equity-free legal, information technology, marketing and sales support."[16] So far this does sound like a classy, focused incubator.

But then Reichert mentions the "network effects" that Greentown Labs provides. Housed during its early life in Somerville in a single 40,000 square foot space with no internal walls, the common elements—Cleantech thrust, manufacturing orientation, mechanical and electrical engineers, a cluster of corporate sponsors who are major energy companies or public utilities, the pool of investors who have put their startup funds into one or more of the Greentown inhabitants—interact and combine to generate substantive benefits to the firms. And Emily adds a comment about Greentown Labs mentoring:

> We do have very specialized mentoring programs in two areas. One is to help companies connect with corporate strategic partners, because that's what our type of startups need. Also, we have mentors around manufacturing issues, because they also are needed by our startups.

To me, those network effects and the specialized mentoring sound like accelerator talk!

In recent years Greentown Labs has expanded dramatically, into three adjacent buildings with more than 100,000 square feet of multi-faceted space. It has hosted more than 200 companies, which have created around 2,800 jobs and raised several hundred million dollars, obviously with much more to come. Greentown Labs "accelerator" (my call) now is creating even greater impact on early-stage manufacturing firms with a sustainability message.

REFERENCES AND NOTES

1. *MIT: The Impact of Innovation,* BankBoston, March 1997.
2. *Ibid.*
3. Edward B. Roberts & Charles E. Eesley, *Entrepreneurial Impact: The Role of MIT,* Kauffman Foundation, February 2009.
4. Charles E. Eesley & William F. Miller, *Impact: Stanford University's Economic Impact via Innovation and Entrepreneurship,* Sequoia Capital and the Kauffman Foundation, October 2012.
5. Edward B. Roberts, Fiona Murray & J. Daniel Kim, *Entrepreneurship and Innovation at MIT: Continuing Global Growth and Impact,* MIT, December 2015.
6. *Id.* at 14.
7. Antoinette Schoar, "The Divide Between Subsistence and Transformational Entrepreneurship", in *Innovation Policy and the Economy* 57–81, University of Chicago Press, 2010.
8. Governor Baker made a video presentation at MIT's entrepreneurship celebration on November 12, 2016.
9. Roberts *et al., op. cit.* at 15.
10. More details are provided in the 2017 *Annual Report of the Martin Trust Center for MIT Entrepreneurship,* entrepreneurship.mit.edu/annual-report/, pp. 14–21.
11. This information is from Brad's discussion at MIT's entrepreneurship celebration on November 12, 2016, supplemented by his interview with Michelle Choate on July 25, 2016, and updated later by personal communication.
12. To watch an exciting video, see John Harthorne's interview with the London StartupGrind at https://www.youtube.com/watch?v=F9iiXMPttyU, accessed on February 23, 2018.
13. John spoke at MIT's entrepreneurship celebration on November 12, 2016, updated by personal communication.
14. Jean's remarks were made at MIT's entrepreneurship celebration on November 12, 2016, updated by personal communication.
15. Emily's remarks are from her discussion at MIT's entrepreneurship celebration on November 12, 2016, updated by personal communication.
16. Zach Winn, "How Greentown Labs became the epicenter of clean tech", *MIT News,* June 25, 2019.

7

MIT Entrepreneurship Goes Global

When I was a graduate student in 1959, in Jay Forrester's new System Dynamics Group, Professor Forrester called us to a staff meeting in which he indicated that an important group of European leaders (the Club of Rome) would be visiting us in the next few days for two weeks of learning. He asked (!!) that we pull together all of our internal memos and copies of our computer models to give them. I was a bit panicked and questioned my boss.

> **ED:** Professor Forrester, if we give them all of our internal materials, won't that help them to catch up with us?
>
> **PROFESSOR FORRESTER:** Ed, you need to understand that at MIT we work very hard to be the leaders of our fields. But then we are responsible to help others to learn what we know. If they catch up with us, it's a sign that we aren't working hard enough!

Over time I have learned that that attitude permeates MIT. Where we lead is an indication that we are obligated to share our insights with others. That practice has dominated our behavior, throughout the MIT entrepreneurial ecosystem, in spreading to the world what we have developed.

MOVING MIT PROGRAMS TO THE WORLD

I already described the early moves of the **MIT ENTERPRISE FORUM (MITEF)** into global chapters, then to serving all of its members as well as worldwide

MIT alumni clubs with satellite broadcasts of major entrepreneurship-related sessions held at MIT's Kresge Auditorium. Its alumni leaders have also entertained visitors from all over the globe who seek to replicate the MITEF concept, and they have even made presentations in many countries on MITEF accomplishments. Similarly, the E-Center's **MIT ENTREPRENEURSHIP DEVELOPMENT PROGRAM** has attracted a large fraction of its 100+ registrants each year since 1999 from abroad, and more importantly, many countries have built their own entrepreneurial growth strategies based on clustered participation in the EDP. Bill Aulet's *Entrepreneurship 101* MITx video series has attracted several hundred thousand viewers from outside of the United States, a number of whom have been encouraged to apply and get admitted as MIT undergraduates or graduate students. The **MIT LEGATUM CENTER**, described in Chapter 5, while primarily internal to MIT with regard to the students it reaches, is wholly external with regard to the countries it seeks to impact. It is responsible for encouraging and helping to fund many MIT students who want to start companies outside of the United States, especially in emerging nations. Our alum Brad Feld's **TECHSTARS** has already spread its wings globally to attract young startups into its accelerating and investing network. And John Harthorne's non-profit accelerator spinoff, the **MASSCHALLENGE**, is going global with a big bang—four countries already and more underway to accelerate their new enterprise formation and impact.

It's hard to keep up with all of the MIT entrepreneurship clubs, classes, and programs that have important global activities. I'll start with those that are worldwide in scope and then examine those targeted to individual countries.

MIT Global Startup Workshop. Student leaders of the then MIT $50K Business Plan Competition decided that they could and should help other students and their universities to replicate on their own campuses the excitement, learning, and outcomes experienced at MIT. They created the MIT Global Startup Workshop, a weekend event held annually, anyplace in the world, but open to attendees from everyplace. In those sessions, MIT students and their invited guest speakers teach others how to organize and run their own student entrepreneurship competitions. The first session was held at MIT in 1998, and then moved over the next four years respectively to Singapore, Spain, Australia, and Italy, and in the 17 years since then to a different country each year, all over the globe. Annual attendance has been as many as 250, and is no longer limited to enthusiastic student would-be organizers, but also includes university faculty and officers, and regional and national economic development officials. No doubt, 60 or more countries now have student startup competitions that flow directly from the MIT $100K. As noted previously, during 2007, John Harthorne headed the Global Startup Workshop, an ongoing MIT student club, carrying his lessons from the activities done that year in Norway into the underlying concepts for the MassChallenge. The MIT $100K (and its $1K, $10K, and $50K predecessors) is truly the "granddaddy" of all university entrepreneurship competitions around the world.

MIT Global Entrepreneurship Lab (G-Lab). As described in the Appendix, Professors Simon Johnson and Richard Locke took our team-project subject, **ENTREPRENEURSHIP LAB (E-LAB)**, and transformed it into a global entrepreneurship working experience for thousands of MIT students. Breaking all kinds of MIT traditions and prohibitions, they created a course that started in the fall, brought student teams into working internships with young firms worldwide during the January MIT Independent Activities Period (IAP), and finished the projects and the course during the spring term. **G-LAB** has given international work experiences to nearly half of the MIT Sloan graduate students for many years. And it has further generated three follow-up country-targeted subjects, with somewhat compressed logistics, in **CHINALAB**, **INDIALAB**, and **ISRAELLAB**, each with specific country learning, travel, and work experiences in young entrepreneurial firms. Professor Yasheng Huang and Dean Jacob Cohen have been instrumental in the development and operation of these latter offerings.

The ChinaLab experience started in a rather unique way. "It occurred to me that our students could help small and medium-sized entrepreneurs in China who otherwise couldn't afford the consulting advice that would make a real difference in their businesses", Professor Huang said.[1] That insight, and Huang's persuasive intervention with Goldman Sachs, led to the global relationships among MIT Sloan's ChinaLab, Kunming's Yunnan University, and Goldman

Project team members of the Fudan-MIT ChinaLab

Sachs's innovative 10,000 Women initiative, which provides business education to women entrepreneurs in developing areas of the world. As a result, in spring 2013, eight MIT Sloan students arrived in a remote corner of China to work with the country's most promising women entrepreneurs, kicking off ChinaLab in its own special manner.

All of these efforts have had impacts in two different directions. Our large number of participating MIT students have become at least somewhat internationalized in their understanding of countries, cultures, people, work, and opportunities, and our students have brought their knowledge and energy to bear in helping many young firms everywhere to grow and prosper. Of course, we have gained increased satisfaction from the many business schools and universities that have adopted these models into their own curricula.

The Regional Entrepreneurship Acceleration Program (REAP). The gradual and then increasingly rapid rise in interest in MIT entrepreneurship brought visitor groups from all around the world to inquire as to what MIT was doing to stimulate entrepreneurship development, and how they might learn from our experiences. Our key faculty members and E-Center leaders were barraged with what almost never was more than a one or few days visit at most. (Due to lack of space and supportive resources, we have had to turn down all but one or two requests each year from colleagues around the world to visit us for a semester or year.) In meetings during 2011, Fiona Murray, Scott Stern, Bill Aulet, and I concluded that we might serve this growing constituency far better and much more efficiently by creating a program to transfer our understandings to various regions of the world. We conceived of **REAP** as a two-year commitment by regional (or large city or small country) teams who would each assemble five "stakeholders" into a dedicated working group: A science and technology-based university as a cornerstone; a government agency focused on economic development; a source of risk capital, public or private; a large corporation interested in stimulating the local economy; and, of course, a representative of the entrepreneurship sector, however meager that sector might be at the outset. (It has been very informing to observe how many parts of the world have great difficulties in even initiating the cross-sector discussions needed to assemble such a group!) They would then, so we hoped, "reap" the benefits of building a more entrepreneurial economy in their regions! Our capacity constraints determined that the program would be limited to not more than eight to ten teams from different parts of the world in each two-years cohort, with four working sessions envisioned during that time period — two at MIT and two at member sites — to work collectively on education and project work for each region. The 2016 "graduating cohort" illustrates the variety of interests that are brought together by REAP: London, Morocco, Moscow, Puerto Rico, Qatar, Singapore, Seoul, and Valencia. And we observe how entrepreneurship commitments build unanticipated conversations, for example, when the Israeli and Saudi teams are recently at adjacent tables.

The four of us co-creators collaborated in kicking off the first of these programs in 2012. Professor Stern (who had done earlier and continuing studies of the factors that influence the development of regional clusters of different industries; e.g., the Cambridge biotechnology cluster) has since taken on the leadership role, with Fiona Murray and Bill Aulet as key contributors, and with Phil Budden adding his foreign service experience to the group. Do note that through REAP we have expanded the concept of an "accelerator" from speeding up and improving the likelihood of success of individual startup teams to doing similar things for regions of the world that seek to develop more and more successful entrepreneurial communities.

In a "scale-up" move, MIT has created the **GLOBAL INNOVATION NETWORK** for regions that have completed the REAP program and are interested in collaborating with regions from their own or other REAP cohorts. Murray and Budden are now also leading a new MIT project subject, **REAPLAB**, based on the G-Lab model, which invites student teams to work with REAP regions. REAP moved administratively in 2016 from the Trust Center to the MIT Innovation Initiative (MITII) as part of MITII's global reach.

An important aside is that the creation of REAP has not lessened the flow of visitor requests for information and help in replicating in some fashion our

Graduates of MIT REAP Cohort 3 in 2017; also pictured are the entire faculty team—Bill Aulet, Scott Stern, Phil Budden, and Fiona Murray—and Sarah Jane Maxted, Executive Director of MIT REAP

"MIT entrepreneurial ecosystem". If anything, it has increased the level of visitor to now being presidents of universities rather than just faculty members, and to city mayors and government officials from both the United States and abroad.

The Venture Mentoring Service (VMS) Global Outreach Training. The MIT VMS organization was also experiencing a similar influx of visitors seeking to learn and possibly replicate the extensive mentoring help that VMS provides to MIT students, staff, and nearby alumni and faculty. About 10 years ago, the Kauffman Foundation approached VMS with encouragement and helpful support grants to engage in outreach education of other institutions, here and abroad. Since then the **VMS GLOBAL OUTREACH TRAINING PROGRAM** trained close to 100 organizations around the world, including about 40 colleges and universities. VMS doesn't do the mentoring but teaches others how to adapt what is done at MIT to their own needs. Sherwin Greenblatt, the VMS Director, smiles: "We're on every continent but Antarctica, and we're looking for opportunities there!"

MIT "COUNTRY PROGRAMS" IN ENTREPRENEURSHIP

Starting with research. Long before the founding of the MIT Entrepreneurship Center, and prior to multiple entrepreneurship classes or clubs, MIT faculty were carrying out research programs aimed at understanding and improving the levels of entrepreneurship and innovation in various countries. These were heavily influenced by the 1972 creation of the **MIT CENTER FOR POLICY ALTERNATIVES (CPA)**, initiated by Professor **HERBERT HOLLOMON** '40, a distinguished scientist with a long career in industry that led to him becoming Assistant Secretary of Commerce for Technology under President John F. Kennedy. (Hollomon's closest colleague and friend in Washington D.C. was MIT Professor Jerome Wiesner, who served as Kennedy's Science Advisor and later became President of MIT.) Hollomon had chaired the Commerce Technical Advisory Board (CTAB), which brought industry, academia, and government together to work on resolving key national issues that significantly involved science and technology, e.g., removing lead from gasoline! I was a member of CTAB from 1967 to 1972, and had become a good friend of Herb. Upon his establishment of the MIT CPA, he and I generated a working partnership in which Herb would identify and "sell" major policy studies for foreign countries and my MTI faculty group (MTI), supplemented by faculty from other MIT departments, would work with him to carry out the needed policy studies and to prepare recommendations for senior country officials. Some of the countries with which we collaborated were India, Brazil, Sweden, and Israel, the latter two being focused on entrepreneurship and innovation.

Herbert Hollomon

The CPA's 1977–1979 project in Israel was sponsored by its Chief Scientist of the Ministry of Industry, General Yitzhak Yaacov, and was led by Herb Hollomon, with Professor Jim Utterback and I carrying the main loads. I launched the first study ever of Israeli high-tech firms, adapting my own U.S. research formats, with on-the-ground support from Professor Baruch Raz of Tel Aviv University.

Israeli entrepreneurship was not yet meaningfully developed. Herb returned from one extensive exploratory trip, annoyed with the attitude that he described as "too many academic entrepreneurs who only want to build their companies up to $1 million in revenues in order to sell out". Those were the same attitudes documented in a detailed study of Cambridge, U.K. entrepreneurs, where many firms were founded out of Cambridge University, but none grew to significant size and impact. Herb said he had met only three "real entrepreneurs": Stef Wertheimer, Uzia Galil, and Efi Arazi. Herb's taste and judgment were excellent: Stef's Israel Carbide (ISCAR) became the first foreign company that Warren Buffett ever purchased, years later, for $7 billion; Uzia Galil built his Elron Industries into the launch-pad for multiple major Israeli corporations, including Elbit and Elscint; and **EFI ARAZI**, an MIT EE alum ('65), created pioneering firms in graphic design and electronic printing, including **SCITEX** (founded in 1968 and identified as the first high-tech firm in Israel) and **ELECTRONICS FOR IMAGING (EFI)**, among others. The Israeli officials respected the rigor of our research and the data we developed. Consequently, we were able to influence a number of early governmental policies for the development of technology-based entrepreneurship.

We shifted next, from 1979 to 1982, to a major CPA effort in Sweden. We did a groundbreaking study of Swedish entrepreneurs, with Professors Dorothy Leonard and Jim Utterback as my collaborators. Swedish entrepreneurs were still small in number, and as we learned, were very different from Sweden's base population. The sponsoring government officials strongly resisted our data, which showed that many of the Swedish founders were immigrants—in what our Swedish sponsors argued was an essentially "immigrant-free society"! Dorothy and I carried out a comparative study then of Boston-area computer entrepreneurs to try to somewhat match the Swedish group. The two country cohorts were nearly opposite in many ways. For example, the Swedish entrepreneurs tended to be solo founders, and seldom even knew more than one other entrepreneur in their country. Boston entrepreneurs formed founding teams, and could readily list several other entrepreneurs with whom they often associated. The aspirations and the growth rates of the two groups were quite different. To impart our recommendations to people of influence in Sweden, we had to carry out a three-day course in the Swedish Royal Academy!

Professors Tom Allen, Harvey Sapolsky, and others joined with Professor Hollomon to do more of these country analyses. But except for the MIT Enterprise Forum and the alumni seminar programs, at that time we were not yet able to demonstrate MIT entrepreneurship programs that worked, and which might be transferred to those countries.

Adding education. The MIT Industrial Liaison Program (ILP) has long been the largest university-industry linkage organization in the world, with some 200 major companies as its subscribers. During all of this time, when we primarily had E&I research at MIT but no programs, the ILP was very active in running seminars and conferences for its U.S. and foreign corporate members, which featured our MIT Sloan faculty group's studies on research, development, technological innovation, and entrepreneurship. Our **MANAGEMENT OF TECHNOLOGICAL INNOVATION (MTI)** group became ILP's single most visited entity at MIT because of the centrality of our research to the R&D heads who were the typical ILP clients. For the most part, they were receptive to our R&D organization and management studies, but skeptical about the relevance to them of the entrepreneurship research, except for the direct corporate venturing projects that covered firms like them. The European and Asian member companies were even more puzzled about technological entrepreneurship, which they saw as a peculiar American phenomenon, but they were of course respectful of MIT research. The ILP somewhat aggressively set up multiple seminar programs in London, Paris, Brussels, and Tokyo to expose our group's research work and findings to its foreign members, so the facts of U.S. and especially MIT-related entrepreneurship were finding outside global audiences. And we accompanied that by establishing at MIT Sloan the **INTERNATIONAL CENTER FOR RESEARCH ON THE MANAGEMENT OF TECHNOLOGY**, jointly run by MTI and the Marketing group, with nine corporate sponsors as active associates — three each from the United States, Europe, and Japan. They became an important diffusion mechanism for our increasing findings on managing innovation and entrepreneurship. One meeting each year of all the members was held at a sponsor's organization, with plant and lab tours of the host company and with many of their key employees invited to participate in our sessions.

Moving into action. When one moves from research, policy making, and education into action, projects become far more complex and favorable outcomes and impact are less certain. I review the various efforts undertaken, more or less in sequence of when they started, to bring MIT's entrepreneurship culture and practices to other countries. Some of these efforts have been more effective than others. Some have essentially failed, demonstrating how difficult it is to bring change to other countries and cultures.

Israel. The CPA project preceded a continuing stream of related efforts in Israel, some individual and some institutional. In 1985, for both personal and professional reasons, I began working with my former student **WALTER WINSHALL** '64 (who had become an entrepreneur and later a significant venture investor and advisor) to create a new non-profit organization, **TECHNION ENTREPRENEURIAL ASSOCIATES (TEA)**, consisting of Boston-area technology-oriented entrepreneurs, the majority being MIT alumni, who were interested in helping Israel develop its entrepreneurship. The Technion-Israel Institute of Technology, "the MIT of Israel", indeed has many of its alumni and faculty closely connected with MIT, and was a natural ally in our mission. With the help of Professor Richard Rosenbloom, my colleague and co-teacher from the Harvard Business School (HBS), we assembled a stack of HBS cases that in one way or another related to entrepreneurs, or at least to young companies. Our TEA group then hired a young former HBS faculty member, Dan Isenberg, recommended as a "good case teacher", who was moving with his family to Israel, to become Israel's first lecturer on entrepreneurship, at the Technion. At the outset, Isenberg knew essentially nothing about starting and building new enterprises! But indeed he was a very good "case teacher", and Isenberg generated large classes of very enthusiastic Israeli students for their first exposure to entrepreneurship education. Dan then became the TEA's local "search" agent to identify startup companies, which we flew to Boston, where we held our own versions of the MIT Enterprise Forum sessions, accompanied by our attempts to mentor, help fund, and/or find partners for these young Israeli firms. Dan later developed an incubator in Israel and, after returning to the United States, has become a well-known lecturer and writer on global entrepreneurship development. Next, as a group, the TEA organized and carried out in Israel for the first time ever our well-received version of the MIT alumni seminar on "How to Start Your Own Company". This was followed by our collaboration with the few leading Israeli venture capitalists in organizing the very first venture capital conference in Israel, to which we invited many U.S. investment groups. Back home in Boston, several of us became actively engaged with the New England–Israel Chamber of Commerce to collaborate with Ed Mlavsky, the Director of the Israel-U.S. Binational Industrial Research and Development Foundation (BIRD)2 and former co-founder of Tyco Labs in Waltham, Massachusetts, to help Israeli high-tech startups find joint venture partners among Greater Boston medium-to-large U.S. corporations. Mlavsky's insights from running BIRD generated the first set of binational Israeli companies, with their technical groups always in Israel but with marketing arms and sometimes even their headquarters in the United States, and sometimes in Europe. And some of us worked closely with a newly created Israeli incubator that housed six to ten Israeli startups in a small space in the Boston Seaport district, then far different from the booming high-tech area it has become, to help them develop and engage in U.S. commerce. When Mlavsky completed long years of service as head of BIRD, he helped form and led Gemini Ventures, one of the very earliest Western-style venture capital firms in Israel, in collaboration with Boston VCs.

AUTHOR'S NOTE

I was surprised to learn from the leaders of the Israel Trek, MISTI-Israel, and IsraelLab that in all three cases, very few of the students who go to Israel in these programs are Jewish. The participating diverse array of students are apparently intrigued by Israel's economic and entrepreneurial growth, and want to learn more about that "Startup Nation".

All of these efforts produced many different (but all vital) contributions, the most important being the kickoff of greater visibility and interest throughout

Israel in entrepreneurship, and accompanying cultural change. In 1982, Stef Wertheimer began building a series of industrial parks with entrepreneurship training programs as their root. Dick Rosenbloom and I became key faculty in Stef's endeavors in 1987, especially in Stef's home area of Tefen in the Galilee, which I continued for the next decade. In 1991, Professor Shlomo Maital of the Technion (also our MIT summer faculty member for 20 years in the MIT Management of Technology Program) and I started activities to create the **MIT ENTERPRISE FORUM OF ISRAEL**, helped greatly by MIT alum **HAIM ALCOLAY** '61. It took us two tries, several years apart, before we generated a sustainable critical mass of MIT alumni engaged in the MITEF of Israel. From 1990 to 1992, joint efforts proceeded between the Technion and MIT Sloan, with strong support of Dean Lester Thurow, to develop a world-class business school in Israel with a featured collaborative mid-career executive education program focused on Israeli high-technology leaders. That admirable attempt failed, but its follow-up, the Technion Institute of Management (TIM), did move forward, with Dean Thurow as Chairman of the Board and an active faculty member, and our long-time associate Shlomo Maital as its Academic Director. Shlomo became a major researcher and teacher of high-tech entrepreneurship in Israel, and later lectured all around the world. He describes his book, *Technion Nation: The Technion's Contributions to Israel and the World* (SAGE Books, 2009), as his "replication" of our 2009 MIT alumni entrepreneurship study, but based on the faculty and graduates of The Technion.

Shlomo Maital

In 2006, several MIT students, both Israeli and Palestinian, organized a new summer program in Israel, called **MIDDLE EAST EDUCATION THROUGH TECHNOLOGY (MEET)**, to bring together exceptional Israeli and Palestinian high school students in equal numbers to study and work together. In the first summer, the curriculum, taught entirely by MIT graduate students from all over the world, was limited to computer science and computer programming. At the end of the summer, the students asked for a second year's program, which was developed to focus on applying computers to business problems. By the third year, the program's emphasis was on creating business plans for new ventures. During those three years, the first- and second-year summer programs were still continuing, so the "faculty", still all MIT grad students, was growing as the student population grew. The outcome since 2017 is that MEET operates from two locations, one in Jerusalem (along with its own incubator in the center near the YMCA) and one in a Stef Wertheimer building in the north of Israel, each location with three years of summer classes ongoing and a total of more than 200 students in attendance. MEET had to recently stretch its faculty to include some recruits from other universities in addition to MIT. And the overall curriculum has now switched entirely to entrepreneurship, with the accompanying name change to **MIDDLE EAST ENTREPRENEURS OF TOMORROW**! In his 2013

Jerusalem speech President Obama cited MEET as the type of organization that is needed for the future of the country.

For several years, the MIT Sloan student-run **ISRAEL TREK** has been the largest of the many annual end-of-year student foreign travel and learning activities, with 240 students participating in the 2019 trip. **MISTI (MIT INTERNATIONAL SCIENCE AND TECHNOLOGY INITIATIVES)-ISRAEL** is the largest of the MIT international internship programs, which are conducted in more than 25 foreign countries, and MISTI-Israel includes many young entrepreneurial firms among its list of internships. Recently, MIT Sloan Associate Dean Jacob Cohen initiated the very popular **ISRAELLAB** subject, which places student team internships with Israeli firms. Finally, as seen previously, **MASSCHALLENGE ISRAEL** is already fully underway, with 100+ companies annually participating in its accelerator. No doubt, all of these MIT-based engagements have contributed vitally to Israel's present prominent global positioning in high-tech entrepreneurship.

The most recent related effort was the June 2015 MIT faculty study tour that I helped organize to better understand Israel's dramatic successes in developing innovation and entrepreneurship as the primary bases of its economy. Ten of us spent an exciting week there, meeting with leading entrepreneurs and large company CEOs, visiting the Technion, discussing the role of the military in stimulating entrepreneurship, and learning from leading Israeli and Palestinian government officials.

Perhaps our most exciting day was our morning in Ramallah with Saab Ereket, the Chief Negotiator of the Palestinian Authority, followed by our afternoon in Jerusalem with Prime Minister Benjamin Netanyahu, recipient of S.B. '75 and S.M. '76 degrees from MIT (see photo below). The Prime Minister invited us to develop a research effort, in possible collaboration with an Israeli and a Palestinian university, to better understand how entrepreneurship can aid in

Left to right: Professors Michael Cusumano, Douglas Hart, Edward Roberts, Retsev Levi, Steve Rosenthal (our travel director), Prime Minister Benjamin Netanyahu, Miri Eisen (our expert guide), Neil Thompson, Dean S.P. Kothari, Steven Eppinger, James Orlin, Yasheng Huang, and Israel Ruiz (MIT Executive VP)

solving unemployment and further economic development issues in Israel and the West Bank. We have not yet followed up on that opportunity.

The United Kingdom. The possibility of a joint effort between MIT and the University of Cambridge "was proposed by former British Chancellor of the Exchequer Gordon Brown in the summer of 1998, who wanted to bring the entrepreneurial spirit of MIT to British universities."[3] This was seen as an important economic development opportunity for the U.K. The original notion was that MIT Sloan would first work with Cambridge to develop prototype programs, with emphasis on undergraduate education, and then we and/or they would branch out to add several more U.K. educational institutions. Ken Morse, as Managing Director of the MIT Entrepreneurship Center, was designated as the MIT Sloan project director, and Professor Tom Allen was appointed as our faculty lead, with Professor **MICHAEL SCOTT-MORTON** especially involved in the Scottish activities that were undertaken. Ken says that the three-part CMI goals were "enhancing innovation, entrepreneurship, and global competitiveness".

BEING CAREFUL to not confuse the British and the Irish ☺, one year earlier Professor Thomas Allen, working closely with Rory O'Shea, initiated the Irish Management of Technology (MOT) Program at University College Dublin, largely patterned after the MIT MOT Program. That program later became the vehicle for bringing in broad entrepreneurship education and activities to UC Dublin.

The program expanded rapidly from its initial concept in two directions. Although still called the **CAMBRIDGE-MIT INITIATIVE (CMI),** it soon included a number of other British universities and science centers across the U.K. And despite its initial intention of being limited to entrepreneurship, it grew instantly to also engage the MIT School of Engineering and its Cambridge University engineering counterpart. The CMI scaled up to a $100 million U.K.-funded effort, with monies from both the government and major U.K. corporations. Professor **ED CRAWLEY** '76 of MIT Aero-Astro was appointed Executive Director of the overall program, which generated many different education, research, and action-oriented elements up through about 2006. Ken Morse visited several times each year for five years, and succeeded in creating some mirroring in the U.K. of MIT Entrepreneurship Center features. Ken conceived and helped run several large and enthusiastic "celebrations of entrepreneurship" among generally more reserved groups of U.K. collaborators. The MIT $50K was introduced there, and the MIT $50K winners would travel over to join their U.K. counterparts in a finale competition. The VMS also worked to replicate itself among U.K. institutions. U.K. follow-up activities at MIT include very heavy and continuing enrollments in the MIT Entrepreneurship Development Program.

Unrelated to CMI, in which she was an active participant, is Professor **FIONA MURRAY**'s personal role as member of the U.K. Prime Minister's Council for Science and Technology. There she brings her research and understanding of innovation and entrepreneurship to bear upon the U.K.'s policy formulation and implementation.

MIT School of Engineering (SoE) "capacity building" programs. Before turning to multiple more limited engagements in other countries, let's examine the array of international programs that have generally been initiated by the MIT School of Engineering, sometimes with active participation of other parts of MIT. I introduced Professor **CHARLES COONEY** earlier in Chapter 5 in regard to the founding and development of the Deshpande Center (and we'll see him again in Chapter 8 as a pioneering biotechnology entrepreneur). He has been involved in almost all of the SoE "country programs" in which entrepre-neurship and innovation have played a key role. Charlie relates his side of these stories, covering much of what has come from the SoE (with some supplemental help ☺) to impact the rest of the world:

> Over the recent 15 years or so, many governments have come to us and asked, "How can we replicate the kind of success you've had at MIT around innovation and technology-based entrepreneurship? MIT, unlike many other prominent universities, decided many years ago that we do not desire, nor will we build, a physical extension of MIT any place else in the world. But we recognize that a number of features of our system—our research, education, and innovation processes—could benefit other institutions, and we do have a sense of responsibility to help make those benefits happen. So, on many occasions we have embarked not only on helping institutions in other countries, but even helping to design them. We call our role "capacity building" for those institutions and countries. Without exception, in all those cases, the governments and the universities want innovation and entrepreneurship to be central to this new institution. As a consequence, I've become involved in most of these new exercises. I'll give you four different examples in four parts of the world:
>
> One that has been very successful is in Singapore—the creation of **SINGAPORE UNIVERSITY OF TECHNOLOGY AND DESIGN**. In that example we tried to take our best practices in stimulating innovative and entrepreneurial behavior from across the Institute, not just the Deshpande Center or the Trust Entrepreneurship Center. And we have built them into the curricula, the operations, and the organization of the institution.
>
> Another example is at the **MASDAR INSTITUTE** in Abu Dhabi, with which I was involved from the very beginning. This month it will graduate its sixth class of students. And they again have various activities, not simply duplicated, but rather adapted from MIT practices into their local environment, culture, and behavior. But it has achieved much less in E&I per se.
>
> An example where success has yet to be achieved, and where I was very involved beginning in 2011, was "**SKOLTECH**"—the Skolkovo

CHARLIE AND I CO-CHAIRED the Skolkovo project's internal Council of Entrepreneurship & Innovation, intended originally to be the cornerstone of the entire university. Additional MIT Sloan participants from the very beginning were Bill Aulet, representing the MIT Entrepreneurship Center, and Professors Murray and Stern. A key addition to the senior leadership of the SkolTech project was Professor Maurizio Sobrero '97, former head of the School of Management, University of Bologna, Italy, who became a heavy-time consultant on Skolkovo's entire educational program.

> Institute of Science and Technology outside of Moscow. The vision was to create a university around education, research, and innovation in which the three were inextricably intertwined, much like a triple helix. This model is different in nearly every aspect from the traditional significant Russian university. It has been much more challenging to carry out that vision. Russian culture is not one that historically has lent itself to innovative behavior. History will eventually show whether or not we've had a successful impact there.
>
> A final example is Portugal. There, beginning in 2006, MIT was not asked to help design a new university, but rather to help develop a multi-university PhD program across all the major universities of Portugal. So, our target was to create a multi-disciplinary, multi-organizational, multi-institutional structure in which innovative and entrepreneurial behavior was central to the design of the curricula and the operating principles of the institution.[4]

Professor **DOUG HART** has succeeded Professor Cooney in leading the entrepreneurship and innovation components of many of these Engineering School programs. He had worked with Luis Perez-Breva and me in creating the first E&I subject for SkolTech, which we pilot tested at MIT with a group of SkolTech and MIT students. Doug later co-taught that same course in Moscow. He adds his own continuing experiences with Russia:

> **ILIA DUBINSKY** '98 is our counterpart there, an MIT PhD who became a serial entrepreneur in the United States before returning home to Russia with his wife. Ilia heads the entrepreneurship working group at SkolTech and is a pleasure to work with. [Ilia unfortunately left SkolTech in 2018.] I see SkolTech as still an interesting experiment and of course a very ambitious undertaking. . . . Many things have changed in Russia, partly due to the economic drop and political strife. But I was shocked when I went there at just how starved the students are to receive this kind of education. Their needs are much more than our students, who have a "candy store" of classes and activities for E&I exposure and assistance. We may not be successful in changing the faculty attitudes

> in Russia, but certainly among the students we have filled a void that was hugely important. I think that will be a lasting influence for many years to come.[5]

Doug Hart adds his more recent experiences in Portugal:

> We now have many programs embedded in Portugal. It has taken off, and the Portuguese welcome us with open arms. Portugal now has the equivalent of our $100K competition that's doing extremely well. Many companies have already spun out of that activity.
>
> Through all this, I think there's an underlying realization in many countries that are attempting to develop an entrepreneurial ecosystem patterned after MIT, but in their own style. Let's put it this way—invention without innovation is really somewhat pointless. You should realize that I would never have thought this way when I arrived at MIT with my PhD from CalTech! All of these countries that we have touched are striving to achieve what MIT has been steadily developing for at least 50 years. These programs are a two-way street: We do help those economies to move forward, but in turn MIT finds many fantastic students who join us later. And we're also learning how to better teach entrepreneurship and innovation to everyone.

MIT Sloan School "capacity building" programs. MIT Sloan has also engaged in institution building in other countries, much the same as the Engineering School. A major difference is that as the Sloan School had entrepreneurial faculty and related programmatic strengths early on, many of its initiatives were limited to E&I. Also, the School, with a rather different management style, often provided only initial demonstration examples in the partner country, and then turned over follow-up responsibilities to its foreign partner.

"The Chinas Vision". Shortly after Lester Thurow became Dean of the Sloan School in 1987, he enunciated a vision that the School could become a "flagpost of leading thought about management and economics under which all of the Chinas would be willing to assemble", referring explicitly to mainland China, Hong Kong, Taiwan, and Singapore. By the end of his deanship in 1993, Lester had achieved major MIT Sloan programs with all four, most with strong roots in MIT entrepreneurship and innovation.

Take Singapore as an example. In 1985, the leader of Singapore's Economic Development Board (EDB), Philip Yeo, who visited MIT regularly, began sending multiple rising stars to the 12-month MIT Sloan Fellows Executive Development Program. Of the three first-year attendees, **MING-KIAN TEO** '86 rapidly moved up Singapore's governmental system, becoming head of its National Research

Foundation (similar to our NSF) and then Permanent Secretary of Finance of the Cabinet. He later became head of the EDB, and still later a major global venture capitalist, **VERTEX VENTURE HOLDINGS**, investing parts of the Singapore Sovereign funds. Having been our student, Ming-Kian was quick to call for help by bringing Sloan faculty and their research ideas to the attention of Singapore's executives. Professor Arnoldo Hax, Michael Cusumano, and I gave the first MIT seminars there, nominally sponsored by the just-started MIT Alumni Club, which already included many Sloan School alumni. Ming-Kian soon followed up by trying to move entrepreneurship ahead in Singapore, quite counter to its culture. He and I organized and ran Singapore's first seminar on entrepreneurship, which included the one prominent Singaporean entrepreneur he could identify.

Later, MIT Sloan undertook "capacity building" there in a project headed by Professor **DONALD LESSARD** to try to modernize the management department of Singapore's "Chinese university", **NANYANG TECHNOLOGICAL UNIVERSITY**, among other changes being the introduction of E&I education to its curriculum. That project was not at all as broad in scope as the later effort by the MIT SoE to develop the Singapore University of Technology and Design, but did achieve significant improvements. Singapore EDB continued to sponsor Sloan Fellows for many years, and expanded its commitments to MIT management education by sending others annually to the Management of Technology program, and then to the regular S.M. and then MBA degree programs. Now, the Sloan alumni in Singapore constitute a critical mass of the country's leadership.

Relationships with Taiwan started early too, but were more modest. The new **EPOCH FOUNDATION** was created to support the MIT Sloan School and to bring modern management ideas to the CEOs of Taiwan's 20 major company sponsors. In 1994, the new Dean, **GLEN URBAN**, plus Mike Cusumano and I, did the first MIT seminar in Taiwan for those CEOs, and visited individually with several of them. In the seminar, we all talked about strategic change from differing perspectives, with my focus deriving from MIT's innovation and entrepreneurship activities. The first seminar of that Taiwan CEO group at MIT was in 1998 and emphasized corporate entrepreneurship, led by **ALEX D'ARBELOFF** '49, co-founder and former CEO of **TERADYNE** and at the time of the seminar Chairman of the MIT Corporation. His leading challenger among the Taiwanese executives was **MORRIS CHANG** '52, founder and CEO of **TAIWAN SEMICONDUCTOR MANUFACTURING COMPANY**, a good customer of Teradyne. In 2016, Morris became the naming donor of the newly redone former Alfred P. Sloan Building (E52), now the **MORRIS AND SOPHIE CHANG BUILDING**.

MIT Sloan actually did do capacity building, in some ways similar to that carried out by MIT Engineering, but different in other ways. In 1996, we began the **MIT-CHINA MANAGEMENT EDUCATION PROJECT** in collaboration with **TSINGHUA UNIVERSITY** and **FUDAN UNIVERSITY**, the two most respected universities in China, to help them develop modern management curricula modeled after the Sloan School. This task was accomplished by an intensive long-term program during which large numbers of visiting faculty fellows from China spend a year at MIT as understudies of the faculty member(s) whose subjects they want to master. While at MIT, they redesign the subject for use in China, with the targeted MIT faculty member acting only as a mentor. This effort expanded to include three other major Chinese universities, and the program still exists. As a result, the management curricula throughout China's best schools of management are Chinese versions of what is taught at MIT Sloan.

Professor **DELIN YANG** of Tsinghua came to MIT as a Fulbright Scholar in 2006, to study our entrepreneurship subjects under my tutelage. In our first meeting, I reviewed the various research projects underway by our faculty, encouraging Delin to meet with them and learn more about their studies. Last on my list was mention of my then data analyses of our first study of MIT alumni entrepreneurs. I stopped, essentially in mid-sentence, and hesitantly asked, "Would you be interested in working together on a similar study of Tsinghua's alumni entrepreneurs?" That triggered exciting discussions for the next week, after which Professor Yang flew back to Beijing to discuss with his Dean and President the possibility of this joint research. We undertook that research, with key participation of my graduate student **CHARLES EESLEY** and a Chinese PhD student at MIT, **YANBO WANG** '09. I persuaded **CHARLES ZHANG** '94, co-founder with me and the CEO of **SOHU.COM**, an alumnus of both Tsinghua and MIT, to fund the Tsinghua budget for that research. (See more about Charles in Chapter 9, The Internet.) The resulting large-scale survey was the first comprehensive study of a foreign university's entrepreneurial outpouring. Eesley took on primary responsibility for most of the work in analyzing the data, and included it in his PhD dissertation.[6] As a result, Chuck became very involved with Tsinghua, especially after he moved to Stanford as a new Assistant Professor, and he has since spent much time on research and teaching of entrepreneurship in China. (Incidentally, in September 2017, Chuck (now a tenured Associate Professor) married a young woman whom he met during his work in China, his wife expecting to soon finish her PhD program in California ☺.)

Sloan School activities in Portugal. From the outset in 2007, these activities were focused on entrepreneurship, trying to help Portugal to develop curricula and action programs beyond that. Fiona Murray and I were the initial Co-Directors of the **MIT SLOAN-PORTUGAL PROGRAM**. In my first lecture in Lisbon, to a large audience, I pushed my strongly-held belief about the importance of interaction between engineering and management students, as well as my data on how mixed teams outperform founder groups that come from only one discipline. A very polite member of the audience came up to me after the talk and said, "You do realize that you are speaking in a business school, with no connections to any technical college!" That caught me by surprise, and I asked if there was a nearby technical university with which the business school might collaborate. He said there was one a block away, but there was no possibility that they would work together. My quick response was that as a professor from MIT, I would have credibility even in a Portuguese engineering school and I would be glad to act as an intermediary to bring them together. My questioner looked at me as if I was totally naïve, and repeated that there would be no chance of making that work!

In fact, because the MIT School of Engineering had its own separate project underway in Portugal, Charlie Cooney, Fiona Murray, and I were able to bring together a broader group of academics from an excellent business school and two technological universities, along with an important government officer who was a potential funding source, and the cross-institution collaborations in Portugal began in earnest. At the first finals of the all-Portugal $100K equivalent, Charlie and I sat in a conference room of the MIT Trust Center, participating in the final presentations on Skype, interacting with the local judges in two cities of Portugal.

The United Arab Emirates (UAE). Here is an example of "sometimes you win and sometimes you lose" in undertaking "capacity building" programs in other countries. In 2003, the assistant to the Minister of Higher Education of the UAE met with me to discuss the possibilities of a joint degree program in entrepreneurship between the UAE and MIT. I immediately informed him that MIT does not create new joint degrees with other institutions, and the conversation quickly switched to the possibility of a joint entrepreneurship program, with a UAE degree. MIT at that time had no significant activities in the Persian Gulf, so several of us saw the idea as interesting but potentially controversial, largely because of long-held concerns at MIT about issues of human rights and equal treatment of women and religious minorities. Much of a year was devoted to discussions at MIT and visits to Dubai to discuss the concept and details of a potential five-to-seven-year effort to help develop UAE entrepreneurship faculty and curricula, while a special cross-Institute task force appointed by then Provost **ROBERT BROWN** considered all implications of such a program. Finally, all internal approvals were received from both sides, and MIT President **CHARLES VEST** approved our movement forward with an initial pilot entrepreneurship conference in Dubai and a related short executive education program there for corporate and government executives from throughout the Middle East.

Several of our faculty participated in both activities in Dubai, headed by Ken Morse and myself. The March 2004 conference was seen as a great success, as was the brief ExecEd program on Strategy and Innovation. The Sheik of the UAE attended the opening, and in a private meeting with MIT Chancellor **PHILIP CLAY** '75 gave his enthusiastic blessings to the anticipated MIT-UAE partnership. But MIT internally did not move forward quickly in processing our large proposal due to administrative conflicts arising about whether this would be treated as an educational activity, which would carry very low overhead, or as a contract "work-for-hire" project, which would require very high overhead recovery on our quite large proposed budget. Not surprisingly, by the time this issue was resolved with MIT's government auditors, our proposal was forwarded quite belatedly to the UAE, much to their disappointment. By then, their officials had already been offended by the long delay and turned down the proposed program.

However, the good relations established with the UAE Minister of Higher Education and the Sheik, both of whom have continued in their leadership positions, were instrumental in establishing the later **MASDAR** program with the MIT School of Engineering in Abu Dhabi. That program includes minor aspects of entrepreneurship in its courses and related student activities.

The Asia School of Business. Professor **CHARLES FINE** became President and Dean of the new **ASIA SCHOOL OF BUSINESS (ASB)** in Kuala Lumpur, Malaysia, a major "capacity building" program undertaken by MIT Sloan, in which entrepreneurship and innovation are playing a key role. That project started in early 2015 in collaboration with **BANK NEGARA MALAYSIA**, Malaysia's central bank, which had been led since 2000 by Dr. Zetti Akhtar Aziz. Her vision was: "The program will foster entrepreneurship, innovation, and hands-on-learning through an active interaction among industry, government, faculty and students." The close continuing collaboration involves joint curriculum development efforts with ASB's first faculty members, and included multiple Sloan faculty doing initial core teaching in a summer session for the first class of ASB students held at MIT in 2017. Additional MIT Sloan faculty provide occasional teaching in Malaysia, but primarily follow the same approach to mentoring Malaysian and other Asian faculty members as has been successfully used in the long-running MIT-China Management Education Project described above. MIT Senior Lecturer **RAJESH NAIR** '14, my former student and assistant who has worked in many roles in MIT's entrepreneurship undertakings, including the Tata Foundation program in India that was mentioned previously, is the Director of the Innovation and Entrepreneurship Center at ASB. His first program at ASB was a joint MIT-ASB-India Institute of Technology (IIT) week-long bootcamp on social entrepreneurship for students from all three participating institutions.

The Tokyo University of Science. Professor **MICHAEL CUSUMANO** has carried out a one-man "capacity building" activity in Japan, serving as Dean of the Tokyo University of Science's business school, dramatically changing its undergraduate and graduate programs and bringing as much as possible of MIT entrepreneurship to the institution. Babson College assisted the university in implementing its core undergraduate entrepreneurship model as a required subject. The undergrads were doubled in size from 250 to 500 in 2016, and now occupy a new building.

The university is the host for MIT REAP's Tokyo cohort, and its major task is the development of a Center for Innovation and Entrepreneurship. As part of that mission, Mike has worked on introducing several new courses, drawn directly from MIT: iTeams, a new ventures lab course, a research seminar in E&I, and a mentoring system for student entrepreneurship projects. The university has also created a million-dollar venture fund to compensate for the significant shortage of startup venture capital in Japan, and has already invested in one faculty-led company. Professor Cusumano observes:

> Essentially, I'm modeling the activities of the Center here around several complementary activities that go on at MIT but are not formally connected. I'm formally connecting them here, creating one Center that combines the Trust Center for MIT Entrepreneurship, the Deshpande Center for Innovation, the Venture Mentoring Service, and the $100K business plan competition. . . . The investment fund will be part of the Center, and we're also partnering with some of the private incubator centers that have been established around Tokyo.
>
> I'm also redesigning the graduate school Management of Technology curriculum (copied from the MIT MOT program many years ago) to make it a bit broader in management training for Japanese engineers, and also to put a new emphasis on corporate entrepreneurship. To support that, I'm introducing a new required course, Corporate Entrepreneurship, which Ed created at MIT, as well as some other classes in strategy, venture creation, and design thinking. . . . We definitely should make an impact at Tokyo University of Science, which has 21,000 students, the largest engineering university in Japan. The government, particularly the Ministry of the Economy, Trade, and Industry, suggests that what we're doing is a possible model for other Japanese universities.[7]

Kyushu University. A second Japanese impact came about with much less formal effort by us! Our MIT Sloan alumnus, **ROBERT HUANG** '79, founder of **SYNNEX CORPORATION**, had done his undergraduate studies at Kyushu University in Japan. In 2009, he asked us to host for about one year its Professor Megumi Takata, to help him develop and launch an entrepreneurship center. Because of our space limitations at the time, Professor Takata had to share an office in the MIT Entrepreneurship Center itself, rather than in our academic office spaces. That turned out in Professor Takata's own views to be the most important influence on his understandings of what was required to build a new and effective entrepreneurship center. He was in the midst of our student startup teams and entrepreneurship club meetings, as well as close to our Entrepreneurs-in-Residence and all of the activities that occurred in our Center. With those experiences, combined with attendance in several classes and seminars, and informal conversations with many of our faculty, Professor Takata returned home. He now is Director General of the Robert T. Huang Entrepreneurship Center of Kyushu University, which engaged with over 6,000 students in 2018 and offered 32 entrepreneurship-related subjects and lectures in 2019, and is already recognized as one of the leading entrepreneurship programs in Japan.

Academic Alumni Global Impact. Before concluding this section, I must describe a very different way by which our academic alumni—MIT Sloan PhD graduates, former faculty, and visiting faculty—have been instrumental in the gradual and worldwide diffusion of the research findings, courses, student activities, and many programs of MIT Entrepreneurship. Our academic alumni have gone on to careers in important institutions everywhere, where their professional roles have been to teach and lead entrepreneurship efforts.

Before moving abroad, let's start first with a domestic U.S. example that then went global. **MARC MEYER** (PhD '86) was one of our early doctorate recipients, then in technology and innovation. But during his graduate school years he co-founded his first software company, followed later by several serial entrepreneurial startups. Yet Marc's career focus was on building and leading the entrepreneurship program at Northeastern University in Boston. Over 300 ventures have emerged from his technology-oriented incubator, raising over $200 million in the past five years. That program has now been transplanted to Andhra Pradash in India, to reflect Marc's own global thrust, with enthusiastic responses especially from young people there. In August 2019, Professor Meyer was awarded a prestigious prize from the Academy of Management for his "impact upon management practice", consistent with our *mens et manus* goals.

Marc Meyer

Koenraad Debackere

Let's turn to an example where the education was local at MIT but the targets of impact were foreign. Take Belgium as an example. In his doctoral dissertation, **JEAN-JACQUES DEGROOF** (uniquely a Sloan Fellow '93 and PhD '02) studied the entrepreneurial spinoffs from all Belgian universities, and assessed what challenges they encountered and sometimes overcame.[8] He found that the needs of universities in Belgium, a country with "weak external supportive infrastructures", were very different from what we experience in the now rich external environment of Cambridge and the United States. The best performing Belgian university by far was Katholieke Universiteit (KU) Leuven, for which our frequent academic visitor **KOENRAAD DEBACKERE** had become the faculty leader of a growing and successful entrepreneurial program. Since going back to Europe, Koenraad has become very sensitive to the differences that arise from both size and especially from internal and external resources that affect new company formation in an academic setting. Professor Debackere has significantly reduced that problem by creative collaborations across multiple nearby regions:

> We now have four cities that work very closely together: Aachen, Eindhoven, Heidelberg, and Leuven. In each region, a number of core institutions really try to push entrepreneurship and entrepreneurial activity around its local key university and in helping to build our broader university community ecosystem.... In Leuven, two institutions have

played a major role: KU-Leuven Research and Development [which Professor Debackere had headed], which includes the university's tech-transfer activities, and IMEC, the large nano-electronics center funded by the government, but with lots of collaboration with private industry. We had some successful entrepreneur role models, but we needed to put more emphasis on mentoring, inspiring, and achieving entrepreneurial success, by patient interweaving and interlocking institutions and actors that help us to build and support that ecosystem.[9]

PROFESSOR DEBACKERE thanks MIT Professors Tom Allen, Jim Utterback, and especially **MICHAEL RAPPA**, with whom he collaborated extensively, for providing the bases of the insights he gained as an extended visitor during the midst of our building our entrepreneurship programs.

Our "innovation", the MIT entrepreneurial ecosystem, has been copied and adapted by our own academic alumni (and others) in many university communities throughout the United States and worldwide, producing effective diffusion and resulting impact. We have not yet properly surveyed our own doctoral alums to measure that spread and the consequences.

WRAPPING UP ON BRINGING MIT ENTREPRENEURSHIP TO IMPACT THE WORLD

Chapters 6 and 7 began by showing the clear evidence of dramatic MIT alumni company formation, growth, and economic impact on the United States in particular, but also on the rest of the world. The number of companies, jobs provided, and economic outcomes have been growing exponentially by decade, as shown in our past 60 years of data. MIT living entrepreneurial alumni alone are cumulatively as large in their economic consequence as a major country. And I again emphasize that this empirical finding does not take into account companies formed by alumni now deceased, or companies that have been merged into others, or companies formed by non-alumni faculty or staff, or non-alumni companies based on technologies licensed from MIT. These analyses also do not even begin to consider the vast innovative but non-entrepreneurial impact produced by MIT's graduates, nor the massive benefits flowing continuously from MIT's scientific and technological contributions to the world.

I next turned to the early efforts by the MIT Enterprise Forum to include non-MIT folk in its nationwide expansion, and its continuing participation as a co-founder and collaborator in the "Birthing of Giants" program addressed to young entrepreneurs, regardless of background.

MIT alumni have actively promoted more effective growth and results of startups through pioneering accelerators of various forms, beginning with Brad Feld's early Techstars, going from multiple sites within the United States to now being engaged throughout the world in entrepreneurship development. Then I described John Harthorne's MassChallenge, already the largest accelerator in the world, but continuing to expand to more countries each year. I then followed up with more specialized accelerators, such as Jean Hammond's LearnLaunch, dedicated to advancing education-oriented entrepreneurs, and Emily Reichert's Greentown Labs, focused on clean energy. Of course, we included discussion of Bill Aulet's development of what now is MIT's delta v accelerator, with the recent addition of its NYC Summer Startup Studio.

MIT activities that strive for a global impact on stimulating successful entrepreneurship began with such MIT-related endeavors as the outreach activities of the Enterprise Forum, the Entrepreneurship Development Program, the Legatum Center, and MassChallenge. The first MIT focus on the rest of the world was by our students who kicked off the MIT Global Startup Workshop, which has educated hundreds annually for 21 years, with a different country as its base each year, teaching others how to create business plan competitions like the MIT $100K. That has inevitably been the source of entrepreneurship competitions in at least 60 countries. Our internal MIT Global Entrepreneurship Lab subject, for years sending about half of the entire MIT Sloan MBA population to internships in young firms all around the world, has educated our students in international settings, served the interests of now hundreds of foreign startup firms, and encouraged imitation by numerous other universities. Within MIT, G-Lab has been followed by ChinaLab, IndiaLab, and IsraelLab, furthering our global entrepreneurial impact. We then went from accelerating firms to accelerating regions and countries entrepreneurially by our launch of REAP (Regional Entrepreneurship Acceleration Program), which instructs and aids task forces of stakeholders from up to ten geographic areas per cohort group, now furthered by the creation of REAPLab, which allows our students to follow the G-Lab model in regional internship efforts. The Venture Mentoring Service has developed its Outreach Program to convey MIT approaches to mentoring and new company assistance to 60 different sites.

The last part of Chapter 7 was devoted to the large number of "country programs" undertaken by all of MIT and by the Schools of Engineering and Management separately, in which enhancement of innovation and entrepreneurship were among the primary objectives. That started with policy study programs of the MIT Center for Policy Alternatives, especially in Israel and Sweden. The company education seminars of the MIT Industrial Liaison Program throughout Europe and Asia brought further attention to MIT entrepreneurship programs and achievements. But the action programs in a number of countries have expended the greatest efforts of MIT faculty and hopefully have generated vital impact. Alphabetically, the country action-programs described were in Belgium, China, Israel, Japan, Malaysia, Portugal, Russia, Singapore, Taiwan, the United Arab Emirates, and the United Kingdom.

In all of these efforts to encourage other countries to meaningfully increase their attention to and effectiveness in developing and then growing entrepreneurial startups, the primary challenge to overcome is the usually dramatic change of culture required. Consider the comments of both Professors Charles Cooney and Doug Hart about the Russian Skolkovo effort above. Koenraad DeBackere added a comparable final observation:

> Last year, we started a program for entrepreneurship and innovation cooperation with the leading universities in Central and Eastern Europe. We already have a good relationship with Charles University in Prague, and we can find fertile ground. But 10 years ago Charles University was not ready to do so. We have to take into account these time delays that sometimes can be huge if the institutional environment is not ready for it.[10]

Michael Cusumano made a similar comment about his Japanese experiences with corporate entrepreneurship:

> Big organizations [including universities!] generally don't like to do things that are too new or will alter their business model. We tend not to see really new ideas or technologies come out of these Japanese internal ventures. Japan has been stuck in fairly incremental innovation. The Japanese leaders know they've got to shake up the economy and get bolder, but this takes a long time.[11]

Chapter 7 lends added testimony to how long it has taken, even at MIT, despite our founding *mens et manus* ideals, to build our entrepreneurship ecosystem.

Overall, the continuing efforts to bring MIT entrepreneurship to the world have a fine batting average, and we keep trying to improve our help to others.

REFERENCES AND NOTES

1. Comments made at MIT, November 12, 2016.
2. By extreme coincidence, Mlavsky's predecessor in that role for only the first year of BIRD was Wade Blackman '66, my Sloan Fellow thesis student! Wade much later became Managing General Partner of ARD, discussed in Chapter 11, "Modern Finance".
3. *Wikipedia*, "Cambridge-MIT Institute", accessed on February 23, 2018.
4. Interview by Michelle Choate on May 9, 2016.
5. Interview by Michelle Choate on May 6, 2016.

6. Charles Eesley, *Essays on Institutions and Pre-founding Experience: Effects for Technology-based Entrepreneurs in the US and China,* PhD Dissertation, MIT Sloan School of Management, 2009.
7. Interview by Michelle Choate on May 6, 2016.
8. Jean-Jacques DeGroof, *Spinning Off New Ventures from Research Institutions Outside High Tech Entrepreneurial Areas,* PhD Dissertation, MIT Sloan School of Management, 2002.
9. Koenraad Debackere's remarks are from his 2016 presentation at MIT. He now serves as the Algemeen Directeur of KU Leuven, the equivalent of Provost and Executive Vice President.
10. DeBackere, *op. cit.*
11. Cusumano, *op. cit.*

(overleaf) top left
Helen Greiner, Michael "Mick" Mountz, Jon Hirschtick, and Harry Lee during the panel on "From CAD-CAM to Robotics", which took place at "Celebrating A Half-Century of MIT Entrepreneurship", November 12, 2016.

top right
Robert Van de Graaff explaining his electrostatic generator to Karl Taylor Compton in 1931. This was the basis for forming High Voltage Engineering.

bottom right
Noubar Afeyan, Robert Langer, Charles Cooney, Phillip Sharp, and Susan Hockfield during the panel on "Life Sciences and Biotechnology , which took place at "Celebrating A Half-Century of MIT Entrepreneurship", November 12, 2016.

bottom left
A young Jay Forrester in front of the Whirlwind computer, with his best friend Bob Everett by his side, circa 1951. Whirlwind was the predecessor of Digital Equipment Corporation and many other computer companies.

PART TWO

Entrepreneurs Who Built Innovative Companies that Pioneered New Industries

Significant MIT-Based Enterprises that Survived the Past Half-Century

Over the years since MIT's founding, it has produced tens of thousands of entrepreneurs who have created and built companies in every field of endeavor and in most countries of the world. This entire Part Two is a tribute to all of them, and their achievements and contributions to society. Part One told how MIT as an institution moved forward from its clear tradition of creating knowledge and bringing it to impact. The past 50+ years have been especially remarkable in developing the organizational capacities to accelerate that entrepreneurial productivity, via education, research, counsel, and stimulus. Part Two testifies to the primary output of those years—the great entrepreneurs who have founded and built countless innovative firms, many of which pioneered wholly new industries.

We start Part Two with brief tributes to those few unique MIT alumni who a half-century ago created their own firms and are still leading those companies towards greater and greater accomplishments. Perhaps surprising, ONLY three firms seem to qualify: Koch Industries, Analog Devices, and Meditech, and of course their entrepreneurial founders.

These firms and founders provide a backdrop to the more detailed examination that follows in each of Part Two's chapters on four industries, all pioneered during this half-century by MIT faculty and alumni whom we honor: Life sciences and biotechnology, the Internet, the evolution from CAD-CAM to robotics, and the world of "modern finance".

Koch Industries

KOCH INDUSTRIES is the result of outstanding entrepreneurship by two generations of MIT graduates who leveraged their MIT technical educations to create a uniquely successful corporation with current annual sales in excess of $110 billion.

Patriarch **FRED KOCH** graduated from MIT in 1922 with a bachelor's degree in Chemical Engineering Practice. He started working in Texas in the rough-and-tumble field of oil refining. In 1925, he joined his MIT '22 classmate, Percival "Dobie" Keith, and ended up by creating Winkler-Koch Engineering. That company focused on developing oil-refining technology, and in 1927, created a breakthrough thermal cracking process for turning crude oil into gasoline. The process was especially helpful to small oil producers, which caused the large companies to do everything in their power to harass Fred Koch and his company and to try to shut them down. Fred survived the ensuing Depression years by turning to the Russian market, where he facilitated the development of several oil refineries. In 1940, Fred co-founded **WOOD RIVER OIL AND REFINING**, which was renamed **ROCK ISLAND OIL AND REFINING**, and steadily continued its growth into a medium-sized oil firm — early 1960s sales were estimated to be in the tens of millions of dollars.

AUTHOR'S NOTE

Throughout Part Two, I identify for each entrepreneur the year (or years) they attained their MIT degrees when I first mention her or him. I do not suggest that their earlier or later education at other universities, or their experiences in other firms and government agencies, were not vital contributors to their entrepreneurial achievements. Instead, these MIT data are intended to show pride in those persons who have passed through the Institute, contributed so much to society via the founding and growth of significant firms in pioneering industries, and hopefully benefited from MIT. And to demonstrate that pride, I place an MIT founder's name and company in bold font when initially identified!

Fred and his wife Mary had four sons, brought up by explicit efforts to instill in them a strong work ethic, including working summers on their ranch baling hay and cleaning out the barns. Two of them (Charles and Bill) were sent to Culver Military Academy to help "shape them up"! Three sons attended MIT, following their father into Chemical Engineering, obviously gaining strong technical backgrounds. Each received multiple MIT degrees and became entrepreneurs and company builders: **CHARLES**, **DAVID**, and **WILLIAM** (Charles — '57, '58, '60; David — '62, '63; and William — '62, '63, '63, '71).

In the 1960s, Fred's health worsened, and in 1966 he turned over leadership of the company to his son Charles, who was only 31. When Fred Koch died the next year, his sons renamed the firm **KOCH INDUSTRIES** to honor their father. Under the leadership (and principal ownership) of Charles and David, Koch Industries has avoided the "second generation pitfalls" that kill off many enterprises built by a brilliant and visionary parent. Instead of coasting on their laurels, Charles as CEO and brother David have been instrumental in making Koch the second largest privately held company in the United States. On their own, the two brothers seemingly discovered how to apply entrepreneurial concepts internally to build Koch, first in its base business of oil refining, and subsequently by diversifying into countless other areas of manufacturing and service. Charles Koch proved to be singularly adept at attracting upcoming executives from other corporations, which he did by giving them entrepreneurial freedom and financial incentives to grow whole new businesses under the Koch umbrella.

In the 1970s, William worked for Koch Industries by running its **KOCH VENTURES** entrepreneurship investment arm in Cambridge, and actively participated in the MIT Enterprise Forum. Bill later started his own company, **OXBOW GROUP**, which also focuses on energy development.

Charles Koch

In recent years, Koch Industries has generated annual revenues of more than $110 billion, and now employs over 120,000 people worldwide. In his writings, Charles espouses strong entrepreneurial principles of management, applauds Schumpeter's call for "creative destruction", discusses "disruptive innovation", and advocates strategies and incentives that encourage internal entrepreneurial behavior in all organizations.[1] David became one of the nation's (and MIT's) most generous philanthropists in science, technology, and the arts. David was a Life Member Emeritus of the MIT Corporation, its governing body. In addition to funding the MIT Koch Institute for Integrative Cancer Research, among other major projects, he also named the David Koch School of Chemical Engineering Practice, from which his father, he, and his twin brother Bill all received degrees. Unfortunately, David died on August 23, 2019.

One of William's notable entrepreneurial achievements was to form and lead the America[3] sailing syndicate that won the America's Cup in 1992, the first time in the Cup's 140-year history for a first-time participant. He broke with many traditions of the sailing field in boat design, as well as in his efforts to have an all-female crew repeat his win the next year, though they ended up coming in second. Bill was strongly supported in this endeavor by Professor Jerry Milgram and others from the MIT Department of Marine Engineering. In appreciation, Bill funded the W.I. Koch Professorship in Marine Technology, which Milgram now holds.

SCHUMPETER'S CONCEPTS of "creative destruction" and today's comparable phraseology of "disruptive innovation" in their most simple interpretation refer to new ideas or inventions that when implemented in new products or new companies drive out the old, replacing it with the new.

Analog Devices

ANALOG DEVICES is a case in which the serial entrepreneurs do much better in their second firm than in their first new enterprise. That trend is identified in our research, not as a certainty but as a strong probability. Three MIT Course 6 (EE) grads had worked together at the MIT Instrumentation Lab (I-Lab) under Professor Charles Stark Draper: **WILLIAM LINKO**, **MATTHEW LORBER**, and **RAYMOND STATA** (Linko—'57, '58; later completing his '66 MIT Sloan Fellows thesis on entrepreneurship under my supervision; Matthew Lorber—'56, '58; and Stata—'57, '58). Following in the footsteps of many who had been encouraged by

Draper's love for entrepreneurs flowing out of his I-Lab, the three in 1962 created **SOLID STATE INSTRUMENTS**. To quote Ray Stata: "We said, 'Hey, let's just do it.' We didn't have a strategy of any kind. We didn't have any money. We just had an urge. We figured we'd find some way to exploit our common knowledge of instrumentation and control systems."[2] In less than two years they sold out to Kollmorgen Corporation's Inland Controls Division for $50,000 each in stock, and with two-year employment agreements. That gave them plenty of time to think about what they might do better in the next company.

AUTHOR'S NOTE

Much of this section is based on my long association with my MIT EE classmate, Ray Stata. Both Solid State Instruments and Analog Devices were included in my very first entrepreneurship study of the spinoffs of the MIT Instrumentation Lab.

In 1965, Stata and Lorber founded **ANALOG DEVICES (ADI)**, initially to produce discrete transistor operational amplifiers, self-financed with the small funds left over from Kollmorgen. They were profitable from the first year, grew fast, and went public in late 1968. In that IPO, Matt Lorber sold half of his stock. He then left the company in 1970 to start **PRINTER TECHNOLOGY**, which soon failed, and then later founded **COPLEY CONTROLS**, successfully sold to **ANALOGIC CORP.** (founded by **BERNARD GORDON** '49). Ray stayed on at Analog, but an executive was brought in to be CEO while Ray maintained responsibilities for business development and marketing. Said Ray:

> We survived [because] I looked ahead and then decided what to do. Not too long after we started Analog, the first integrated circuit semiconductor operational amplifiers came on the market, and I could see the point of inflection in moving to this very sophisticated form of technology. It was a huge deal. You could see the strategy and the need to change, but the courage and wherewithal to do it were key. Many people in the company fought that need to change.... I applied my "frequently wrong but never in doubt" philosophy, because in my mind we had no option but to make that major transition.[3]

To accelerate that transition, Ray wanted to invest in a startup. The Board of Directors thought he was crazy, but when Ray pledged his own stock to secure the company's investment, they let him move ahead. Conflicts between Ray and the imported CEO were finally resolved when Ray became President in 1971, and CEO and Chairman two years later. In 1971, ADI acquired **NOVA DEVICES**, co-founded by **MODESTO "MITCH" MAIDIQUE** '62, '64, '66, '70, which became a key contributor to the ongoing years of ADI's growth and success.

Today, Analog Devices is a global company, specializing in data conversion and signal processing products. It generated $6.1 billion in estimated 2019 revenues, employed more than 15,000 people, and had a market cap of $40.9 billion.[4] Ray is still Chairman of the company, and has been married to his wife Maria for nearly 60 years, with whom he had two children, both of whom are serial entrepreneurs. (My research shows a far greater likelihood of a person founding a company if he or she is following a father's entrepreneurship example.) His son **RAYMIE** '91, '92, '96 founded **STATA LABS** and sold it to Yahoo, where in time he became CTO, and then later became founder-CEO of **ALTISCALE**. Ray's daughter Nicole was founder-CEO of Deploy Solutions, which was sold to **KRONOS** (founded by **MARK AIN** '64), and then became founder-leader of Boston Seed Capital. In the meantime, Ray also built and sold **STATA VENTURE PARTNERS**, a major early investor in high-tech startups. Ray and his wife Maria donated substantial funds for the MIT Stata Center, that houses much of the EECS Department. Ray has led several industry and community organizations, and became a Life Member of the MIT Corporation. At the Stata Center dedication, Ray said, "MIT taught me that no problem is too difficult to solve. All you need is to be willing to work hard enough to get it done!"

Ray Stata

In Analog's 50th anniversary celebration book, *The Innovation Engine* (2018), Ray indicated his continuing entrepreneurial look-ahead perspective: "ADI has reached a tipping point where combinatorial innovations can foster radical discontinuities that no one could have anticipated. It will take judgment and sometimes deliberate experimentation to decide which . . . will have the greatest impact on the world."

Medical Information Technology (Meditech)

AUTHOR'S NOTE

As co-founder of Meditech where I remain a board member, I have written thi "case" in the first person!

In mid-1968, **A. NEIL PAPPALARDO** was fuming about his boss at the Massachusetts General Hospital (MGH) Lab for Computer Medicine. He was talking about leaving to start a medical programming company based on the computer language he had developed, lovingly called MUMPS (i.e., MGH Utility Multi-Programming System!), which became one of the very few U.S. Department of Commerce standardized computer languages. At the same time, while then an Associate Professor at the MIT Sloan School of Management, I was searching for Boston-area development groups who were working on any aspect of medical computing. During my preceding few years of research in various medical areas, I had observed the absence of dedicated medical computing companies, and decided that would be a great entrepreneurial opportunity. One of several researchers whom I had contacted to potentially collaborate with was Frank Heart '51, who was leading efforts at **BBN** to develop a medical information system. But our discussions didn't go anyplace. (See the later section on BBN in Chapter 9, The Internet, to learn of Heart's key role in ARPAnet development.) Based on the suggestion of a mutual MIT friend, Steve Lorch '59, I "cold-called" Pappalardo to chat, not realizing that he had attended a much earlier MIT entrepreneurship seminar that I had led. Neil invited his lab sidekicks **CURTIS MARBLE** and **JEROME**

GROSSMAN, M.D., to our first meeting at MGH. (Except for Grossman, who had been a biology major at MIT prior to a medical degree, the rest of us had MIT Electrical Engineering degrees with both software and hardware backgrounds, among other things—Pappalardo—'64; Roberts—'57, '58, '60, '62; Marble—'63; and Grossman—'61). While getting to know each other, we explored the projects underway at Mass General to which they were trying to apply computers, such as patient admissions and record-keeping, taking a patient's medical history, and automated medical laboratory data processing. But we quickly conflicted on the kind of medical computing firm we might create. In meetings over the next several months, the four of us, all MIT alumni, evolved a plan to launch a medical information systems software company that might eventually cover all aspects of hospital clinical and administrative functions, and we named the firm **MEDICAL INFORMATION TECHNOLOGY**, **MEDITECH** for short. (I remember joking with Neil: "With M I T as the company's initials, we'll have a great trading symbol should we ever go public, despite the screaming from both the real MIT as well as Massachusetts Investors Trust", with obviously the same initials!) To further build our team's skills and perspectives, we agreed to add to our team a marketing-sales co-founder, identifying and recruiting Morton Ruderman, an EE alumnus of Northeastern University who was the cross-products manager for medical sales at Digital Equipment Corporation (DEC). We also decided to complete our initial team as soon as the company was funded by hiring Lawrence Polimeno as operations manager. Larry, after a half-century at Meditech, is now Vice Chairman.

Neil Pappalardo

Ed Roberts

While all of this startup planning was taking place, Neil quit his job at MGH, becoming what he called "gainfully unemployed" for eight months! Without any money, he managed to order a PDP-9 computer from DEC and made a deal with a landlord to rent 5,000 square feet of office space, which was in need of total renovation, right behind MIT. The space would hopefully be ready in August 1969, with the computer scheduled to arrive then too. To afford the space, at $8 per square foot, my small consulting company, **PUGH-ROBERTS ASSOCIATES**, agreed to lease the back 1,000 square feet of that office.

I wrote the company's business plan, including a computer model of Meditech's projected development and growth, and also identified prospects for investment in us. Mort Ruderman had insisted that his boss **KEN OLSEN** '50, '52, co-founder and CEO of **DEC**, be given the opportunity to provide Meditech's financing. So, Mort arranged for a meeting with Olsen for us to pitch Meditech as a potential software affiliate of DEC. Olsen instantly rejected the proposal, asserting that software was insignificant. "Iron is the name of the game", he exclaimed, echoing attitudes similar to those displayed then by IBM and other early computer firms. (Oh, how wrong they all were!) Fortunately, two venture staff members from another successful all-MIT, all-EE company,

EG&G INC. (**HAROLD EDGERTON**—'27, '31; **KENNETH GERMESHAUSEN**—'31; **HERBERT GRIER**—'33, '34; and **BERNARD "BARNEY" O'KEEFE**, no degree, as its co-founders), were taking an advanced management course on technology and innovation that I led at yet another successful MIT spinoff, **BBN**. I mentioned Meditech as an example of the type of startup that was increasingly of interest to large companies as a potential strategic alliance partner. In less than one week, the Meditech team gave its pitch to the top management of EG&G. Barney O'Keefe, the CEO, asked for a 20-minute break in the midst of the intense presentation meeting. The staff explained later that they needed to give a briefing to their senior execs on what a software company might do to make money ☺. EG&G "leaped in" for this future diversification opportunity, investing both startup and later follow-on funding, and for many years provided active and significant counsel by O'Keefe and other key executives.

Meditech pioneered the hospital information systems business in 1969, along with two other startups in the same year. They were McAuto (a division of **MCDONELL-DOUGLAS** aviation, the Douglas portion founded by **DONALD DOUGLAS** '14), which lasted for only a few years, and Shared Medical Systems (SMS). Both of them focused upon the financial side of hospitals while Meditech started with the clinical aspects, later broadening to cover the entire hospital system. SMS grew with some degree of volatility, sold out to Siemens in 2000, which in turn closed down its hospital software activities and sold SMS to Cerner in 2015. Meditech began with the then-unique approach of selling time-shared access to its DEC PDP-9 computers (similar in concept to "the Cloud"), allowing the hospital customer to "try before you buy" at very low cost—i.e., no need to purchase the software and especially no need for the more expensive computer hardware. Initially, a single PDP-9 computer could handle up to 16 lines or customers simultaneously. Gradually, the software sale approach became more acceptable, and eventually Meditech dropped time sharing. Within Meditech's early years, Neil expanded his role from CTO to CEO, and successfully led the company's technical and strategic growth from then until 2010. He then turned over the job of President and CEO to long-time employee Howard Messing '73, though Neil has continued serving as the full-time Chairman of Meditech. Throughout its half-century of operation, Meditech has remained wholly focused on healthcare organizations as its clients, gaining over time the industry's largest number of hospital customers in the United States, Canada, and overseas. Meditech's partially owned subsidiary, Meditech South Africa, has brought advanced healthcare information technology to all of southern Africa, as well as to the Middle East, now expanding into the U.K. We estimate Meditech's 2019 revenues at just under $500 million, employing about 3,500 people in the United States. We have now in a sense returned to our time-shared origins by introducing a "cloud" version of our comprehensive healthcare information systems, initially for smaller hospitals but soon rolling out for larger customers as well.

In addition to Neil, I am the only other co-founder who has continued with Meditech since 1969, but as a very active Board member rather than as a company employee. During this half-century, Neil and his wife Jane have become major supporters of many art and cultural organizations in the Boston area. Neil is a principal donor to MIT in particular, a Life Member of the MIT Corporation, and served as a key member of its Executive Committee for 10 years and as Chair of its Audit Committee. So Neil has been an instrumental part of MIT's leadership team, through several MIT Presidents.

Three anecdotes do not constitute a meaningful base for generalization. Yet it is intriguing to note the common characteristics: All of these successful and long-lasting alumni founders formed partnerships (rather than doing it alone!) and surrounded themselves with other MIT alumni. When successful, all of them gave back to society in many ways, especially by demonstrating their appreciation of MIT—by guest lectures, active participation in governance, and significant financial support. And all continue to see hard work, passion, and entrepreneurial behavior as keys to their own successes and as primary values to impart to others.

FOUR INDUSTRIES PIONEERED BY MIT FACULTY AND ALUMNI

Many MIT alumni have founded great companies and pioneered new industries, and deserve to be honored. Time and space limits obviously prevent the inclusion of all of those many significant entrepreneurs in this book, and I settled on selecting just a small sample of industries, and their firms and founders.

The software industry, packaged or specific applications or broad-based enterprise software firms, generated by MIT alumni, is one obvious candidate for elaboration. Indeed, both our 2009 and 2015 reports on alumni entrepreneurship identify software as the most popular industry chosen by MIT company founders (e.g., Meditech, above).[5] The electronics industry is another strong area of MIT engagement, reflecting the continuing excellence and size-dominance of MIT's Department of Electrical Engineering, which now includes Computer Science too (e.g., Analog Devices, above).

Instead, with apologies to all of the MIT entrepreneurs and their firms that are being omitted, I selected four industries for the chapters of Part Two, each quite different from the other, yet all involve MIT faculty and alumni entrepreneurs as the primary pioneering founders and builders, my key criterion for selection. They are: Life sciences and biotechnology, the Internet, the evolving industry from CAD-CAM to robotics, and the world of "modern finance". Each of these four industries and its key MIT-founder firms strongly display the role of *mens et manus*: discoveries stemming from scientific research, technologies flowing from engineering development, and knowledge and skills transferring from education were combined with the vision, passion, and energies of MIT faculty and graduates to form and build great companies and to pioneer these new industries.

Until now, in Part One, I and other key MIT organization builders told stories of how MIT has achieved greatness in fostering and nurturing entrepreneurs, both within MIT and then more broadly for the world. Chapters 8 through 11 relate many more stories, but these cases reveal how great firms and new industries were formed and developed by MIT entrepreneurs. And as much as possible, each of the entrepreneurial founders tells his or her own story. I hope you enjoy hearing their voices.

I devote different amounts of space to each of the entrepreneurs, but not because of differences in their success. Rather, I find in each one's tale key points about entrepreneurship that I might have said myself. But the entrepreneur says it better, and with perhaps a clearer identification of her or his experiential reasons for the comment. I hope these chapters are instructive for current and future entrepreneurs, as well as enjoyable.

8

Life Sciences and Biotechnology

This industry most strongly illustrates how university-based scientific advance becomes the basis for industrial revolution through entrepreneurship. And MIT-linked people are at its roots. I begin with biotechnology's very first company, follow up with other key early firms founded by MIT persons, and then bring the story up to its more current manifestations.

Genentech and Robert Swanson

"In 1976, **ROBERT SWANSON** and Herbert Boyer created the biotechnology industry over a couple of beers at a San Francisco bar called Churchill's."[6] Swanson had received two MIT degrees in 1969 (S.B. in Chemistry and S.M. in Management). While at MIT, Bob was a student in what was then the sole entrepreneurship course, New Enterprises, taught by retired entrepreneur Richard Morse. After graduating, Bob had a few years of venture capital experience at Citicorp and then at **KLEINER-PERKINS**, headed by **THOMAS PERKINS** '53. At age 29, Bob was on temporary leave from Kleiner-Perkins, exploring the potential of the new discoveries he had heard about in the biosciences. On his own hook, Bob "cold-called" Herbert Boyer, a 40-year-old biochemistry and biophysics professor at UC San Francisco, who had recently co-discovered a new method to splice DNA from one organism into the genome of another, which was called recombinant DNA. Together they invested $500 each, created **GENENTECH INC.** (for "Genetic Engineering Technologies"), and founded an industry! At the time, Swanson was surviving on $410 per month of unemployment benefits.

Herbert Boyer (left) and Robert Swanson (right)

Phillip Sharp, MIT Institute Professor and 1993 Nobel Prize winner in Medicine, adds some background:

> Here's how entrepreneurship changed my life. It was 1977, I was 33 years old, an Associate Professor of Biology, sitting in my MIT office, having a fabulous afternoon reading and thinking. The phone rang and someone named Raymond Schaefer asked me to fly to San Francisco to consult on an investment. I didn't know Ray Schaefer, and I had never consulted for anyone. Another MIT faculty member told me that Ray was an MIT alumnus, had started a venture department at International Nickel Company (INCO), and was going around the country looking for possible investments. Working with Kleiner-Perkins, he had the first shot at Genentech. A few days later in San Francisco, Swanson and Boyer laid out the fundamentals of their first planned activities at Genentech. I listened, then walked into the next room and told Ray, "I don't know if you can make a buck out of this, but they're going to do the science and will synthesize the insulin A and B chains and the growth hormone genes. They have the knowhow and relationships to make this happen."

Kleiner-Perkins invested the first $100,000 for 25% of Genentech, with INCO's money constituting a substantial part of that angel round.

With Genentech now launched, Swanson became CEO and Thomas Perkins became Chairman of the Board, two MIT alums, neither with a background in biology, together driving the first biotech firm in the world, from 1977 to 1990, with co-founder Herb Boyer serving as CTO and Vice President. In 1979, Genentech became the first major biotech company to show a profit. In 1980, it went public. Phil Sharp remembers that the Genentech IPO was priced at $35 per share, then jumped within an hour to $88 per share, suddenly catapulting the biotechnology industry to the forefront of investor attention. In 1982, the FDA approved Genentech's "synthetic human insulin", the first-ever approved genetically engineered human therapeutic.

As Genentech grew, it formed additional close ties to MIT. Professor Charles Cooney, an expert in pharmaceutical manufacturing processes (more about him later in this chapter), is one of those connections:

AUTHOR'S NOTE

Quotes throughout this chapter are primarily from those individuals' presentations in a session led by Susan Hockfield, MIT President Emerita, at our November 2016 MIT entrepreneurship celebration, integrated with interviews conducted by Michelle Choate in 2017 and other supplemental sources.

> My initial deep dive into the modern world of biotechnology was with Bob Swanson. In January 1980, Genentech had made progress and was up to 30 employees. Bob came into the office after I had spent the day there, meeting with various people. In the middle of the conference table, he put a large bottle of white powder. In California, you could get suspicious of a large bottle of white powder! But I got very excited because it was completely filled with the world's largest supply of human growth hormones that had ever been put together in one place at one time. That was a pivotal moment with Bob, and I said, "Yes, I will sign on." I became, for the next decade, a commuting consultant to South San Francisco. Never again do I want to take a red eye flight from San Francisco.

Following a 1990 $2.1 billion purchase of majority shares by Hoffman-LaRoche, Genentech became an operating subsidiary of the combined firm. In 2009, Roche bought the remaining shares for about $47 billion. In 2019, Genentech employed close to 14,000 people. A more detailed history of Genentech, its early struggles, and later successes, is available online.[7]

Bob Swanson died after a long battle with brain cancer at age 52 in 1999. Tom Perkins died after a prolonged illness in 2016 at age 84, having been one of the stalwarts of Silicon Valley and a pioneer of the venture capital industry. (Much more about Perkins is in Chapter 11, The World of "Modern Finance".) Many of his investments turned into gigantic hits, but Perkins always said that his favorite investment was Genentech.

Biogen and Phillip Sharp

Phillip Sharp

Relationships count big in entrepreneurship. Within months after **PHILLIP SHARP** and Ray Schaefer collaborated in getting Genentech off the ground, they were working together to assemble leading scientists into another biotech startup.

Phil recalls those beginnings:

> We established **BIOGEN** by combining the East Coast and Europe into one large biotech company. Little did we know that there were going to be thousands of biotech companies. Everyone told us we would not last two years, as no successful large integrated pharmaceutical company had been started for decades. Biogen in Geneva began in 1978, and then one year later Biogen Inc. was founded in Cambridge, Massachusetts.

The panel on "Life Sciences and Biotechnology". From right to left: MIT President Emerita Susan Hockfield (chair), Professor Phillip Sharp, Professor Charles Cooney, Professor Robert Langer, and Dr. Noubar Afeyan.

Biogen's key co-founders were Phil Sharp (who served on the Biogen Board of Directors for 29 years) and Walter Gilbert, a leading biochemist at Harvard University and winner of the 1980 Nobel Prize in Chemistry (who served as the initial Chairman of the new company). Startup funding came from Schaefer's INCO ventures group, which worked with Kevin Landry of Boston's TA Associates. The same investors continued to help create and build Boston's early biotech industry with a 1981 investment into ImmunoGen, and later in other startups.

ANYONE WHO has not seen Binney Street since 2014 would not recognize it, with its high-rises and block-upon-block of impressive glass and steel office buildings, filled by IT and biotech companies.

Sharp:

> In considering where we would open our site in Cambridge, we walked around the neighborhood. There was nothing to the east of MIT for several blocks. You had to go around Binney Street before you got out of the Cambridge Redevelopment zone. We were going to have to hire young people out of universities, and they would only come to organizations close to universities where they could keep their contacts. We wanted to be close to MIT, and felt we had to be. So, Biogen opened its first lab on Binney Street, a founding unit of the now extraordinary Kendall Square world center of biotechnology and pharmaceuticals. And that's where we got the first recombinant DNA license in Cambridge.

Biogen's new laboratory building, in the same but now wholly revitalized area, is dedicated to Phil Sharp!

Sharp:

> It suddenly struck us egghead molecular biologists that we had all of this science and technology, but we needed to produce something. We immediately reached out to **DANNY WANG** and brought him on the Scientific Advisory Board so we had someone who was familiar with

Kendall Square area in 1971

> fermentation. [Wang was MIT '59, '61, and Professor and founder of the MIT Biotechnology Process Engineering Center and several companies.] That facilitated increasing conversations between MIT engineering and biological science. Out of that, with lots of great leadership across the Institute, increasing integration and appreciation have evolved between those two parts of MIT that have benefited us all, and the world at large.

Professor Sharp concludes:

> Recognize that all this came out of research done in the interest of basic science—learning how genes work. Harvard's recruitment of Jim Watson of *Double Helix* fame and MIT bringing in Salvador Luria (academic investments in the 1960s that were motivated simply by scientific curiosity) are what created the science that began our story of entrepreneurship that saw Biogen happen. Fortunately, that basic science combined with the spirit of MIT: Let's solve problems, let's get it done, let's make an impact.

In 2019, Biogen's revenues were $14.1 billion, with about 7,500 employees, and a market cap of $43.5 billion. Not to be outdone by Genentech, Biogen stock soared from $3 per share to $18 the first day it went public ☺. In 2002, Professor

Sharp also co-founded **ALNYLAM PHARMACEUTICALS** (market cap of $9 billion)[8] with his MIT faculty colleague **PAUL SCHIMMEL** '67, co-founder of several other biotechnology firms such as **ALKERMES**, **CUBIST**, and **REPLIGEN**.

Bio Information Associates, Genzyme, and Charles Cooney

Charles Cooney

CHARLES COONEY '67, '70 came to MIT in 1966 as a graduate student in the biochemical engineering program, established as a collaborative effort between chemical engineering and biology, and physically existing within the then Department of Nutrition and Food Science. Charlie reports:

> With that PhD and a post-doc in industry, I returned to MIT, excited by the opportunities to help bring scientific discoveries from biology into practice.
>
> A decade after I became an MIT faculty member, a group of related MIT faculty [an astonishing ensemble of scientific and entrepreneurial achievers] formed a consulting company called **BIO INFORMATION ASSOCIATES (BIA)**. This was a consequence of the close ties we had in National Science Foundation programs, the MIT Biotechnology Process Engineering Center, consulting work that I and others had done with Biogen and Genentech, and other connections we had established across the campus.

The "associates" were: Charlie Cooney, **HARVEY LODISH** (MIT faculty since 1968 and co-founder of **GENZYME** and **MILLENIUM PHARMACEUTICALS**, among others), **TONY SINSKEY** (MIT faculty since 1968, co-founder of **METABOLIX** and many other companies, identified in Chapter 5 and in the Appendix relating to his role in the MIT-HST Biomedical Enterprise Program), **GEORGE WHITESIDES** (MIT faculty from 1963 to 1982, then Harvard; co-founder of Genzyme and 12 or more other companies), **CHOKYUN RHA** (MIT faculty since 1969), **BILL ROUSH** (MIT faculty from 1978 to 1986, and co-founder of **IFM THERAPEUTICS**), **GRAHAM WALKER** (MIT faculty since 1975), and later Chris Walsh (who became director of the Harvard-MIT MD-PhD Program). Charlie observes:

> The eight of us each had a different lens on what we thought biotechnology was. It was the classic view of the elephant with a bunch of blind folks trying to figure it out.

> Our mission was to help people and companies figure out what to do. The scientists in those startups were struggling with the challenge of translating science into practice. That led us to come together in 1982 with the venture capitalists who were forming Genzyme and had begun to assemble some assets as the bases for the company. Those assets included manufacturing capabilities in the U.K. for biochemicals, plus a research project at Tufts New England Medical Center for glucose ribosidase. We realized that this was a pivotal opportunity to integrate those assets and for BIA to become part of Genzyme's creation. As a consequence, BIA got a founding seat on the Genzyme board, which I occupied for 30 years, representing the initial interests of BIA and helping through consulting and counsel to take this vision of what might be a company to what became a very substantial firm. BIA became essentially Genzyme's scientific advisory board over this long duration. Out of our classrooms and research labs, we had given birth to BIA, a new company creation facilitator, and BIA just continued in its role year after year. As a consequence, most of us and other MIT colleagues ended up being co-founders of one or more biotech companies, both as part of BIA and independently.

Genzyme itself identifies two principal co-founders, Sheridan Snyder and George Whitesides, MIT Professor of Chemistry until 1982 and a founding member of BIA. Henry Blair was also a scientific founder of Genzyme, working at the time as a technician at Tufts Medical School. Genzyme's first location was next door to Tufts Med in an old clothing factory in the midst of Boston's "red light district"! Henri Termeer came in as CEO in 1983 and focused the company on finding solutions for rare diseases, leading the firm to impressive growth over the next 30 years. Sanofi acquired Genzyme in 2011 for $20 billion, and operates it as a wholly-owned subsidiary. In the year prior to the acquisition, Genzyme Corporation was the world's third largest biotechnology company, then employing 11,000 people around the world, with revenues of $4 billion.

Charlie adds a comment that helps us understand what has happened at MIT regarding entrepreneurship in biotechnology and life sciences:

> I am proud that during my years at MIT I was on the PhD committees of many graduate students who have become distinguished achievers, such as Bob Langer and Noubar Afeyan. That and other academic and intellectual connections have served us, MIT, and the world of biotechnology very well. We have all shared in this wonderful adventure of starting and building great companies.

Langer Lab: The Source of Several Dozen New Life Sciences Companies

ROBERT LANGER, '74 in Chemical Engineering, is an MIT Institute Professor in the David Koch Institute for Integrative Cancer Research. Among other distinctions, he has the largest number of patents ever issued to an individual, and is the most cited engineer in history. With former students and lab scientists, Bob has co-founded over 40 startups based on biotechnology and materials science, and that number increases somewhat continuously. Bob Langer:

Robert Langer

Let me relate some aspects of my own evolution, as well as that of Cambridge. I arrived in 1970, and the area around MIT was terrible. Not just no companies, but no hotels and no real restaurants—my special love! There was a sub-shop, the F&T Diner, and lots of bars, but it was rather dangerous to go out at night, or even at 5 pm!

Despite having Harvard and MIT, Cambridge had some incredibly poor areas. While working on my thesis, I got very involved in seeking to do some good. I helped start the Group School for local poor kids and spent a lot of time working on new chemistry and math curricula. That made me think about how I might use chemical engineering to help people. When I finished my doctorate in 1974, most of my classmates went to the oil industry. They had great high-paying jobs. I got 20 job offers, but I wasn't very excited about that.

I ended up doing post-doctoral work at Judah Folkman's lab at Boston Children's Hospital as the only engineer in the hospital. It was by far the lowest paying job offer I got, but I loved the idea that I might possibly do something that might help people. I found it really hard to read those biology journal articles. But I liked it and made some findings about how you could use plastics to deliver molecules. The research got good academic acceptance, but I wanted my work to lead someday to products that might matter.

One day I got a call from a big animal health company that wanted to hire me to help figure out how to deliver animal growth hormones. I said, "Would you be interested in licensing my patent?" The caller said, "Yes. We want you to be a consultant, we're going to pay you, and we'll give you a grant of $200,000 to further your research. We're going to really develop your work." I thought all that was incredible. The very next year a major pharmaceutical company did something similar. This was so wonderful. In fact, I even finally went from a Ford Pinto to a much better car.

But all this turned out to be disappointing! I got the grants and the better car, but the companies didn't do much with my work. After an experiment or two, they kind of gave up. A couple of years later, **ALEX KLIBANOV** [MIT faculty since 1979], one of my friends and colleagues, said, "Bob, we should start our own company." We did. Children's Hospital owned the initial patent and asked the companies to give it back! We started **ENZYTECH**, licensed the IP from Children's, and developed the technology. Enzytech was on the fifth floor of a nearby building in Cambridge and **ALKERMES** was on the fourth floor. I soon sensed that we had a good technology but didn't have a very good CEO. Alkermes had a technology that wasn't working so well but it had a really good CEO, Rich Pops. So, we merged the companies. Alkermes developed and sold our microspheres, and now lots of them are used all over the world for different clinical applications. And I had my first lesson: In addition to great science, a successful company might require good investors who are patient and thoughtful and good management people to lead and run the company. I think it's really the combination of those things that matters.

I strongly agree with all aspects of Bob's observation.

The first four people in Enzytech were my students who had worked on this in the lab. Their passions were so different from the people at the two large companies we had dealt with previously. Our guys would walk through walls to get our stuff out to the public. From this, my very first experience as an entrepreneur, I could see that new companies could really make a difference in getting scientific discoveries to the market and eventually to the patient.

Bob now turns to the gradual outpouring of new companies from his lab:

Gradually people began asking me and my students, "Could I start a company on this? Or on that?" So, we did start those companies and we keep doing it as our MIT lab continues to grow. But when anyone asks me what he or she should do in his career—pursue academia, industry, or entrepreneuring—my answer is always the same. You should do something because you love it, because you have a passion for it. Don't do it because it's about money. Don't do it because your parents told you to do it. My advice is that simple—find something you love.

When I get asked what are the keys to those companies becoming successful, I tell them that I don't know any specific lessons. But some general lessons that can be shared relate to intellectual property, leadership, and trying to thoughtfully select targets. But every company is

> different and every person is different, so every situation has its own unique set of challenges.

Elicia Maine '97, now a Professor at Simon Fraser University, did a "deep dive" study of Langer Lab: There were 1,476 papers, 363 issued U.S. patents, and 30 ventures that spun off of this lab by the time of her research, uncovering other aspects of Langer's "secret sauce"!

> What we found first was superb technology-market matching. Bob Langer is an exemplar in that, and he can start either from the technology or the market. It's well known that Langer steers his students in his lab towards unmet market needs. But what may not be so well known is that he often will found several ventures from one technology platform. For example, in the case of controlled release polymers, his most famous platform technology, he has ten ventures that stem from that. Bob delineates each company by field of use and applications. Essentially, it's a way of giving oneself many chances at success.[9]

Bob Langer continues:

> Personally, my number one turn-on has been to do the research and create the solutions that will get out and benefit the world. And my second goal is to help my students realize their dreams. It was not my early intention to found companies per se. But that certainly became my intention after a while. Naively, when I started, I thought I would publish papers and the impact would happen. And it didn't. And then I thought that if I worked with large companies, the impact would happen. And it didn't. And then I was involved in some startup companies, and I could see that they and the people involved would almost live or die based on these ideas. And that was great. I've had the good fortune of being involved in companies with MIT colleagues, friends, and former students. We have had great fun, and success as well.

Terry McGuire, co-founder and general partner of Polaris Venture Partners, has been the key venture capitalist in many of Langer Lab's offspring. He frequently shows a slide that has two Langer-Polaris trees, its branches and leaves being the underlying technologies and the 16 companies that have been formed by Langer and his alumni in which Polaris has invested. The slide shows more than 33 therapeutic areas of contribution, with claimed potential impact upon 2.5 billion people. Indeed, that is success as measured in global impact on health and well-being.

Bob Langer concludes: "Now I look at Cambridge and the area around MIT, and what Susan Hockfield has said is clearly correct: 'This is the most entrepreneurial square mile I've ever seen. It has the highest concentration of biotechnology companies in the world.' . . . And many of Boston's best restaurants are within a few blocks of my office."

Flagship Ventures: A Company that Creates Great Companies

Noubar Afeyan

NOUBAR AFEYAN '87, co-founder and CEO of **FLAGSHIP VENTURES**, was born to Armenian parents in Lebanon. At age 13 he and his family fled to Canada, where Noubar attended McGill. In 1987, at age 24, he received MIT's first ScD in Biotechnology Processing. After graduating, he has been concurrently an entrepreneur, venture capitalist, and builder of major bio-pharma companies. Since 2000, he had also been an MIT Senior Lecturer in entrepreneurship until his recent appointment as a member of the MIT Corporation. His primary role is as co-founder and CEO of Flagship Ventures, and as head of its VentureLabs unit, which has created numerous major new companies.

During my MIT graduate studies, by chance at a conference to which Professor Daniel Wang had sent me, I met somebody who affected the course of my life profoundly. He told me how he and an MIT alum had started a company 30 years earlier in the field that was then called electrical engineering. I was taken by his story and came back and thought I might want to try that in biological engineering. That person was David Packard of **HEWLETT-PACKARD** [co-founder with **BILL HEWLETT** '36].

Close to completing my thesis at MIT, I realized even more clearly that I was not going to live a life in academia. My impatience and unruliness were two of the contributing factors. At the time—1986—the biotech industry was searching for engineers who knew a little bit about biology and biotechnology. Large companies recruited me heavily. Merck actually proposed that it would set up a separate lab and give me money to do whatever I wanted because they wanted entrepreneurial spirit within their company. ☺

For a bunch of chance reasons I decided to start a company. [There are many parallels here to Bob Langer rejecting the big job offers from major companies to do what he really wanted to do.] That had a lot to do with Ed Roberts. I had "snuck over" [??] to the Sloan School, and

> took Ed's course called "Corporate Entrepreneurship". That was the closest thing to anything to do with innovative entrepreneurship that I could find at MIT. He had a requirement that I had to know something about management to be able to complete his big project assignment. But I persisted with him, and he let me in the class, telling me that I would probably flunk the course. But he ended up giving me an A+! Ten to 15 years later, I was a guest lecturer in the same course. Ed likes to tell that story too, which was the beginning of our more than 30-years relationship.

Indeed, I do tell the story, but from my perspective as his professor! With no background in management, but infinite smarts and dedication, Noubar did a *tour de force* for his term paper in my course, studying the strategies of a number of major chemical and pharmaceutical companies as they attempted to enter the field of biotechnology. That project no doubt served him well as he advanced as an entrepreneur, corporate strategist, and later investor.

Noubar continues:

> Danny Wang, Charlie Cooney, and Bob Langer, remarkable academics and serial entrepreneurs, were on my dissertation committee. Ed was not. But he was on my "thesis committee" when I started a company. I came to see him the summer after I graduated, and gave him my business plan for what eventually became **PERSEPTIVE BIOSYSTEMS**, my first company, on the instrumentation side of the biotech business. The first time Ed edited my business plan, he marked it up severely, and said it was garbage and full of bad logic. On the second pass, six months later, Ed was far more encouraging, and his "seed fund", **ZERO STAGE CAPITAL**, became our initial investor. So, I really owe a great debt of gratitude to Ed, but also to MIT.

AUTHOR'S NOTE

Paul Kelley, Gordon Baty, and Jerry Goldstein were my principal partners at Zero Stage Capital. More on that pioneering seed fund appears later in Chapter 11, The World of "Modern Finance".

In response to Noubar's generous comment, I must say that being the first investor in his first company reflected my overall attitudes to startup investment. The ideas and plans of startup entrepreneurs contain great uncertainties, even as shown in the shift of Noubar's own initiative after six months. I have always sought the greater certainties of the entrepreneurs' personal attributes—their drive to achieve, their openness to criticism, their adaptability to needed change, their persistence, and their trustworthiness, and of course their personal brilliance. Noubar impressed me. In the last section of the final chapter of my 1991 book *Entrepreneurs in High Technology: Lessons from MIT and Beyond* (Oxford University Press), just three years later, I discussed him as portending the future of technological entrepreneurship—a striving Lebanese immigrant, a student but still pioneer of the biotechnology field, a daring young man founding a company just as he is departing from his formal MIT education. All of these seemed to forecast the future of entrepreneurship, as I wrote, despite PerSeptive Biosystems then having only 26 employees.

Back to Noubar:

> Anyone who's been leading a life of entrepreneurship would say that MIT provides students with a sense of technology prowess – i.e., being at the forefront of any field—and the courage and confidence that come with that prowess. But you also gain discipline. Maybe that's not the right word to use, but the MIT disciplined way of thinking, not just about problem-solving and engineering but about management, organization, objectives, and even people, has been a huge influence on me and my thinking. I devoted my first ten alumnus years to building PerSeptive Biosystems and becoming involved in a number of other companies that I co-founded in the 1990s. In 2000, I found myself thinking, "Okay, what does one do as an entrepreneur if you are not really serially-oriented?" Most entrepreneurs tend to be serial entrepreneurs, going into one thing and when they either complete it or get kicked out, they go to the next one, and they continue like this. I got interested in engaging with the notion of parallel entrepreneurship, as opposed to serial entrepreneurship.
>
> I always felt that if you think about starting companies as an innovative process—not as a kind of "beginning and an end", but as a continuous stream, where you could think about this as a discipline, not as some voyage—you'd approach it differently.
>
> In 2000, Chuck Vest [MIT's President at the time] said to me, "Noubar, you should really establish some ties with MIT where you can do this thinking further!" At Ed Roberts's invitation, I started to co-teach New Enterprises, which taught me more about entrepreneurship than I ever taught other people. And then I got deeply involved in co-creating and co-teaching iTeams [Innovation Teams], putting together teams of engineering and management students to work on MIT faculty research ideas that have advanced to the stage of possible serious assessment for commercialization and entrepreneurship. Most of those projects came from Deshpande Center sponsorship, which strives to move faculty ideas to impact. In iTeams, the professors agree to have their lab, post-docs, and themselves be available as counterpoint to the teams we deploy. But generally the class students do the work.
>
> By the way, at the start the students usually don't know anything about that invention. They may not even know much about the field of the invention. But what I found is that while you may need to be an expert to invent, you definitely don't need to be an expert to innovate. I think you need to be more of a generalist, much more of a connector

of the pieces, as opposed to a highly expert and therefore possibly narrowly-minded person who may not see the unobvious application of something that can be very valuable.

In iTeams, the students systematically bring a professor's research project forward through considerations of intellectual property, alternative potential applications, and issues of financing, manufacturing, and company launch, and end with detailed recommendations of what ought to be the next steps with that research effort, including possible startup of a new enterprise. I've dedicated my latest 18 years to that notion of thinking about entrepreneurship differently and systematically. It underlies what we have done with our VentureLabs efforts inside Flagship Ventures, where I now have a fairly large group of people who practice what I was teaching at MIT!

Noubar turns his attention further to his own company and its unique approach to creating new and great firms:

A number of years ago, we began setting aside a portion of **FLAGSHIP**'s capital investment funds to identify and organize internal seed-stage projects that we thought had huge downstream commercial potential. Our website explains: "**FLAGSHIP VENTURELABS** has originated more than 200 patents [2,500 worldwide as of July 2019] and 40 companies [over 100 as of July 2019]. Some of our notable venture creation successes include Moderna Therapeutics, Seres Therapeutics, Axcella Health, Indigo Agriculture and Adnexus."[10] Our VentureLabs staff frequently comes up with the initial ideas for these ventures. In other cases, the ideas are brought to us by outside scientists from MIT and many other universities. VentureLabs creates initial teams from our own staff, complemented by outsiders we recruit. We provide the initial funding. But we frequently seek early growth funding and especially growth staff, including additional leadership, from outside of Flagship. We then always develop and scale these ventures significantly in major partnerships with a variety of large pharmaceutical firms. To the extent possible, VentureLabs has been practicing our best understandings of systematic disciplined entrepreneuring, but we still have lots to learn.

To that point, Flagship Ventures recently renamed itself as **FLAGSHIP PIONEERING**, to emphasize its creative new venture initiation and development practice. By 2015, Flagship had become the largest venture investor in companies based out of Massachusetts, and it maintains that unique status. By July 2019, Flagship had "founded more than 100 science-based businesses, worth more than $30 billion in aggregate value. . . . [which] have filed more than 12,750 patents."[11]

The similarity in the underlying principles between what I taught in iTeams and what we practice in Flagship VentureLabs makes me want to comment on some aspects of how we are handling entrepreneuring education at MIT.

First, my own ethics about conflict of interest strongly matches the way that the MIT Entrepreneurship Center [now the Trust Center] operates. I don't allow myself to get involved in any of the things, including many new company startups, that come out of the iTeams class. Not because I couldn't, but just because I don't need to do things with my students that might raise questions. I know that we are different from even some other very prominent institutions in that belief and practice.

Second, I'm also an engineer, but I don't do "engineership". I do "engineering"—the focus is not on me as the person but rather on the act of what engineering actually involves. So, I take issue with the word "entrepreneurship" and strongly prefer "entrepreneuring", the act of being an entrepreneur. Call it whatever you want, but what I seek is the mindset of saying this is a profession, a discipline. I think a massive shift has occurred among "professional entrepreneurs" to identify ourselves not merely as people who are entrepreneurs, but rather who are practicing the science, art, and craft of entrepreneuring.

Finally, I am extremely happy that MIT is in this collaboration primarily between the School of Engineering and the Sloan School of Management, and that the School of Science is also beginning to accept responsibility for getting students to think seriously about starting and building companies. Across MIT, let's move away from seeing entrepreneuring as a risky game versus a difficult, long, challenging activity for our best and brightest.

A FINAL VOICE ON MIT'S LIFE SCIENCES ENTREPRENEURS

PAUL SCHIMMEL, former MIT MacArthur Professor of Biochemistry and Biophysics, and co-founder of several biotech companies, provides a bottom-line:

> The life science educational enterprise spreads across five departments at MIT. None of the extensive commercial and residential real estate development, restaurants, hotels in the Kendall Square area . . . nor the founding and locating of major biopharmaceutical enterprises would have happened . . . and none of the robust economic impact would have occurred if not for MIT's life sciences.[12]

And the beat goes on! The newer generation of MIT's life science academic leaders continues to pioneer scientific breakthroughs, while also moving them rapidly to the marketplace via company startups. Increasingly they are crossing gender and racial lines that had earlier seemed to pose barriers to significant entrepreneurial achievements. Professors **KAREN GLEASON** and **SANGEETA BHATIA** (Gleason—'82, '82; Bhatia—'93, '97) are serial entrepreneur examples of multi-faceted MIT faculty careers coupled with innovative formation and development of major firms, establishing more impressive role models for junior faculty and students.

The future of MIT-based entrepreneurship in the life sciences and biotechnology is promising and assured. For example, in the recent annual meetings of Flagship Pioneering, Noubar Afeyan showcased a large array of advancing projects in agriculture, energy, and medicine, including concepts for new firms focused on the microbiome as well as yet unexplored areas of DNA.

The life sciences and biotechnology industry is rather different from the others that I discuss in the next three chapters. It illustrates strong dominance by faculty of MIT who became entrepreneurial founders, and is a wonderful illustration of how *mens et manus* can work at MIT. Here an extraordinary entrepreneur can concurrently be a Nobel Prize winner, or run the largest single laboratory at MIT, or pioneer MIT's relationships with one country after another in transferring MIT's entrepreneurship and innovation understandings. At many

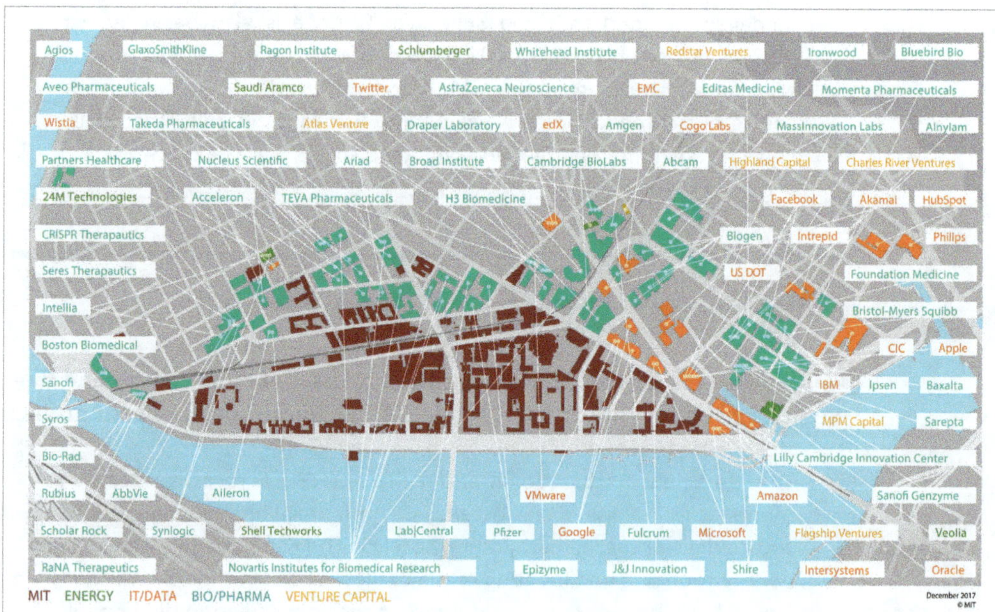

Cluster of high-tech companies in Kendall Square (as of December 2017)

other universities, this practice of faculty entrepreneurship is prohibited, or not encouraged, or doesn't happen anyway!

The three industries of Chapters 9 through 11 present the more typical situation, where faculty may well be providing the underlying scientific or technological base, but their lab associates and students more frequently become the prime movers in founding new firms. And of course, in many cases illustrated among these four industries, the original ideas for the startups came from the students and alumni themselves.

REFERENCES AND NOTES

1. Charles G. Koch, *Good Profit: How Creating Value for Others Built One of the World's Most Successful Companies,* Crown Publishing, 2015.
2. Christopher Vaughan, "Interview with Ray Stata", *Kaizen*, February 8, 2010.
3. Interview with Kavita Chhibber.
4. Accessed on August 12, 2019.
5. Edward Roberts and Charles Eesley, *Entrepreneurial Impact: The Role of MIT,* Kauffman Foundation, 2009; Edward Roberts, Fiona Murray, and Daniel Kim, *Entrepreneurship and Innovation at MIT: Continuing Global Growth and Impact,* MIT, 2015.
6. Arlene Weintraub, *BloombergBusinessWeek,* October 18, 2004.
7. Funding Universe, http://www.fundinguniverse.com/company-histories/genentech-inc-history/, accessed on March 29, 2018.
8. Data on Biogen and Alnylam accessed on August 13, 2019.
9. From Elicia Maine's presentation in a research session on November 12, 2016 at MIT.
10. Flagship Pioneering, http://flagshippioneering.com/about-us/, accessed on March 29, 2018.
11. Flagship web site, July 7, 2019.
12. Elizabeth Chadis, *Science at MIT* 11, Spring 2015, accessed at science.mit.edu on February 20, 2017.

9

The Internet

"In the beginning, MIT created the Internet!" Well, that is a bit of an overstatement. But indeed, the Internet as we know it was conceived, technically developed, and first implemented primarily by MIT faculty, staff, and alumni, some of whom were also entrepreneurial founders of new pioneering companies. Or as **BOB METCALFE** '68 puts it, again with some exaggeration: "You've all heard 'success has many fathers, but failure is an orphan'. It turns out that all of the 'fathers' of the Internet came from MIT!"

The November 12, 2016 MIT panel on "The Internet": (right to left) Bob Metcalfe (chair), Tom Leighton, Charles Zhang, and Frederic Kerrest

This chapter relates how MIT faculty and alumni essentially developed all key aspects of the Internet, founded its first companies, transported the Internet to China (the largest Internet marketplace in the world today), and made feasible the Internet's amazing continuing traffic growth. The chapter concludes by presenting one particular firm that is helping to pioneer the Internet's journey into the clouds.

A BRIEF HISTORY OF INTERNET DEVELOPMENT

Beyond possible conceptual credits to Vannevar Bush '16, the founding and early development of the Internet depended importantly on **LEO BERANEK**, co-founder in 1948 and CEO of **BOLT BERANEK & NEWMAN, INC. (BBN)**, and on many of BBN's key employees. (In addition to Beranek, BBN's co-founders were **RICHARD BOLT**, MIT Professor of acoustics, and **ROBERT NEWMAN** '49, Bolt's student.) Beranek was an MIT professor from 1947 to 1958. The first series of memos that outlined the ideas for an Internet came from **J.C.R. LICKLIDER**, an MIT faculty member in the 1950s and then again from 1968 on. He authored those memos while he was Vice President of BBN, from 1960 through 1962. Licklider followed them with more work at MIT Lincoln Lab on the Whirlwind computer and with the SAGE system. In October 1962, he was appointed the first head of the Information Processing Techniques Office (IPTO) in the Department of Defense Advanced Research Projects Agency (DARPA), then became Director of DARPA's Behavioral Sciences Command & Control Research. In an April 1963 memo to his colleagues, Licklider outlined the challenges in establishing a time-sharing network of computers with the existing hardware and software. Ultimately, his vision led to ARPAnet, the precursor of today's Internet.[1] Ivan Sutherland '63, a great pioneer of computer graphics, succeeded Licklider as head of IPTO.

AUTHOR'S NOTE

Quotes throughout this chapter are primarily from those individuals' presentations in a session led by Robert Metcalfe at our 2016 MIT celebration of entrepreneurship, integrated with interviews conducted in 2017 by Michelle Choate as well as supplemental sources. Bob Metcalfe and Larry Roberts, two living experts and both MIT alumni, were especially helpful in providing the details. Many historical details come from Steven Hartley, "History of the Internet", December 1996, accessed at www.securenet.net/members/shartley/history/ on February 21, 2017.

The next step in the MIT-to-Internet chain was through **LAWRENCE "LARRY" ROBERTS** '61, '63 (and not related to me!). "After talking with Licklider", Larry said, "I concluded that computer networks would hold enormous potential, so I went to Lincoln Lab and began experimenting. In 1964 I was drafted by the Pentagon, much against my resistance, into IPTO to become the program manager for ARPAnet." Larry was later named one of the "founding fathers of the Internet" for his funding and leadership of the overall ARPAnet development program. Wesley Clark '55, also from Lincoln Lab and with strong Whirlwind connections, came up with the idea of using small "host" computers at each node of the intended computer network, which he called Interface Message Processors (IMPs), and identified **FRANK HEART** '51, '52, then at BBN but previously at Lincoln Lab, as the "only" one who could build them. Paul Baran and Donald Davies, independent of one another and neither from MIT, were both concerned that a possible nuclear attack would seriously interrupt military communications, and had developed the idea of packet switching as the mode for more assured messaging over multi-channel communication lines. With tight-knit connections among these individuals, Larry Roberts incorporated both IMPs and packet switching concepts into the Request for Quotation sent out to 140 companies in 1968. With 12 companies responding, ARPA awarded the contract to BBN. Its 200-page proposal was submitted by Jerry Elkind '51, with lead contributions made by Frank Heart and several others. Frank became the program manager and ran the entire BBN development of the ARPAnet system. Frank comments on the importance of his MIT background:

"Jay Forrester was very concerned with reliability issues. . . . I learned this lesson well, and many years later . . . I believe that my emphasis on reliability made the difference between success and failure of the ARPANET."[2]

JAY FORRESTER '45 developed MIT's Whirlwind computer and headed the computer and systems aspects of MIT Lincoln Laboratory's SAGE system program. He later created the System Dynamics program at MIT Sloan.

The tight BBN team was frequently called "the IMP guys". It included Robert Kahn '58, an MIT EE Assistant Professor who had moved to BBN, was later hired by Larry Roberts into IPTO, and still later was one of the co-developers of the TCP/IP protocol that lasts to today. Leonard Kleinrock '59, who had been Roberts's MIT office mate during their PhD studies, joined Kahn in the TCP/IP development. (Most of the key people mentioned here came out of and contributed to the advancement of MIT's Electrical Engineering Department.)

In October 1969, the first message was sent over the network, which connected four universities along a telecommunications line from BBN, and thus ARPAnet was born. By the summer of 1970, MIT, RAND, System Development Corporation, and Harvard received their IMPs and a second cross-continent high-speed (for that time!) line was added from BBN to RAND. (More on this is in the later section of this chapter that focuses on Bob Metcalfe and **3COM**.) After ARPAnet became operational, over the next several years BBN developed the defense data network called "Milnet", and then built a gateway between it to the 4-node ARPAnet, calling the connector between those two networks "the Internet". BBN also developed the first router, the TCP/IP protocol, and the first person-to-person email system, further cementing the great contributions it had previously made to the field.[3]

Bob Metcalfe was very active during this same time period. He remembers early versions of the Internet-to-be:

> ARPA had an early idea that we would use the Internet to log into computers using teletypes around the world. Such an Internet was demonstrated at the International Conference on Computer Communications in 1972. Because I had gone to MIT Sloan and knew how to wear a suit, even though I had a big red beard, I was given the job of escorting the AT&T executives around the demonstration so they could see the various Telnet-ish applications. The Internet (as it was then) crashed during the demo to the AT&T execs. I remember vividly and with pain that they all laughed. Clearly, we recognized that our own data needed to be available for you to do your computations when you logged into someone else's site. So, we came up with what we called the File Transfer Protocol [FTP] to be able to move our data.

Bob continues: "Then email came about a year after these operations began, becoming the dominant application unanticipated by ARPA. So we moved from the Telnet Internet to the email Internet very quickly." Also in 1973, Ray Tomlinson '65 at BBN created the "@" symbol to separate the user name from the computer name in every email address, based on the little-used symbol on his Model 33 Teletype!

MORE ABOUT BBN AND LARRY ROBERTS

As soon as the U.S. government legalized "value-added carriers", BBN set out to create a private sector version of the ARPAnet, incorporating **TELENET, INC.** (NOT Telnet), the first packet-switched network service available to the public. That was in 1972, and BBN invested $550,000 of its own funds as the founding investor during 1973 and 1974. Its co-founding leaders were **LARRY ROBERTS** as President and **BARRY WESSLER** 65, '67, also from ARPA. AT&T declined to invest in BBN's proposal, reflecting the skepticism regarding the future importance of what became the Internet. AT&T also indicated that if any commercial potential did develop out of BBN's venture, it was sure that Bell Labs could provide the needed technology! BBN struggled to raise venture funds at that time, eventually bringing in a total of $4.8 million from multiple sources during 1975 and 1976, with BBN adding $1.4 million of its own. GTE acquired Telenet in 1979 and later sold it to Sprint, which renamed it Sprintnet and transitioned it into the Sprintlink IP network, which is still part of today's Internet.

Lawrence Roberts

When questioned about why he became a Telenet entrepreneur, Larry replied:

> My orientation all along was to do something that would change the world significantly. I did not want to teach. That's why I went to Lincoln Lab in the first place, and why I gave in and went into ARPA. That worked out great, because suddenly I had the money to really change a lot of things in computing, including funding work on speech recognition and on artificial intelligence. Only after the ARPAnet was up and running did I decide I really needed to take the next steps and move out into starting and running companies. Telenet became very successful, and is still in use today. The finance industry uses it because it is much more secure than the rest of the Internet.
>
> I then went on to become a leader of several firms and to form a number of companies—some successful, some not. I became CEO of DHL and put in an airline, which in a way is like a packet network! Then I started several companies: **NETEXPRESS**, then **ATM SYSTEMS**, and later **CASPIAN NETWORKS**, which failed to get the needed funding to

make it realizable. I created **ANAGRAN** in 2004, and most recently I have started **FSA TECHNOLOGIES**, working on new products to speed up the Internet. All of these have been outgrowths of the technical and managerial tasks I undertook in leading ARPAnet development and implementation.

It's certainly clear to me that MIT is the center of the tremendous amount of innovation that is taking place in the country. But I am most proud that I was a major part of MIT being the primary inventor of the Internet, because of so many MIT people who were involved. The Internet is probably the biggest overall change that has happened in the world.

ROBERT METCALFE AND 3COM

Robert Metcalfe

ROBERT METCALFE received his undergraduate education at MIT (dual degrees in EECS and Management '69). He went on to get a PhD at Harvard, but was not willing to give up his attachment to MIT. He recalls those earliest years, and after:

I started as an MIT freshman in the fall of '64. The next year I began a job at **RAYTHEON** [co-founded years before by **VANNEVAR BUSH**], and thereafter was employed full time while being a student. I worked from midnight to 8 am every day. During my next four years, I started three consulting companies that integrated my studies in EE and Management, named **MANAGEMENT SYSTEMS CONSULTING**, **DATA CONCEPTS DESIGN**, and **PROFESSIONAL DATA SERVICES**. Each was successful for a year or two, and I paid my tuition. I stayed a fifth year to get a degree in electrical engineering.

During that fifth year, I took some courses from Professor Don Troxel '60. He taught us how to build things out of integrated circuits, which were brand new. I remember helping build a computer by build-ing its memory. I mention this because the device I built then evolved to become 3Com. The memory for the class project was an acoustic- delay line that stored things by launching the bits down a long cable. They'd spin around out there and come back a little later to the same place from which they were transmitted. You could keep circulating them and that served as a memory.

Metcalfe discusses how he came to be an Internet pioneer:

When I graduated from MIT, I enrolled at Harvard for a PhD. Then an unexpected opportunity arose. The Department of Defense had a new project called ARPAnet. DARPA gave both Harvard and MIT opportunities to build devices to connect to ARPAnet, and I enthusiastically proposed to Harvard that I build its device as part of my doctoral program. But Harvard said that I couldn't take on that project because it was much too important. That annoyed me, because I had just finished getting an MIT EE degree, and I was all excited. I turned around and went back down Broadway to Tech Square. Despite my being a Harvard PhD student, MIT hired me as a part-time member of the research staff to build a device to connect its computers to ARPAnet. I then turned again to Harvard and said, "Hey, MIT has agreed to let me build two of these devices and I can give one to you." Harvard still rejected the offer. The powers there said, "This is much too important for a grad student." Harvard gave the contract to BBN to build its device. It would send bits one at a time, serially, down a really long cable. Does that sound familiar? That experience strongly affected me. At MIT you were encouraged and supported to go and do what you wanted to do, and you weren't discouraged or told that you weren't experienced enough. No limits were put on you at MIT.

It took me a year to build MIT's ARPAnet connector. My project advisor was MIT Professor J.C.R. Licklider! I still have the device. It's called IMP [Interface Message Processor]. In 1972, I finally left Harvard and MIT for Xerox Palo Alto Research Center [PARC], where I then built yet another one of those devices to connect Xerox's computers into the growing ARPAnet.

Now Bob's opportunity grew, as he describes:

After putting Xerox on ARPAnet, we decided to build the world's first personal computer and put one on every desk. This was outrageous at the time. Not one computer per building, but one on every desk. Because I was a networking guy, I got the job of building the network to connect all these computers. And it had to be as fast as we could possibly make it. The first Ethernet was devised, with a big cable that connected all the computers. You sent bits down one at a time, or in the then new world, you sent packets of bits down the cable, one packet at a time!

David Boggs and I co-invented and built this first Ethernet, which ran at 2.94 megabits per second, 10,000 times faster than the bandwidth I had at my desk before. On one day it went from 300 bits per second to 3 million bits per second, because semiconductors allowed us to build this network to be as fast as we practically could make it. Then David and I filled the Xerox Corporation with an Internet of personal computers, and with a private network called Ethernet.

interconnected the computers with routers around the world. This was the Xerox Ethernet, developed slightly before and in parallel with the real Internet, the big one outside. But despite our pioneering, Xerox management repeatedly opposed trying to commercialize what we had done in-house. [Do see and consider the parallel of AT&T rejecting the investment opportunity in the Internet!]

And then came entrepreneurship:

In 1978, I read about an MIT alumni luncheon at Ming's Restaurant in Palo Alto. This was a local follow-on to the MIT Alumni Entrepreneurship Seminars that Ed Roberts had led all across the country. On the panel was **DUBOSE MONTGOMERY** [three MIT degrees, '72; much more about DuBose in Chapter 11, The World of "Modern Finance"] who had founded **MENLO VENTURES** in 1976, Dave Anderson '66 who was a partner in Sutter Hill Ventures, and a few other MIT venture people. I went because DuBose had been the manager of the MIT Tennis Team in 1968-69 when I was the captain, so we knew each other pretty well. Now my friend DuBose was telling MIT alums how to start companies.

That provoked me to leave Xerox soon after in 1979 to start my own company. But I wasn't really sure exactly what to do and how to do it. So, I went back to MIT and worked for a few weeks for Professor **MICHAEL DERTOUZOS** '64, who was in the process of creating the MIT Laboratory for Computer Science. Mike was already a successful entrepreneur, and was very helpful in guiding me. I went back to Palo Alto and decided to move ahead, basically to recreate all we had started to do at Xerox on the Ethernet and related networking. I called the company 3Com Corporation, short for "Computer Communication Compatibility".

A wondrous event happened just after we incorporated. Steve Jobs tried to recruit me to his startup. "Steve, I just started my own company last week. So, I have to decline. What is the name of your company again? Apple? What a funny name for a company!" Steve did something that surprised me. Instead of getting upset with my turndown, he decided to help me start my company. He introduced me to a few people, including Bob Noyce. You would think I might already have known **ROBERT NOYCE** '53, an MIT alumnus and the founder of **INTEL CORPORATION**. But I met Noyce through Steve Jobs, and then Noyce became an angel investor in 3Com. Steve Jobs later became a customer, buying networks from us. When I turned him down in 1979, he hired a guy who worked with me at PARC to be head engineer for the Macintosh project. I think Steve wanted to be successful with these networks, because someday his PCs would be in such networks.

> A few weeks after I incorporated, **GREG SHAW** '77 joined me as a co-founder, and then a bunch more of my MIT fraternity brothers and friends came on board.
>
> Together we built a series of these high-speed network interfaces, first with mini computers, and later for the IBM personal computer and the Macintosh, and so on. We grew very rapidly, went public in 1984, and hit a peak $5.8 billion in revenues, with more than 13,000 employees, in 1999.

THOSE EARLIEST EMPLOYEES INCLUDED, in order of Metcalfe's recollections, Ron Crane, Howard Charney, J. "Pitts" Jarvis, and Ken Morse (later the first Managing Director of the MIT Entrepreneurship Center).

Hewlett-Packard acquired 3Com in 2010 for $2.7 billion.

Bob:

> When I came back to Boston, I had the delight of annually sponsoring a "soiree" the night before the finals of the $50K and then the $100K MIT Business Plan Competition. All of the finalists would come to my home and set up small booths or stations to chat with so many Greater Boston entrepreneurs, VCs, and just old friends. That was a fascinating social way to bring together the larger entrepreneurship community around young MIT would-be entrepreneurs.

At one of Bob's soirees, I met Howard Anderson, who joined the MIT Entrepreneurship Center the next year and stayed for a decade (see the Appendix: MIT Entrepreneurship Faculty).

Bob concludes:

> I am a Trustee Emeritus of MIT, and have various opportunities to give back. I gave a professorial chair in writing, to celebrate what Professor Jay Forrester taught me when I was in his Undergraduate Systems Program. And we are honored that Tim Berners-Lee occupies the 3Com Founders Professorship. Now I am trying to get all who claim to be an inventor of the Ethernet to contribute to another chair in that name!

MORE INTERNET COMPANIES AND PROLIFERATION

"Internets" of different configurations, for a wide range of purposes, began to be created. To diversify its base from strong dependence on BBN, DARPA brought in even more MIT alumni to help develop Internets for various military organizations. **LINKABIT INC.**, co-founded by **IRWIN JACOBS** '57 and **ANDREW VITERBI** '56, and employing a flood of MIT grads, was given a contract to handle some of the development needs. (Linkabit's most significant follow-on was **QUALCOMM**, also co-founded by Jacobs and Viterbi, along with five more of their Linkabit colleagues. Both firms are discussed in greater detail in Chapter 12.)

Following the new government regulations that permitted privatization of the Internet, many firms in addition to Telenet were created, including the bevy of Larry Roberts's initiatives mentioned previously. One early firm was **QUANTUM COMPUTER SERVICES**, co-founded in 1985 by Jim Kimsey as CEO and **MARC SERIFF** '73 as CTO, which was soon joined by Steve Case who took over as CEO. In 1989, they changed the name of the firm to **AMERICA ONLINE**, which grew very rapidly, simplifying its corporate identity to **AOL, INC.** As a side note with which other early MIT alumni might sympathize, Marc actually started as a freshman at MIT:

> However, the shortage of female classmates and parties at the Massachusetts Institute of Technology produced what Seriff called "a miserable year" at MIT, so he returned to Austin to attend the University of Texas as an undergrad. Once he got the true college experience out of his system, a subsequent return to MIT for graduate school gave him the connections and inspiration to get his technology career back on track.[4]

Coming out of MIT with his EE master's at the right time, Marc immediately became one of the first dozen employees at Telenet. He says he was strongly influenced in that decision and in his later entrepreneurship by his MIT advisor Professor Licklider and his Telenet boss and friend Larry Roberts. The AOL co-founding followed Seriff's years at Telenet.

A later key addition to AOL and the Internet was a different kind of MIT "alum". **TED LEONSIS** was in the first one-week class of the "Birthing of Giants" executive program (described in Chapter 6) in 1991, co-sponsored for many years at MIT Endicott House in Dedham by the MIT Enterprise Forum of Cambridge, **INC. MAGAZINE** (founded and led by **BERNARD GOLDHIRSH** '63), and the Young Entrepreneurs Organization. I was the official faculty sponsor of the program (with several other MIT Sloan faculty as participants) and gave the kickoff lecture. In the coffee break immediately after that talk, Ted Leonsis approached me with great urgency. He was concurrently trying to raise money for his Redgate Communications Company and had just received an offer to buy his company from a young firm named AOL. Our lunch-time personal discussion explored the pros and cons of Ted growing his own firm against the prospect of selling out. Shortly after the course ended, Ted sold to AOL, and over the years rose to become its Vice Chairman, the number two executive in the firm. Ted today is very active as the owner of multiple sports teams in Washington D.C., a venture investor, and a philanthropist, but he remembers fondly his brief and helpful period as an MIT "student"!

In 1985, the same year that Quantum/AOL was founded, Nick Negroponte '66 and Jerome Wiesner, MIT's President, created the MIT Media Lab, which became the source of large numbers of Internet applications and spinoff companies.

SOHU.COM, CHINA'S FIRST INTERNET COMPANY

China's first global Internet transmission occurred nearly a decade later in 1994, between Stanford University and Beijing's Tsinghua University, which calls itself "The MIT of China". **CHARLES ZHANG**, a Tsinghua distinguished alumnus, had in 1993 just completed his MIT Physics PhD. Remaining temporarily in the United States, Charles was working part-time for the MIT Industrial Liaison Program, escorting the increasing number of Chinese visitor groups around MIT to help them meet faculty and learn about the forefronts of science and technology being explored at MIT. Those visits carried Charles on several occasions into my MIT office, as many of the Chinese visitors were quite interested in my entrepreneurship research and in the development of the MIT Entrepreneurship Center.

AUTHOR'S NOTE

As co-founder and board member for 20 years, I speak for myself in this section.

One day in September of 1996, Charles stuck his head into my office and asked if he could have a brief chat. I welcomed him and asked how I might help him. Charles responded, "I want to go home to China and start an Internet company". Both parts of that statement were entirely unusual notions at that time. Essentially all Chinese graduate students at MIT then were searching for ways to delay the end of their visas and be required to return home to China! In probing Charles during the next two hours, I was impressed with his sincerity and passion, qualities I have long come to desire, even demand, in would-be entrepreneurs. When pushed about going home, Charles said: "China is going to become a great nation. And I want to be a part of making it great!" Four months of arguments and discussions led to the two of us incorporating **INTERNET TECHNOLOGIES CHINA, INC. (ITC)** in December 1996. In providing the meager angel funding, totaling $225,000 deposited in the First National Bank of Boston, Nick Negroponte and one other MIT person joined me, somewhat reluctantly. ITC was incorporated in Delaware in my hopes of somewhat enhancing the credibility of the firm—the idea of starting any kind of company in China in 1996 was seen by most Americans as extremely risky and foolish.

Edward Roberts and Charles Zhang

Charles went home to China with $25,000 deposited in the Bank of China to get him started, with another $200,000 back in Boston that needed to be co-signed by Charles and me! We had not yet determined what kind of Internet firm Charles was trying to create—a basic entrepreneurship violation from my perspective—but frankly, my mental objections were overcome by my fascination with pioneering in China.

Charles began to learn fast, after his eight years away in the United States. He recalls:

> We were the first real Internet company in China. Nobody there understood what the Internet was about. [As pointed out above, the very first Internet message, from the United States to China, had happened

just two years before!] No rules yet existed to define our business, or what we could or could not do. It was even unclear as to which government ministry would regulate the Internet—the Ministry of Electronics, or the newly formed Ministry of Information Industries. So, we had to submit all our applications to both ministries.

I began running around trying to do things to help figure out what our focus should be. Some infrastructure had already been built. But I realized that the first thing needed was to build a website. I was trying to put some content onto sites, and some ISPs were emerging in China that provided services. On my website I put some information from traditional data providers, collecting various kinds of information—some newspapers and magazines. It took a lot of work to type in that content or even to use email to enter the content. The whole year of 1997 I tried to study what the Internet was really about. Then when I finally opened a site, I realized that the Internet is really an open plan. Of the 500 daily hits I got, half of them would go to the list of connections, the ISPs, instead of reading the newspapers or the other content I had put in with so much effort. I just needed to list some things, and I'd get half of the traffic. I decided that was the way to go.

Then I read a book about the first 1,000 days of the Internet, and found one chapter describing Yahoo and its rather primitive search engine, which was really a "connection engine". "This is exactly what I'm doing", I instantly thought. So, I went back to the U.S. to see if Ed and Nick Negroponte could introduce me to Jerry Yang at Yahoo. The first time I met Jerry I said, "In China I'm also doing this directory thing that you have in Yahoo. Maybe we should merge." No real response! A year later Yang came to China and tried to acquire ITC, but then I refused because I wanted to do my own thing. Anyway, we didn't do the deal.

We began to have competition as a news and information source: Netease began in 1997, Sina in 1998, and then the barrage started of many new Internet companies with many different directions! Early in 1999, we raised a more significant investment that included funds from Gerald Chan of Morningside Group in Hong Kong, corporate venture money from Intel (both Ed and Nick provided introductions at the very top) and Reuters, and straight VC from the **IDG** [**INTERNATIONAL DATA GROUP**] Beijing fund (**PAT MCGOVERN** '60 was a good friend of Ed's from when they were undergraduates). That gave us an entirely Western, English-speaking board of directors, except for me, and many years of educating them into China and Chinese ways while we were building major experiences in the new world of a rapidly growing Chinese Internet. As all of this was going on, the Chinese news and magazines began to pay attention. I became almost a movie star in being interviewed frequently as the young man who brought advanced American technology back home to China, with photos on magazine covers and so forth. Every time I spoke, I mentioned my background from MIT, and Ed Roberts as my co-founder. Soon I was very famous and Ed became widely known as "The Godfather of the Chinese Internet"!

As we grew, we entered one after another new application, usually as the first one in China to try it out. After straight news and information, we again followed Yahoo's lead and went from a connection engine to a true search engine that we developed internally, and that was very important for us. We called it "Sohu", which in Chinese means "search fox"—a fox being admired as a smart and fast animal! On the first day the Sohu search engine went online, our website crashed from the huge number of hits we received. Fortunately, one call to our Intel investors and the next day a team arrived from the West Coast and installed all of the hardware and software we needed to support our new traffic! After a while we realized that we didn't need to promote two names, Internet Technologies China and Sohu, so we changed our company name to **SOHU.COM**.

In July 2000 we went public, but our timing turned out to be terrible. It was the death-days of the Internet bubble and we went from opening at $13 per share to less than half that in three weeks, on our way steadily down to 50 cents per share by April 2001. Our stock price stayed very low, and we just avoided being delisted from NASDAQ by its change of rules during the prolonged market collapse. It took about two years for both our business and the stock market to recover. Then for both years of 2002 and 2003, SOHU became the stock with the highest rate of price growth on NASDAQ, and we were back on our way as a company. By the way, NASDAQ honored us by having Sohu.com open the market on our tenth anniversary as a company. Ed shows the photos of that day on the walls of his MIT office!

Different from Charles, I obviously have to look at Sohu's history from the view of a management school professor, but one who has been an active co-founder and a Sohu director from day one. Because Charles is very smart, insightful, and daring, we were the primary mover and innovator in one after another Internet market. We were the first in China to do online shopping, delivering products by a bicycle fleet in Beijing and collecting cash payment from our customers, because China had neither a meaningful delivery system nor credit cards. We were the first to do online stock trading, but it had to be done with each regional bank separately as our partner, and we were very restricted on the terms and conditions of who could buy and what we could offer. We were early in entering online gaming on PCs, and that has now nearly died, but we have fortunately switched over to mobile gaming on smart phones that proliferate in China! Sohu spun-off Changyou, its gaming division, as a public company many years ago, but retains control. (Changyou had a market cap of $2 billion as of October 16, 2017, but dropped precipitously to about $500 million by June 15, 2019.) We were early entrants to providing online video entertainment, including doing our own video production effectively, but have had to cope with government policies that strongly restrict our licensing of foreign films and TV programs. For example, we brought "Big Bang Theory", Charles's and my favorite TV show, to China and it was a great hit. But after one year the government censors decided it contained too much sex and banned it! In all of these areas initiated by Sohu, the enormous growth of the Internet market in China, the largest in the world by far,[5] has made possible much later entries by new firms that raised huge investment funding, both privately and in the public markets, such as Alibaba, Baidu, TenCent, Youkoo (founded by Victor Koo, who earlier had been President of Sohu, under Charles who was CEO and Chairman!) and many others. Each of those new and well-funded entrants focused on a single market while we were still defending a broad-based portal covering multiple fields. We let ourselves be spread too thin!

Charles observes these same phenomena from the view of the entrepreneurial chief executive in China for these past 20-plus years:

> Through all of these years, and especially in the first decade, I didn't have any business experience, and Ed helped me a lot. Also, he was important in managing the board of directors, and getting help from them in building the business. They were all Westerners and I was not always comfortable with dealing with them. After we went public, the board gradually shifted toward all being Chinese, with the one exception of Ed, but we kept our global telephone board meetings going in English. We had a constant flow of new issues to treat, all the way through today, with a broad mix of successes and failures. The slowdown of the Chinese economy during the past four years has significantly impacted our revenues and profitability. Nevertheless, we are still competing and still leading in our traditional area of online news and information, while holding a reasonable position in gaming and in the video marketplace. And we have fought our way based on new technology to be second and growing in online search. Our search division, Sogou, went public as SOGO on NASDAQ on November 9, 2017, but we still retain control of the firm. [Sogou had 2018 revenues of $1.1 billion, and had been valued at approximately $5 billion at its 2017 IPO. Despite its growth and superb products, its value is now considerably lower.] Our joint laboratory with Tsinghua has given us remarkable advances in artificial intelligence and speech recognition, which have helped." [Sohu now employs about 10,000 people in China, and generated $1.9 billion in revenues in 2018.].

Charles concludes: "But there's no question. Just as Ed showed that MIT created the original Internet in the United States, it's fair to say that MIT created the Chinese copy as well ☺."

THE FOUNDING AND GROWTH OF AKAMAI

Thomas Leighton

Professor **THOMAS LEIGHTON** '81, who later co-founded and became CEO of **AKAMAI**, provides his background and more:

> I never left MIT after getting my PhD in 1981. I became a post doc, then joined the faculty in Applied Math. My background is very theoretical. It's mathematical models and analysis and proofs for problems in computer science and networking.
>
> In 1995, the Internet had been around for a long time. We'd been doing email forever, but the Web was still sort of new. Tim Berners-Lee [later "Sir"] had created the World Wide Web, built the first Web browser, and the first server in 1989 while he was at CERN in Switzerland. Professor Mike Dertouzos, as head of MIT Computer Science, had the good judgment and perseverance to persuade Berners-Lee to join MIT in 1994, where he has continued his Internet leadership. Professor Berners-Lee's office in CSAIL (Computer Science and Artificial Intelligence Lab) was right down the hall from mine. He gave a talk to our seminar about what he felt was going to become a big problem. Tim asked, "What happens when you put up a website, add some popular content, and suddenly a lot of people go there at one time? That would create a 'flash crowd' or a 'hotspot' and it would melt down the Internet". [Charles Zhang mentioned above that this is exactly what happened to Sohu.com on the day it launched its new search engine.]

Leighton's reaction was that the hotspot problem was perfect for his group.

Daniel Lewin

> We started thinking about how we would distribute content on the Internet in a way that was scalable and reliable and secure. We began working on that, and the next year **DANIEL LEWIN** '98 came to MIT as a graduate student, a brilliant, brilliant person from the Technion [Israel's MIT!] who ultimately wrote a prize-winning MIT master's thesis on the subject, developing what's called "consistent hashing". This is a way of deciding where you store what on the Internet, and on what server you put what content so you can quickly get it.
>
> We produced a series of papers that came out of the research on better ways of delivering content. All that would have stayed as just

AUTHOR'S NOTE

How similar! Ken Olsen, the founding CEO of Digital Equipment Corporation, said he wrote in one night the required business plan for DEC by taking a toothpaste company example from Paul Samuelson's first edition *Economics* textbook and just substituted numbers that seemed better for computers than for toothpaste. The officers of American Research & Development Corporation (ARD) commented to Ken that it was the best business plan they had ever seen, and they then invested in DEC—the best mistake (☺) ARD ever made!

research papers, except that in 1997 an MIT Sloan grad student named **PREETISH NIJHAWAN** '98 was drinking beer with Danny, his apartment house neighbor. Danny was distraught because he was facing bankruptcy. He was a graduate student not making much money, had two kids in private school, and his loans were mounting. Preetish said, "There's this thing called the MIT $50K Business Plan Competition [now the MIT $100K]. You're doing some very cool research on the Internet. Why don't you enter the contest? I'll help you, and if we win you can pay off your debts."

Leighton comments:

> Neither Danny nor Preetish knew that if you won, you didn't get $50,000. The first prize then was really $35K, and $15K went to other award-winners. And you can't use it to pay off your student loans. You've got to use it to help start a company. None of us knew that, and Danny and Preetish needed somebody with gray hair. I was less gray then, but I did qualify. Despite my reluctance, I really wanted to support Danny, so together we entered the $50K. That was a great experience. We got books out of the library on how to write a business plan. We met luminaries in the field who really knew how to start companies and knew what they were doing. We didn't. We started developing a real plan for how you could take these ideas that were in theses and papers and make a difference.

Of course, getting Akamai off the ground entailed major difficulties for this group of total novices. Leighton continues:

> Urban legend is, we won the $50K. We didn't, but we made it to the final round, and that was very cool. We were probably in sixth place of those that presented, because we didn't have much business experience. We did learn a lot during the course of the $50K and met many people, including venture capitalists, who were interested in us, and we did then grow the team. **JONATHAN SEELIG** '01 [Jonathan dropped out of the MIT Sloan School of Management to help found Akamai as its Vice President of Strategy] made some really key contributions early on in helping us figure out how to start and then grow our business. Also Randall Kaplan joined our team.
>
> We actually tried to get the technology into practice by giving it to carriers. We went to see AOL, which was much bigger then than today. We tried to convince them that this technology would help them deliver content. Our sales effort failed—AOL felt that distributed computing, which is what this was based on, was an "ivory tower" concept

> that would never work in practice. They said, "Please go back to your ivory tower", which we did.
>
> We talked to some content providers, people with big websites, and they said "If you build this into a service that we can buy from you, we might buy it. We might use you to deliver our content because you'd make it be faster and cheaper for us". That meant we had to form a company, which we were reluctant to do because we had no business experience at all.
>
> We liked being at MIT. I liked being a professor at MIT. Danny wanted to be a professor at MIT preferably, but if not there then somewhere else. It was a very difficult decision, but we concluded this was a really rare chance, unique in our lifetimes, to do something in mathematics that could really make a difference in the world. We bit the bullet. The five of us [Leighton, Lewin, Nijhawan, Seelig, and Kaplan] incorporated **AKAMAI TECHNOLOGIES** in August 1998. Akamai is a Hawaiian word meaning "intelligent" or "clever"! We obtained an exclusive license to certain intellectual property from the MIT Technology Licensing Office, and began further development efforts in the fall of 1998. Most of our early employees were students who had worked on the project at MIT.

Shortly after the launch, several experienced executives were brought in to help move Akamai forward, in particular: Paul Sagan, former President of New Media for Time Inc., and George Conrades, former Chairman and Chief Executive Officer of BBN and Senior Vice President of U.S. operations for IBM. Conrades became the Chief Executive Officer of Akamai in April 1999, and led the company from startup to sustained profitability and positive free cash-flow before turning the reins over to Sagan in 2005.[6]

Tom Leighton continues to relate the early and rather surprising keys to Akamai's growth:

> Our first big break actually came indirectly from Apple. Steve Jobs had purchased the exclusive right to distribute the first *Star Wars* trailer in early 1999 ahead of the movie coming out. That was a big deal back then. He did it on the Internet because he wanted to help establish Apple's reputation in streaming. We didn't know any of that, but we were approached by a company called Entertainment Tonight to distribute online the same *Star Wars* trailer. We didn't know that it was bootlegged, as were many other copies, by everyone but Apple! We got the trailer on time and we started delivering it. Then we began reading online headlines that apple.com was down. They weren't able to distribute the *Star Wars* trailer they had licensed! All the other companies that had bootlegged copies of this trailer were also down.

The only company distributing the trailer that had not crashed was this unknown thing called Akamai doing distribution for Entertainment Tonight. A reporter who was very tech savvy at CNN dug into this episode, discovered Akamai, and gave us tremendous press that put us on the map.

The first really famous example of a website crash was soon after, on February 4, 1999, when Victoria's Secret was among the first to start its own e-commerce site. Today everybody knows about e-commerce, and a lot of business is done that way, but not then. Victoria's Secret wanted people to know you could go to their website and buy their clothing. They ran a TV ad during the 1999 Super Bowl showing supermodels in lingerie at a fashion show walking down the aisle for 30 seconds. The ad said if you want to see the full fashion show, come to its new website, www.victoriassecret.com, on Tuesday night at 9:00 pm.

A lot of people watched the Super Bowl, and you can imagine what happened Tuesday night at 9:00. Not only was the Victoria's Secret website down, but the Internet was down in Dallas and most of Texas—crushed by the load of people trying to "hit" the website. That got headlines in the newspapers the next day. Suddenly people realized that the idea that you're going to have websites and a lot of people are going to come to a website, doesn't scale.

From then on we grew very rapidly. It was the dot-com bubble, so we were able to raise money. Shortly after we had done the *Star Wars* trailer NOT for Apple, Steve Jobs noticed. He called us up and tried to buy the company. We didn't sell, but we did establish a strategic relationship with Apple.

Apple engaged Akamai for the second round of that trailer. Richard Trenholm reported that it was much improved, with

> 6.4 million downloads within three weeks. Steve Jobs himself described [this happening] as "the biggest Internet download event in history".... But the success of the trailer proved a new technology for handling such colossal traffic much more efficiently. Previously, if lots of people would suddenly visit a site it was likely to become overwhelmed and crash. But a company called Akamai had come up with a way to more efficiently distribute the load. And it worked: Between Entertainment Tonight hosting the *Phantom Menace* trailer and ESPN covering March Madness [the opening of the NCAA basketball tournament], Akamai successfully handled 250 million hits on just those two sites—up to 3,000 hits per second—while other sites covering the same ground crashed under the strain [both events were on the same day, March 11, 1999]."[7]

Back to Leighton: "Apple became our first strategic investor, and we've had a close relationship ever since. That has been very helpful for us." This is very similar to Bob Metcalfe's comment about 3Com's ties with Steve Jobs and Apple.

With the benefits and public acclaim from these victories, Akamai went public on October 29, 1999. After three upward revisions of its offering price during the few weeks prior to the IPO date, Akamai was finally priced at $26 per share. But given the huge demand for its stock, it opened for trading at $110 per share and closed on that first day at $145 per share.

MORE ON Danny Lewin can be found in Todd Leopold, "The Legacy of Danny Lewin, the First Man to Die on 9/11", CNN, www.cnn.com/2013/09/09/tech/innovation/danny-lewin-9-11-akamai (last viewed March 29, 2018). MIT honored Lewin shortly after his passing by naming the intersection of Main and Vassar Streets, right outside of CSAIL, "Danny Lewin Square", and Akamai dedicated a nearby park to Danny's memory. Molly Knight Raskin has authored a fascinating and complete biography of Lewin as well as of the founding, building, and nearly day-by-day history of Akamai: *No Better Time*, De Capo Press, Boston 2013.

After these signal achievements, and with Akamai moving forward very rapidly, just two years later, on September 11, 2001, Akamai and the world lost Danny Lewin aboard the hijacked American Airlines Flight 11 that crashed into the World Trade Center in New York City, the first to die in the 9/11 attacks. Danny was 31 years old, with a wife and two children. He was seen as the underlying and everlasting spirit of the company.

In that crisis, Tom Leighton immediately took a leave of absence from MIT and returned to be CTO of Akamai, as well as to try to provide solace for its many employees. He is now once again CEO of the company. "We've certainly grown a lot since the early days", Tom observes:

> We generated $2.3 billion in revenues last year, and this year we will generate over a half billion in cash. [Akamai had a market cap of $12.9 billion as of June 15, 2019.] We carry most of the major brands on the Internet. We make their sites fast, reliable, and secure, and that's a big effort today. Nobody knows who we are. The joke is we're the biggest company on the Internet you've never heard of, because we're under the covers. You use us every day when you go to major websites. Your browser comes to an Akamai server that is near you, and we give you what you want and try to make it be fast so you have a good experience.
>
> As I look at today and guess at tomorrow, I would say security is one of the biggest challenges now for the Internet. It's our fastest growing business, and the "Internet of things", while wonderful in many ways, is now enabling attackers to do very bad things at a very large scale. I'll end here, with that final mixed message of growth and gloom.

MOVING THE INTERNET (AND EVERYTHING ELSE!) TO "THE CLOUD": OKTA, INC. AND FREDERIC KERREST

The final tribute here to MIT entrepreneurs of the Internet is to the new generation of MIT students, alumna, and alumni who grew up with computers, and increasingly with smart phones in their pockets and certainly at their thumb-tips ☺. They have been users of the Internet in all aspects of life, with apps galore to aid them in pursuing whatever their interests! A major contributor to all this is the development of "the Cloud", which enables storage of huge amounts of information without requiring personal ownership of bulk storage or the costs associated with that.

> **CONCEPTUALLY** "the Cloud" is very similar to time-sharing, in which MIT was among the pioneers. See the discussions of MIT Lincoln Lab's time-sharing contributions to the creation of the Internet earlier in this chapter; Meditech's early use of time-sharing as described in the Part Two introduction; and Lincoln Lab's attractiveness to the Applicon founders in Chapter 10.

> **According to *Fortune* magazine, a *unicorn* is a private company valued at $1 billion or more.**
>
> Source: fortune.com/unicorns, list updated as of January 19, 2016.

And as pointed out by Tom Leighton above, the biggest challenge to today's booming computer use is security. **OKTA, INC.** was a rapidly growing "unicorn" from MIT, and its co-founder and COO, **J. FREDERIC KERREST** '09, provides more insights into today's responses to these security problems.

Freddy begins his story:

Frederic Kerrest

Among MIT entrepreneurs, I am in the company of many who have started firms in the hard sciences, and I am comfortable with that, even though my MIT degree is in management. My undergraduate engineering degree is in computer science from Stanford. Then I wrote enterprise software for a few years, and later I started and ran my first company, a high technology consulting firm. After that I joined a somewhat bigger company, Salesforce.com, at the time called a software company, which had 100 employees. I experienced and learned enormously from its next five years of dramatic growth and success, leaving for MIT when Salesforce had 3,000 employees.

But I always knew that I wanted to start my own company. Obviously, enterprise software is what I have done for the last 20 years. I love it and I'm pretty good at it. But I thought that I had to learn a number of things. One of the co-founders of my first company, and a very good friend of mine, went to MIT Sloan, class of '05, and he loved the experience. He said "It's awesome, you should go check it out". I applied only to MIT and Stanford, because those were the two best entrepreneurship master's programs.

I was at MIT for two years in the MBA Program, but in the very focused and rather intensive Entrepreneurship & Innovation Track. As a result, I am a huge fan of MIT, MIT Sloan, and all that Ed Roberts, Bill Aulet, Ken Morse before Bill, and all of the key faculty have done to fos-ter MIT entrepreneurship and to build up the likes of me. It was nothing short of transformational in my career.

Through my time at MIT I got to do a lot of cool things. I served as the Managing Director of the MIT $100K entrepreneurship competition during my second year, which taught me about encouraging and managing young entrepreneurial women and men. Most interesting for me about managing the MIT $100K was leading numbers of my peers without providing any financial compensation. How do you motivate broad teams to do a lot of things when they are pulled in so many directions, pretty stretched in school? IT IS MIT! A couple of professors presented their studies to us—Scott Stern on how motivated people work much harder than they are paid for, and Eric von Hippel on how many innovators contribute to solving big problems without any expectation of money. They do it because they are challenged or because they think it is important to do, or even just for fun! And running the $100K gave me lots of time to put those ideas into practice ☺.

In my year we spent a lot of time fundraising, because the organization was not in great financial shape. The year before they raised $150,000. During my year as Managing Director we raised $850,000, so we put a lot of money back into the coffers. These experiences were not unlike running a startup with both people and money issues, and I learned from them. I am sure that leading the $100K was key to my winning the Patrick McGovern MIT Entrepreneurship Award [mentioned in the Acknowledgments].

The summer between my two years at MIT, I worked for MIT Corporation member **MARK GORENBERG** '70, an early partner at Hummer-Winblad Ventures in San Francisco [and more recently the founder of a new VC firm, **ZETTA VENTURE PARTNERS**]. Hummer-Winblad only invests in early stage enterprise software. I learned a lot about early stage venture capital processes and operations, first at MIT in the classroom, but also during that summer. Obviously I've used that to my and Okta's advantage. We raised $230 million in venture capital over the last seven years, prior to our IPO, and my MIT and summer learning have served us well.

In all of this I have observed how very common it is for folks involved in any way in the MIT entrepreneurial area and ecosystem to stay in close touch, to come back to the campus or to alumni affairs, and to delight in mentoring students or participating in events as judges or speakers. It is a very close-knit community, no matter how far flung across the world you become. I remember Ed Roberts commenting to our class, "Entrepreneurs love entrepreneurs. Just remember and be part of that!" Over the last eight years, I've also met and now know well a lot of MIT alums in California who are leaders in the entrepreneurial and venture capital industries, such as Doug Leone '88, an investor of mine at Sequoia Capital, and Rich Wong '91 at Accel. They help provide an MIT home away from MIT!

Freddy describes the Okta start:

In the spring of 2009, right before I graduated, I began talking with Todd McKinnon, with whom I had worked closely at Salesforce.com, about the possibility of starting a company together. He was CTO of Salesforce and a great complement to my personal strengths in sales and sales management. Right out of the gate, we saw that more and more companies would want and need cloud technology for financial, technology, and business reasons. Enterprise IT firms needed help in incorporating cloud applications and mobile applications more intelligently into their infrastructure. One big problem was what we called Identity Management, to assure secure use of the remote and presumably primarily organizationally separate cloud capabilities that companies would need to access. Certainly, the business we started then, and the complex software product we started building, were predicated on the deep market and customer insight we had from our previous jobs. But given the early stage of the cloud market in 2009, we were betting that enterprise cloud usage would significantly accelerate. We turned out to be right on that. And as the potential co-founders, we really had enjoyed our years of close personal ties at Salesforce, and the trust we had developed in each other, so we decided to go for it!

SO MANY cute names with hidden "meanings": Genentech, Meditech, 3Com, Akamai, Sohu, Okta—each carrying its own secret message ☺.

We named the company "Okta", the meteorological unit of measure for cloud cover. We provide our software as a service, usually on a subscription basis.

In Okta's eighth year, it filed an S-1 with the SEC to indicate its intent to go public. The filing indicated that Okta had 750 employees and over 2 million people using its products to access cloud applications, websites, mobile applications, and services from a multitude of devices. It had 2016 revenues of about $160 million, about doubling annually for the previous three years.[8] Freddy explains, "We are an enterprise software company that provides a security product to enable large companies safely to take advantage of all the new cloud and mobile technologies."

OKTA was priced at $17 per share at its IPO on NASDAQ on April 7, 2017, with the stock closing on that day at $23.51, valuing this young firm at $2.1 billion. Two years later (on August 14, 2019), with 6,100 employees and annual revenues of $440 million, the stock market valued OKTA at $15.2 billion!

A FINAL VOICE ON MIT'S INTERNET CREATION

In summing up the contributions of MIT faculty and alumni entrepreneurs to the Internet and through that to the world, I enjoy Bob Metcalfe's top off to his earlier remarks: "The five largest market cap companies in the United States are Apple, Microsoft, Amazon, Alphabet [i.e., Google], and Facebook, all of which you could argue are Internet companies. The Internet has been quite impactful on all of us, and its creators certainly deserve the tribute provided here!"

And the applications that it and the cloud have made possible are already legion. Clearly, another complete chapter might have been devoted to the Internet application enterprises that have been founded by MIT alumni.

REFERENCES AND NOTES

1. "J.C.R. Licklider", *Wikipedia*, https://en.wikipedia.org/wiki/J._C._R._Licklider (last accessed March 29, 2018).
2. *A Culture of Innovation: Insider Accounts of Computing and Life at BBN 120,* Waterside Publishing, 2011.
3. "Levy Led Internet Creator BBN Through its Heyday", http://www.bizjournals.com/boston/blog/mass-high-tech/2002/06/levy-led-internet-creator-bbn-through.html (last accessed March 29, 2018).
4. *Austin* (Texas) *Business Journal,* April 12, 2016.
5. Hostingfacts.com reports China at 802 million users and the United States at far less, with 98 percent of China's users mobile (accessed on June 15, 2019),
6. "Akamai Technologies", *Wikipedia*, https://en.wikipedia.org/wiki/Akamai_Technologies (last accessed February 25, 2018).
7. Richard Trenholm, "How the 'Star Wars: The Phantom Menace' Trailer Made Web History", *CNET,* November 28, 2014.
8. Okta, Inc. S-1 filing with U.S. Securities and Exchange Commission, March 20, 2017.

10

From CAD-CAM to Robotics

Evolving from computer-aided design, development, and manufacture (CAD-CAM) to robotics is really part of the tale of how computers have affected everything in life, starting with industry and moving into everyday consumer activities. Look much earlier to all aspects of automation, and then look forward beyond robotics. You already see the continuing extension from simple ground-based "walking" robots to flying ones called drones, driving ones called "autonomous vehicles" like cars and trucks, and of course both underwater "swimming" and underground "tunneling" versions. Ivan Sutherland, mentioned in Chapter 9 in regard to his DARPA leadership, had developed SketchPad at MIT Lincoln Lab in 1960, and is credited as being a "father" of computer-aided design and predecessor of the companies described in this chapter. Following the pattern thus far in Part Two, the MIT alumni founders relate their stories of a few especially significant pioneering companies over this CAD-CAM to robotics evolution.

The MIT entrepreneurship celebration panel on "From CAD-CAM to Robotics": (left to right) Harry Lee, Jon Hirschtick, Michael "Mick" Mountz, and Helen Greiner

THE PIONEERS OF CAD-CAM: APPLICON AND COMPUTERVISION[1]

HARRY LEE '57, '59, '62 provides an introductory perspective on the beginnings of the CAD-CAM industry:

AUTHOR'S NOTE

Quotes throughout this chapter are primarily from those individuals' presentations in a session led by Helen Greiner, serial entrepreneur of iRobot and CyPhy Works, at our 2016 MIT entrepreneurship celebration, integrated with interviews conducted by Michelle Choate, and supplemented by other sources.

Harry Lee

> **APPLICON** was one of two pioneering computer-aided design companies to grow out of the MIT community in 1969. The second one was **COMPUTERVISION**, and together we started a revolution in how electronic circuits and many other products are designed. I am going to tell you only the Applicon story. Four of us, all PhDs in the MIT Lincoln Lab Digital Computer Design Group, were sitting together in its auditorium in May 1969 attending the lecture by MIT Professor Ed Roberts on his studies of companies spun off from MIT labs. When he showed his slide that 80% of the lab spinoffs were still alive after five years, we looked at each other and said, in essence, "What in the world are we waiting for? Those are damned good odds!" In hardly any time at all, we left Lincoln Lab and set ourselves up as what became Applicon, Inc. in nearby Bedford [Massachusetts], to create tools for computer-aided electronic design. [That made-up name was a contraction of "application" ☺.] Gary Hornbuckle [UC Berkeley] served as President, **RICHARD SPANN** '61, '62, '66 as VP of Sales and Marketing (unfortunately with no related experience!), Fontaine Richardson [University of Illinois] as VP of Product Development, and I became Chairman of the Board of our startup. Dick Spann and I had previously been Assistant Professors in the MIT EE Department.
>
> We all had been attracted to Lincoln Laboratory by its extraordinary computer resources. These were centered on the TX2 computer, revolutionary in that it was almost entirely transistorized, which made it very fast, very capable. It also had time-sharing, which meant that multiple users could work on different problems at the same time. They could do it interactively, so you wouldn't have to come in at three o'clock in the morning to get your hours of computer time. You could just go to a terminal, call up your program, and work on it while other users worked on their problems. That seems commonplace today, but it was revolutionary at the time. A third very important aspect of the Lab's capability was that it had really pioneering visual input/output graphics that enabled a user to interact with his problem graphically as he solved it.
>
> The four of us were working, each rather independently, on advancing either computer design or circuit design or microchip design.

All those targets were becoming ever more difficult because of the explosion in microchips. We worked in the same group, but were exploring our different but related topics. Over time we had become friends, all living with young families in Lexington, Massachusetts, and we socialized together. At lunch we often talked about the idea of creating a new company, and how the *Wall Street Journal* seemed infatuated with them. That is how the whole thing began.

Harry shifts to getting Applicon off the ground:

Startups were a rarity for MIT at the time we left Lincoln. The few there were seemed like random events, and they weren't incubated or supported in any way by the Institute. No birthing process was in place at MIT at that time, so we just had to make it up as we went along, doing the best we could. [This was 20+ years before I founded the MIT Entrepreneurship Center ☺.] Soon after that lecture, we resigned our positions at the lab, created something that resembled a business plan, and amazingly found some venture capital to cover our startup expenses. That was very challenging, because venture capital was pretty much unknown at the time. Another hurdle was that our interests were primarily software, and the venture capitalists that did exist didn't understand software, and therefore didn't want to invest in it. They felt it was too ephemeral. [In Part Two's introductory discussion of Meditech's founding in the same year, 1969, see the same comment about EG&G's management and software.]

Through contacts, we fortunately ended up convincing W.R. Grace Chemicals to back us for an initial bank loan, and soon after to invest $400,000 for one-sixth of our company. It was sort of a diversification venture that its CEO thought was a great idea, without many others there in agreement! With money in hand, we hired six outstanding graduates whom we had mentored at MIT while we were their teachers. And we were off and running. We were very happy about who we were and about those we brought on board. In my view, both the faculty and the students at MIT are extraordinary achievers, with leading-edge understanding of technology and where it's going. They're the smartest and brightest – the kind you want to be working with in a startup, because you're going to be competing with others of that type.

The initial stages of Applicon were much like many other firms started solely by technical people, with no managerial inputs. Harry:

The four of us had absolutely no business experience, and that became a near-fatal error for our startup. This is reflected in our first milestone.

Being engineers we were totally focused on product creation, not product sales or product marketing to ensure income, but rather on creating wonderful products.

Our first milestone was to come up with initial versions of four different products that we felt had revolutionary potential. The first three of these were what today we might call "cloud-based programs" for doing advanced design of different types of circuits. In fact, they were time-sharing software programs on remote computers that would be accessed over telephone lines. They would enable users to access design programs that they themselves could not create, and that their companies did not have the resources to create. As I indicated, we had time-sharing at Lincoln Lab, but few in the world outside really understood or used it.

The fourth product was a standalone, self-contained workstation that exploited computer graphics to enable our computer input and output to facilitate the design of microchips. The product, which we named the "Design Assistant", provided a display, a tablet, and a keyboard that would give the user access to a huge virtual, multi-level drafting table for interactively designing advanced chips. An engineering user could do this much faster and more accurately than with the previous hand methods. Being highly motivated and rather talented engineers, we worked and worked and got these products finished in the time frame we had expected.

And then came the first crisis:

Our second milestone came up at that point—to secure a second round of venture financing to sell the products that we had developed. We had assumed that would be quite easy once a venture capitalist could see our products. Unfortunately, what happened was the recession of 1970 that struck with enormous force, so the few VCs that existed at that time went into hiding. They were financing nothing. In addition to that, the companies that we were trying to sell were laying off engineers right and left, and those engineers were supposed to become our customers. We were out of money and we had no prospect for getting new venture financing to continue our operation. Financially, we were up the creek without a paddle.

Our new milestone suddenly became "survival". We had to totally reinvent Applicon. Despite our limited sales experience up to that time, we realized that our most promising opportunity by far was the semiconductor market that was exploding as a result of the challenge of creating ever larger, ever faster microchips. The prior design methodologies for microchips were based on hand drafting, but these methodologies were overwhelmed. They needed computer assistance, and we saw that our interactive graphics design workstation, the Design Assistant, was exactly the kind of solution that the industry required. So, we put our other three products on life support and focused all company resources into the promising Design Assistant.

We also devoted much more effort to sales and marketing than we did previously. Two of us left our homes in Lexington and went out on the road, basically full time for two years, to sell the company's products across the country and around the world. During this year when we had zero money, we were living on financial fumes. Each month we knew where the money was coming from to make that month's payroll, but we had absolutely no idea what would take care of the next month. Amazingly, over the whole year, one or another of our core group would pull some technical or sales miracle out of the sky and we kept afloat.

The company survived the second year from our successful call that the Design Assistant product was where it's at and to go full-bore with that. Secondly, and equally important, was the grit and determination of all the company employees. A very important lesson to us was if we were going to be entrepreneurs, it was going to take a lot of work. It's not, as you might say, a walk in the park. You have to be able to pivot and hang in there for the long term, and also maybe develop some skills you might not have nor ever thought you'd need, like marketing and sales!

After that second year, we began to gain traction. Semiconductor industries started realizing the benefit of our Design Assistant workstation, and sales began to take off. We got new venture capital financing once the 1970 recession passed and VCs could see our progress. VC involvement was important—not just for the money it provided, but it also gave the company access to real business know-how. General Electric invested in 1972 and 1973, encouraged by GE users of Applicon's products. After that, the company's milestones became much more conventional, and we addressed them much more conventionally. Those were such things as building accounts with major companies, enhancing our user features, upgrading our hardware, expanding into adjacent markets like 3D graphing, and fending off a hoard of wannabe competitors that started appearing on the scene. We were able to leave behind the drama of the first three years.

By then, we had finally learned to focus. We just left alone the three other products we first conceived. The future was in the Design Assistant, so we went gung-ho with that. Users could continue using the other products, but we provided very little support and made no effort to further sell those products. We had an IPO in 1980 and continued to grow rapidly. We were up to 800 people by 1981, with about

$100 million in revenues, when we sold out to Schlumberger for $232 million.

One more MIT output helped Applicon greatly. In the early years we needed a capable, but not very expensive, display for our winning Design Assistant product. IBM had a big fancy display that cost $25,000. We wanted to undercut that cost. **COMPUTEK**, an MIT startup founded in 1968 by MIT Professor **MIKE DERTOUZOS** '64, provided the product that filled our needs. We would not have found that display without our MIT connections. Computek's people worked night and day just like we did. If we were on the road and had a problem with the display, we'd call them up at 8pm and somebody would be at work and could handle our problem.

The final aspect of MIT that I'd like to address is the phenomenal networking. Applicon was the first company that I co-founded, and later I did two more that were also successful. In all three companies, at least some of the co-founders were people that I had associated with, worked with, at MIT. Neither of those other companies would have started without that association.

Harry sums up his Applicon story:

Our big failing at the beginning was that we all were in love with our products but had very limited understanding of the real-world markets. We would have benefited enormously if we had put more effort into assessing and trying to quantify those markets before we took venture capital money and put it into developing products for those markets. We were saved by the fact that we had diversified across four products, and one of them fortunately proved to be a winner. I think now that anybody contemplating a startup ought to take a couple of basic business courses. Of course, if their flavor is entrepreneurship, not just straight business, that would be enormously helpful.

PHILIPPE VILLERS '60 is himself a great example of the evolution "from CAD-CAM to robotics". In 1969, in Bedford, Massachusetts, the same time and town as Applicon, Phil Villers started **COMPUTERVISION**! Phil recalls the unusual path that led to the company getting underway:

Philippe Villers

I was born in Paris and fled to escape the Nazis in the early 1940s. This obviously affected me tremendously. To top that off, I got an undergraduate degree in liberal arts from Harvard. So, before I went to MIT I had developed a lifelong ambition to be a significant change agent for a better world. 1968 was the year that Martin Luther King was assassinated, and that following Sunday the preacher in our church in Concord, Massachusetts gave a very powerful sermon on MLK's life. I realized that King was only a few years older than I, at that time 33. I decided that if I was really going to follow my life dream, I needed to do something right then.

That day I literally sat down with a piece of paper and charted how I might do this. I decided that the "direct route", as I called it, of leaving my professional training to start in a non-profit world with no resources, no training, and no experience made no sense. I decided upon what I called the "indirect route"—to start a commercial company that would provide those missing ingredients. That's exactly what happened over not such a long time!

CONCORD CONTROLS was yet another MIT spinoff company, formed in 1956 by most of the engineering staff of the MIT Digital Computer Laboratory, who had been developing numerical control systems for machine tools and, among other accomplishments, the APT language for automatic programming, using the MIT Whirlwind I computer as their base.

With my mechanical engineering background I had by then become the manager for advanced products in a small company, **CONCORD CONTROLS**. I had a concept for the company I wanted to start, but I had no top management experience. [Note that Harry Lee and Applicon suffered from the same deficiency.] To maximize the chance of success I invited Marty Allen, my former boss at Singer-General Precision, to join me. I proposed that he would become President and I would be Senior Vice President, and we would share equally in the equity and leadership of the firm. And that's what we did.

David Friedman, later an MIT Sloan Fellow '87, remembers when Philippe and Marty invited him to become the third co-founder of Computervision:

> I had a wife and kids, and I couldn't take the chance of no salary for a long time. So, I told them, "Sorry, but I would be excited to join you just as soon as you land some capital". That took them a few months, and then I joined as Vice President of engineering and "employee #1". Given the difference in the amount of ownership I received, my earlier reluctance to become a co-founder turned out to be the most expensive decision I ever made in my life!

LARRY POLIMENO, identified in the beginning of Part Two as the initial Operations Manager of Medical Information Technology, makes exactly the same comment about his delay in joining the Meditech founding team. And a significant number of other "Joiners" give economic needs as a primary reason for avoiding "foundership" in preference to slightly later "joinership"!

Villers continues:

> The technical notion came from my earlier days as a Mechanical Engineering grad student at MIT. Ivan Sutherland, as a PhD candidate, using the largest available computers, did a thesis called "Sketchpad" showing how computers could be used to do engineering design, with emphasis on actual engineering drawings. In starting Computervision, we tried moving from the huge computers that Sutherland had used to time-sharing computers, but they turned out not to be very adequate. So, we changed in the first six months to the then-emerging minicomputers, adopted the Data General Nova, and built a commercial system based around that, with an interactive table as both the input and output device.
>
> The industry had no name at that time. We coined the name "CAD", computer-aided design, but were concerned that the spread of this new technology might initially be slow and that we might not survive. So, we came up with the idea of a bread and butter product for the semiconductor industry [the same target industry, but via a different route from that taken by Applicon]. I had become convinced that the process of making integrated circuits, which requires alignment to micron precision, could be done automatically. Large companies such as IBM had tried and failed, but I felt we could do it. In four months we accomplished it by rejecting the conventional wisdom that you had to align on whatever design circuit was in front of you. I'm one of the original patent holders on what we called "auto align", which used micromanipulators to align to a precision of one micron. For the first three or four years of the company, that kept us alive.
>
> Eventually the industry started growing. We decided to dumb down a bit with what is actually a glorified drafting tool, which was the original definition of CAD. Over time, we added engineering features. By 1975, we had our own version of the Data General Nova, and were producing computer hardware and software systems optimized for their graphics capabilities. Specialized applications grew and were adopted in high volumes in several domains.

DATA GENERAL was a spinoff from DEC, which had been formed by MIT alum Ken Olsen and his Lincoln Lab colleague **HARLAN ANDERSON**.

For example, "in 1981 [right after Villers left to form **AUTOMATIX**], the United States Navy awarded Computervision an indefinite quantity, indefinite delivery contract valued at $63,000,000 for its Designer V hardware" for a wide and growing variety of Naval priorities.[2]

> In early 1980 we added improved 3-D design. And it was soon apparent that we were dealing with two different industries, CAD and CAM.

We invented the term "CAD-CAM" because we quickly recognized that we could create a link to computer-controlled machine tools, the beginning of the CAM part. People could move from a design on a screen to actually driving a useable CNC [computer numerical control] machine. In the other direction, our bread and butter product that kept the company alive let us descend into a totally different IC manufacturing industry.

Villers's days at his own company came to an end:

From this recognition, 10 years after I had brought in Marty Allen to handle management questions at Computervision, my main responsibility was focused on advanced products—that is, new concepts. I came up with a plan to enter the robotics industry as a logical extension of the work we were doing in the CAM part of CAD-CAM. I believed that marrying what was predominantly Japanese robotics technology with two other things—minicomputer programming and artificial vision—would make robotics far more robust in industry. The robot wouldn't just have an arm, as it's often referred to, but it would have eyes and computer-based capability to adjust to specific needs. However, my former partner Marty rejected my concept of entering the intelligent robotics field, which is why I left Computervision in 1980 to start Automatix.

I founded it with **VICTOR SCHEINMAN** '63, a couple of key people who left with me from Computervision, plus others from Data General and elsewhere. Automatix became the first company to build a vision-based system that could do welding, which was very difficult to do because welding requires brilliant arcs, and you have to do lots of light filtering. With our robots with built-in machine vision, we could also do inspection. But our key problem was not technical. It was market, in that American manufacturing did not revive as we had hoped. We raised a lot of venture capital, because many others shared our hopes and excitement, and we went public in 1983. I was President until 1986, when I left to form **COGNITION CORPORATION**, my third company. After I departed, Automatix went through a series of mergers, but some of its pioneering products are still available.

The same sort of things happened to Computervision. It merged with **PRIME COMPUTER** in 1988 (**BILL PODUSKA** '59 was co-founder and CTO), and in turn was later acquired by Parametric Technology Corporation (PTC) in 1998, founded by one of Computervision's most brilliant alumni, Sam Geisberg [who had previously worked for Applicon as well].[3] But many of the Computervision early software-hardware packages have continued in use in various industries, regardless of which company was the current owner of the firm's capabilities and products.

I was Cognition's President for three years until 1988, to make a true engineering tool where you could come up with a sketch, change a dimension or value, and it would propagate throughout the entire design. Since then, a number of other companies have gone beyond us and done even more sophisticated work, including our Computervision alumni Sam Geisberg, as well as **JON HIRSCHTICK** '83 at **SOLIDWORKS** [discussed next in this chapter].

But I ended up fine. Given the money I made from the sale of Computervision, I was in a good position to take some of it and start what is today **FAMILIES USA FOUNDATION**. It has devoted 30 years to bringing about healthcare reform and to provide quality healthcare coverage for every American. I also head **GRAINPRO**, a not-for-profit focused upon helping farmers in developing countries to bring products to market, avoiding the disease and rot that often destroy a large fraction of farm output. That organization is headquartered and has its manufacturing plant in the Philippines, where it produces ultra-hermetic packaging for grain bags that tremendously aid the farmer. I suspect that my social concerns have been as deeply held as my product innovation notions, and both have filled my life.

JON HIRSCHTICK: THE MOVES TO SOLID MODELING AND THEN THE CLOUD

Jon Hirschtick

JON HIRSCHTICK, with double MIT degrees in 1983, has spent 38 years in CAD, mostly as a serial entrepreneur, going from running the MIT CADLab, to interning at Computervision, founding his first CAD company while still an MIT student, becoming Computervision's Director of Engineering, founding and being CEO of **SOLIDWORKS**, then selling his company to Dassault Systems and becoming a Group Executive. For an encore, Jon has founded and is now Chairman of **ONSHAPE**. While at MIT, Jon began his career in CAD. But he also served as a player and instructor on the MIT blackjack team, which won fame, money, and notoriety!

As described in Chapter 9, in 1963 Ivan Sutherland began the whole field of computer-aided design with his pioneering MIT PhD research and beyond, launching a 50-year story of computer design. Harry Lee and Phil Villers related the early parts of the CAD-CAM industry. Uniquely, Jon Hirschtick can look at the entire half-century of CAD:

It combines research at MIT and other places, companies founded by several of us from MIT and many other people, and R&D accomplishments through generation after generation of CAD technology and products. The result, not to be immodest, is that our CAD work has improved the way that every manufactured product on Earth gets designed. The standard way products were designed 50 years ago was pencil, paper, and a drafting board, and today it's all 3D models in CAD.

IDENTIFYING SOME but not all of the players, this article describes a very entrepreneurial period of MIT-based activities in a quite different but highly technical field: *The MIT Blackjack Team*, in *Wikipedia*, https://en.wikipedia.org/wiki/MIT_Blackjack_Team, last accessed March 29, 2018.

Most people don't realize that in 1963, few people had yet seen a computer. But Ivan Sutherland visualized a concept of CAD in his MIT PhD thesis. An excellent video shows that work as certainly far more visionary than anything I've done in my career.[4] MIT hardcore nerds like me will be delighted to learn that his thesis advisor was Claude Shannon '40, a real MIT legend known mostly as the father of information theory.

In the 1970s, Applicon and Computervision, the two big companies, were "duking it out" in the CAD business. They were using very expensive room-sized computers, maybe $200,000 for a system, but they produced mainly computer-aided drafting and some 3D wire-frame modeling. I entered the picture in 1981, as a sophomore in mechanical engineering who knew how to program computers. I went into the internship office and they sent me over to Computervision for a summer job. The story of my life is that I've built CAD systems ever since.

In 1982, I had already worked at Computervision for a couple of summers. My grad program advisor, Professor David Gossard '75 in the MIT CADLab, was an incredible visionary. Dave not only had insights into what 3D modeling would be—solid modeling—but also equally important, he had the computer platform vision of saying, "This'll be on every engineer's desk." People thought he was nuts: "What do you mean? You'll use this thing called a mouse to draw? We won't be typing commands?" I was very lucky to be around him. An awesome video on YouTube shows this, "MIT CADLab '82".[5]

RUSSELL OLIVE was a Senior Lecturer who for 20 years taught the New Enterprises subject and others as part of the MIT Entrepreneurship Center programs. The students had to develop a business plan for a new company as their term project. Russ was a master teacher and a wonderful and dedicated mentor to all of his students. Jon Hirschtick endowed a fund at the MIT Entrepreneurship Center to honor Russ.

A couple of other things happened to me in the 1980s that mattered. I took a class in the Sloan School called New Enterprises, and started my

> first company. I learned a lot from Russ Olive, may he rest in peace, a great teacher who gave me a lot of inspiration. Without that class, I don't think I'd be sitting here.

That first company, **PREMISE**, came from Jon's business plan in Russ's class in 1987 with his classmate **AXEL BICHARA** '88 (who went on to co-found **BOLT INNOVATION**). Harvard Management Company invested $1.5 million in the startup, but the market for its main product was too small for survival. Computervision acquired the company and its two co-founders in 1991, and Jon stayed there until 1993, when he quit.[6]

Four months later, in 1994, Jon and several others started SOLIDworks Corporation, whose products today are the most widely used 3D modeling tools in the world. Jon relates the basis for this new firm: "The big idea of SolidWorks was, 'Put 3D modeling on a Windows PC—a platform shift.' People told me, 'Windows? That's ridiculous. You can't run CAD on that.' But we made it work and today, millions of people use SolidWorks products." In 1997, just four years after the SolidWorks founding, the French firm Dassault Systems purchased the firm for stock valued at $310 million.[7] Jon Hirschtick and his key management team stayed on to run the SolidWorks division. At the time the company was sold, SolidWorks was doing just $25 million in revenues, but with high customer acceptance and apparent growth prospects.

Jon continues:

> I loved it and stayed there for 18 years, but then I noticed that things had begun to change. I saw new computing technology–cloud, web, and mobile. I saw that how people worked was changing. Our customers who were designing products were increasingly using agile design pro-cesses. Teams were working differently, fragmented all over the world, with people coming on and off the team. Time constants were shorter.
>
> In October 2012, I left SolidWorks with five of my closest and most senior associates to found OnShape, my new company, where we have again rebuilt the complete CAD system to meet the needs of modern design teams. It's a full-cloud architecture. There's nothing installed. There are no downloads. It runs on mobile devices. We believe that once again, this kind of architecture for CAD will enable product design teams to work faster and better, and once again we will improve the way every product on Earth is built. I am the CEO of OnShape, but I am still doing the same stuff I was doing 35 years ago. And we are back home in Cambridge ☺.

Peter Levine of Andreessen Horowitz provides a vision of the future of OnShape, and moreover of the entire CAD-CAM industry. (Andreessen Horowitz led an $80 million round for OnShape in September 2015, and incidentally is

PETER LEVINE was an MIT student and at Project Mac in the 1980s, worked in several high-tech startups and then VC organizations for two decades, and returned in 2010 to MIT as a Senior Lecturer in entrepreneurial marketing and sales in the Trust Center for MIT Entrepreneurship. https://www.crunchbase.com/organization/onshape-inc-, last accessed March 29, 2018.

also the lead investor in Okta, Inc., presented in Chapter 9.) "With every generational shift in computing, the markets get bigger, because the tools become easier to use", says Levine, now on OnShape's board.

> Just as we saw with the transition from mainframe to PC to mobile, with OnShape I think we'll see the creation of a whole class of micro-designers and micro-manufacturers who will be doing a lot more design work because the tools are readily accessible. If \$8 or \$9 billion is the estimate for the current CAD market—which is already huge—then one can expect that to double or triple.

HELEN GREINER, IROBOT, AND CYPHY WORKS

HELEN GREINER '89, '90, '90 and her colleague **COLIN ANGLE** '89, '91 were key players in the revolution in robotics started by MIT Professor **RODNEY BROOKS**, who headed the MIT Artificial Intelligence Lab and then all of CSAIL (MIT's Computer Science and Artificial Intelligence Lab). Helen explains her early years:

Helen Greiner

> I was born in London as the daughter of a Hun-garian refugee, and came to the U.S. at age 5. My start in robotics was at age 11 when I saw *Star Wars* on the big screen. I fell in love. R2D2 was my muse, because he had character, a personality, and he was really more than a machine.
>
> I've always wanted to build things that were actually more than machines. Something attracted me to MIT, and I thought that would be the place to learn how to do it. We learned wonderful things at MIT, with lots of great stuff. Big emphasis on building things, and not giving up until you solved tough problems, while having fun. But at the time, 1989, no one at MIT really knew how to build commercial robots. If you wanted to do robots, the only place to go after graduation was to a government lab or to stay in academia. Those are two great choices, but I had spent my summers interning at the Jet Propulsion Laboratory—a wonderful place, but it seemed very bureaucratic to me. I obviously have a startup type of mentality.
>
> With Rod Brooks's guidance and guts, Colin Angle and I joined him and we founded **iROBOT** in 1990. When we started, we only knew we

> wanted to build robots. We thought, "Hey, maybe we can do the first robot that steps on the moon." It wasn't a great plan. We were 20, 30 years ahead of our time. We did work in entertainment, in research robots, law enforcement, military research. We did commercial cleaning robots! "How weird", people thought! And we did toys and games. No one was coaching us as to what we needed to do to build a company. And we certainly hadn't heard that MIT had just started an Entrepreneurship Center across the campus that might have tried to help us!
>
> All the time, even though our revenues looked infinitesimally small to others, they were always growing a little. We always felt we were doing well and accomplishing big things—especially when we did things like get a toy on the market, or put a robot a mile down into an oil rig. All this time, we were bootstrapping ourselves for money to keep going. It wasn't until 1998 that we raised venture capital, and brought in a total of $38 million over the next few years. It's not that we were turned down; we hadn't bothered to ask. We had heard bad things about venture capitalists, and even if we had asked, I don't think we would have been funded until we were able to show some successes. Then we put the "Roomba" vacuuming robot on the market, as well as "PackBot" military robots. I can honestly say both were necessary for iRobot's success, because sometimes the Roomba wasn't doing well and sometimes the military robots weren't doing well. Together, they made it so that we had exponential growth.

Colin Angle was CEO and Chairman from the beginning of the firm, and Helen was President and succeeded Colin as Chairman in 2004. Helen explains:

> I've only been describing the revenues up to 2008, when I stepped down from being Chairman and turned to drones. But iRobot is still going strong. I ran the military side and deployed over 6,000 PackBots into action with U.S. military forces, as well as SUGV [Small Unmanned Ground Vehicles] robots. We did lots of robots that kept people a safe distance from danger!
>
> I'll give you a typical example of very strong customer satisfaction. I was visiting the troops in Afghanistan to see how our PackBots worked in the field. One big strapping Marine at a base in Bagram carried up to me a very heavily damaged robot and asked, almost in tears. "Can you fix this?" My answer was "No, it voids the warranty." He really wanted this particular robot, because it had done many IED [Improvised Explosive Device] missions, one UXO [Unexploded Ordinance] mission, one vehicle-born explosive device mission, and he credited it with saving his team many times. Its name was "Scooby Doo", and that's

the kind of feedback I got. What I'm most proud of doing in my life is these robots that saved the lives of hundreds of soldiers and thousands of civilians by remediating IEDs, a big killer in the 2000s conflicts.

Given PackBot's adaptability, it has also been used to go into dangerous non-military places as well, such as the Fukushima nuclear plant.

The entire military business was sold in April 2016 to Arlington Capital for an estimated $45 million, and then re-launched as the independent Endeavor Robotics. But iRobot continues, wholly focused on consumer products. Headed by Angle, the Roomba automated vacuum cleaner has sold over 10 million units worldwide since 2002. "Scooba", a floor washing robot, followed Roomba, and then came "Braava" for floor mopping, as well as an increasing array of home robotic "appliances". Helen goes back to her own original *Star Wars* longing: "Once people have Roomba in their homes, they start to think of it as a little pet—their little guy. Georgia Tech did a study that determined that 63% of the Roomba owners named them. With its little bleeps and bloops, I think we got somewhat towards my goal of R2D2-like robots." Helen didn't anticipate the *Time* magazine article titled "How I Learned to Stop Worrying and Love the Roomba". Its author extolls: "I can talk to my Roomba all day. Our conversations, while short, are always meaningful. I might tell Roomba that it's the best thing that has ever happened to me, and Roomba will reply, 'Error 18, please open the iRobot app for help.'"[8] Helen also didn't anticipate the Amazon advertisement for its Echo product, in which Echo calls on Roomba to clean up the messy floor!

In 2005, we were ecstatic to be able to take iRobot public, raising $75 million for financing our next stages of growth. Now the company has a market value of around $1.8 billion. [$2.5 billion on June 15, 2019.] In my looking-back opinion, it has been the team and the dedication of the team that made all this happen. There were roadblocks and hiccups all along the way. There were numerous product/market failures to match the few but significant successes. There were changes in strategy, and the need to continuously discuss things and be able to come up with a new plan. We needed to pivot often, try to figure out what was best, and go forward as a team. That is what eventually allowed us to be successful: Two guys, Colin and I, who really stuck with it through the thick and thin, led by our professor and stimulus Rod Brooks. iRobot's 2016 revenues were $660 million. [$1.1 billion in 2018.]

Now I'm doing a company that builds drones, **CYPHY WORKS**, which I started in 2008, and I'm very excited about the drone space. It's so much easier than being on the ground! There's always crap on the ground. You have to deal with people and chairs and sodas and bags and all this stuff to avoid if you're a robot! But you're talking about free space in the air. And outside, just above the treetops, there's another, almost a super highway, waiting for these drones to also partake in delivery of all sorts. We did tests with UPS recently in Massachusetts, doing deliveries to islands off the coast. But because delivery drones are not quite legal yet, our flagship product today is what we call a "persistent drone". We tether it to the ground and it's able to stay in the air and do reconnaissance, communications relay, chemical sensing, and radiation sensing for many days at a time. It's a lot different from the hobby drone. We have them deployed and doing pilot tests for the Department of Transportation. The applications are oil and gas and mining and agriculture and any place you have a facility where it's inconvenient to be there 100% of the time. Of course, the military is quickly stepping in to envision and fund development of both tethered and flying drones that would supplement or sometimes replace the earlier ground versions. [Unfortunately, CyPhy Works didn't work out! It pivoted its focus to drone data collection and renamed itself as Aria Insights, but soon closed down entirely on March 21, 2019. Failure is clearly a frequently encountered outcome for startups, even those that persist for a decade!]

My last comment is about today's MIT. I've been a Trustee and serve on various MIT committees, so I see what's going on now. What a fantastic place to become an entrepreneur! There is so much happening, and so many people and courses and organizations to help you. I saw that a drone company won the $100K competition just a year ago. And a young woman is launching satellites with exciting new technology. And there are even robots that have emotions. How exciting! I would love to be an MIT student again today.

A POSTSCRIPT ON ROBOTIC VEHICLES: MOBILEYE

Amnon Shashua

The most rapidly growing category of robotic vehicles is automobiles (and soon after, trucks), with increasing use of advanced Driver Assistance Systems and active on-the-road testing of fully autonomous vehicles. The leading company in propelling this field has been **MOBILEYE**, an Israeli firm created in 1999 to carry out related AI and vision systems research, which was co-founded by **AMNON SHASHUA** '93, its CTO and Chairman. It released its first products to the market in 2007. In June 2015, Dr. Shashua showed a group of MIT faculty, who were on a study tour of Israeli innovation and entrepreneurship, MobilEye's schedule for the next three years of various system installations in 27 different vehicle manufacturers, worldwide, as well as a brief film of him "driving" an autonomous vehicle in Israel. His comment to us was, "Certainly, driving in Israel isn't like handling the Los Angeles freeways, but we're getting there!"

In March 2017, **INTEL** (with **BOB NOYCE** '53 as its founder) acquired MobilEye for $15.3 billion, the biggest-ever acquisition of an Israeli technology company.

Michael "Mick" Mountz

"MICK" MOUNTZ AND KIVA SYSTEMS, NOW AMAZON ROBOTICS

MICHAEL "MICK" MOUNTZ earned an S.B. in mechanical engineering from MIT in 1989 and an MBA from Harvard, and holds over 30 U.S. technology patents. Mick founded **KIVA SYSTEMS** in January 2003 after spending time in high-tech product development, manufacturing, and marketing at Motorola, Apple, and WebVan.

Mick says:

> I got started in thinking about the issues that led to Kiva Systems in 1999, at the time of the first Internet bubble. I was working in the Bay Area at a company called WebVan, online ordering of groceries and other goods. Its real world problem was how to get all of those grocery items into a tote bag cost-effectively. We were essentially taping $20 bills to the totes that were leaving the building, costing us more to pack and ship by far than the margins on the shipments. So WebVan went bankrupt very quickly.
>
> WebVan's crises were my source of insight into the problem. To build a successful company, you've got to be working on a real-world problem. Ours is the classic situation where it all started with fundamental research, then somebody finally cross-fertilized: "Oh, what we were doing all this hard science on applies to this real-world business problem." With a little bit of entrepreneurship thrown in, that catapults off to a market solution. I have heard MIT Professor Eric von Hippel call what we did "user-based innovation", because we owned (or at least shared) the problem before we got underway. This was absolutely true, but in addition we assembled a big team of collaborators working together to get it right.
>
> My step number one was to call my MIT fraternity roommate with the "Hey Pete, I have this idea" phone call, which he had heard from me a million times before. I did have the idea, but I had no clue as to how to build mobile robots or do the software. But my old roommate **PETER WURMAN** '87 was finishing his doctorate and teaching computer science at North Carolina State at the time, and his research was on agent-based systems that could bid for jobs. What we ended up

needing and actually doing, in terms of the computer software architecture, built on a lot of the work that Pete had done.

I described the problem to Pete. I said, "I need a machine that does this: I want to be able to just put my hand out, then have a product show up, and I put it into a tote." We abstracted the problem away using great MIT problem-solving principles and brainstorming too. What's the simplest way we could fill these orders? Then, let's build the enabling technology that we need. So, I started the company with one fraternity brother as a co-founder, and we roped in about six or seven other guys to help build the business, each who knew a piece of the equation. Then the team grew. One of the fun things about being an entrepreneur is you get to reach out to the people that you met at MIT and everywhere along the way.

AUTHOR'S NOTE

In a presentation that I watched at the MIT Technology Breakfast, Mick and his co-founder Pete Wurman showed a slide of them and seven more of their fraternity brothers, all at Kiva, with the titles under the photo showing their key positions in the organization!

When we were students at MIT, we had learned a lot of mechanical engineering, and how to build things and make them work. But we also learned how to think outside the box and approach problems with a fresh perspective. Immodestly, I would say that both Pete and I, in different ways, were thinking outside the box from the beginning, and our guys expanded our capacity to do that even better. That enabled us at Kiva Systems to disrupt the entire industry. [Consistent with all of the other cute startup names, Kiva is a Hopi term meaning ant colonies!]

Kiva ended up deploying mini-armies of mobile robots in the warehouse. But our big idea was very simple: Rather than having humans walk around the factory to go find the red T-shirt you just ordered, we'll send the robots out to pick up the entire shelf and bring the shelf over to the humans who are standing around the perimeter of the building. This is a productivity tool that enables e-commerce fulfillment centers to really crank out the orders faster, better, cheaper.

Looking at what we accomplished technically, I see it as quite analogous to the Internet founders who built upon a number of key tools from the computer and networking pioneers who preceded them. So too, those who came before me in CAD-CAM and in early industrial and military robotics and vision systems had created incredible tools that my company leveraged to generate a mobile robotics solution for the e-commerce industry. Our actual solution even works much like the Internet does. Our robots travel on a grid system. In fact, we stole the "collision back-off retry algorithm" from the Ethernet to say, "If two robots are seeing each other, they take a random number and back off and one of them wins and one loses." It takes a slightly longer time for them to get where they're going, but it works. Also, our whole system was designed with a lot of computer architecture thoughts in mind about what's in the cache in front of the operator. We're always looking for inventory in front of the operator versus out in the field. Then we page and swap memory accordingly.

Many of those ideas came from some of the great people whom we had at the company. The people you bring in and the culture you instill in the company are what make it survive through the thick and thin and eventually grow and flourish. I always emphasize that we were an engineering-driven company, but the secret sauce at Kiva was that two thirds of the engineers were software, one third hardware. We're not exactly the robotics company that people think about.

In a lot of ways, I still see myself as an engineer. So I wish I could show you the hardware engineering that goes into making those robots, which are the key to our entire business operation. I remember walking into our mechanical engineering offices at Kiva, and they were working on the chassis frame for a next generation robot. The engineers had it all detailed out in SolidWorks. They had done the finite element analysis work on the parts, to understand where the stresses and strains were going to be if you started torqueing and bending this piece of the chassis. You could see clearly, through color, where the hot spots were, and they were taking steps to resolve it.

I flash back to my first job out of MIT as a brand new mechanical engineer at Motorola. I was doing some drafting on a brand new **APOLLO** [**BILL PODUSKA** '60, '60, '62, co-founder and CEO] computer system that Motorola had, and we had a competition in the office to see who could memorize more of the hierarchical menu. But when we wanted to do some finite element analysis, we had to put together a file in a batch job, which we submitted to the National Center for Super-Computing at the University of Illinois. Two or three days later, we'd get back the file, and hopefully you had it right, because then it would display the thermal stresses in the parts. Today, our engineers are doing that at their desks, with the push of a button, with tools which MIT alums and others at SolidWorks and elsewhere have developed. All this let us grow very quickly as a company. It goes to show how everything builds on everything else, much from our predecessors, not only from the people we hired.

We ended up deploying our mobile robotics solution with many e-commerce companies around the country. Kiva was placing thousands of mobile robots into pick-pack-and-ship fulfillment centers, tripling productivity, while simultaneously increasing the speed, accuracy, and flexibility of the operation. And we could scale up from a small volume operation to a huge warehouse over the weekend, with no system downtime! We had already captured many of the top high-tech producers and sellers in the marketplace when Amazon tried us out. Ultimately, Amazon decided it wanted to use us across its entire company, and so it acquired Kiva, took us internal and off the market. We became **AMAZON ROBOTICS**, and I and most of our key players stayed on to run this operation.

Mick closes with pride:

> We had built Kiva rapidly and cost effectively, using only $33 million in venture funding to drive the firm up to the point of Amazon's 2009 acquisition of us for $775 million. [In my MIT E&I Technology Entrepreneurship class, Mick showed his financing planning slide from which he had formulated Kiva's growth and finance strategy!] At the time of the acquisition we had 275 people, including a bunch of my MIT fraternity brothers! [Just like Bob Metcalfe's description of how he staffed up 3Com.]
>
> Now I have the pleasure of serving on the School of Engineering's advisory council, as well as on the Mechanical Engineering visiting committee. I'm learning how MIT has changed since I left in 1989. I love the fact that the Institute is embracing the entrepreneurial spirit more formally and more broadly. Students now can actually have a serious shot at starting a business right out of school. When I was there, it was very rare for anyone to say, "Yeah, I'm going to start something right when I graduate." And now it happens all the time, and I think that's MIT embracing a mind shift that is wonderful.

MIT CAD-CAM AND ROBOTICS ENTREPRENEURS CONTINUE TO THRIVE

Aided by dramatic advances in artificial intelligence and machine learning, among other technologies, MIT's history of entrepreneurial pioneering continues apace, from early computer numerical control or automating machine tools to the present. Recent examples include **RIC FULOP** '06 co-founding **DESKTOP METAL**, a 3-D printing company that is making highly automated custom parts manufacturing available at high volume to individual companies worldwide. On the robotics side, Professor **CYNTHIA BREAZEAL** '93 of the MIT Media Lab, founder of its Personal Robots Group, and named by *Fortune Magazine* as one of the most promising women entrepreneurs, has founded **JIBO, INC.**, whose Jibo robot is a social robot for the home that the company claims "looks, listens and learns". And throughout the Institute we have backwards-jumping robotic jaguars and every other form of robotic creatures and applications. Without ques-tion, more and more new enterprises will be forthcoming in this domain!

REFERENCES AND NOTES

1. Helpful perspectives and additional detail came from David Weisberg, *The Engineering Design Revolution,* Cyr Research, 2008.
2. "Computervision", *Wikipedia*, https://en.wikipedia.org/wiki/Computervision (last viewed March 29, 2018).
3. An interesting sidelight: After Applicon, co-founder Richard Spann became the President of **ADAGE, INC.**, yet another company founded in 1957 by MIT alumni, headed by **JIM STOCKWELL** '52. When approached by Geisberg and his proposed Parametric Technology Corporation (PTC), Richard decided that Adage should become the seed investor and also provide space for Geisberg's startup. Spann served as a Director of PTC until after its IPO. What goes around, comes around.
4. "SketchPad", *YouTube*, https://www.youtube.com/watch?v=57wj8diYpgY (last viewed March 29, 2018).
5. "MIT 1982 CADLab", *YouTube*, https://www.youtube.com/watch?v=d6SudJ-nHFE (last viewed March 29, 2018).
6. Weisberg, *op. cit.,* p. 18-1.
7. "Dassault Systemes Signs Definitive Agreement to Acquire SolidWorks", *3ds.com,* https://www.3ds.com/press-releases/single/dassault-systemes-signs-definitive-agreement-to-acquire-solidworks/ (last accessed March 29, 2018).
8. Kristin van Ogtrop, "How I Learned to Stop Worrying and Love the Roomba", *Time,* April 10, 2017, p. 54.

11

The World of "Modern Finance"

Unlike biotech, the Internet, CAD-CAM, and robotics, finance is not a new industry. It dates back as far as trade, and to tell its history would require books upon books. But "modern finance"—including new approaches to assist startup firms in their founding and growth, as well as the new tools and techniques used to create financial instruments and to trade in financial markets—was essentially born after World War II. And yet, the vast breadth of the modern finance field precludes even identification, and certainly not complete inclusion, of all of the MIT alumni who have over the years become major entrepreneurial contributors to these financial innovations. So my selective coverage will need to suffice in this chapter on the role of MIT faculty and alumni in creating new and innovative financial enterprises.

As done in the three earlier industries assessed, only the founding or co-founding entrepreneurs of these firms are treated, not the hundreds or even thousands of MIT alumni who followed as major contributors to those enterprises. As in the other three industries assessed, MIT faculty were not only the creators of new theories and techniques, but as *mens et manus* encourages, frequently joined with their former students to start and to build new enterprises. I will not directly address the splendid array of their breakthrough contributions to the theories and methodologies of modern finance, neglecting even the many who earned Nobel Prize global recognition. And I shall unfortunately limit myself to only a few "sub-industries", including domestic and international venture capital, quantitative investing and trading, and electronic trading.

THE BIRTH AND EARLY DEVELOPMENT OF VENTURE CAPITAL: COMPTON, DORIOT, AND ARD

Karl Taylor Compton

Georges F. Doriot

KARL TAYLOR COMPTON, MIT's President beginning in 1930, and later its Chairman, spent much of World War II in Washington D.C. as a key member of the Office of Scientific Research and Development (chaired by Vannevar Bush '16, and former MIT VP and Dean of the School of Engineering), directing U.S. efforts in radar and in synthetic rubber, among other tasks. Even before the war, Compton felt strongly that science and technology had a huge unexploited potential to aid society. He had had several discussions in 1939 and 1940 with Professor **GEORGES FREDERIC DORIOT** of the Harvard Business School (HBS) and others about creating an organization to help accelerate the transfer of that know-how to the market.

An episode with a group called Enterprise Associates, which in 1940 went on to fund National Research Corporation (founded by Richard Morse '33, who would go on to teach the first MIT entrepreneurship course in 1961), convinced Doriot and Compton that they needed to combine investment funding with an organization that would do planning and development of S&T ventures. But the war demands upon both of them interrupted those conversations.

IT'S IMPORTANT to note that until the 1950s, MIT had only an undergraduate Course XV in Engineering Management. The 1964 founding of the MIT Sloan School of Management generated the gradual development of a full faculty covering the major fields of management including finance, and also including as shown in this volume the field of entrepreneurship.

Almost immediately at the end of the war, Compton and Doriot got together to renew their prewar discussions, both men being even more determined as a result of their wartime experiences to apply technological advance to societal benefit. Doriot's biographer identifies Compton's lead role: "MIT President Karl Compton dusted off his plans to create a new type of financial firm that would finance the development of technical and engineering companies."[1] Doriot was still busily engaged in governmental responsibilities, so in June 1946, Compton moved ahead in launching **AMERICAN RESEARCH AND DEVELOPMENT CORPORATION (ARD)** (note the emphasis suggested by the name on technology development, rather than just finance!). It was incorporated by MIT Treasurer **HORACE FORD** '31, '32 and three heads of manufacturing companies who were close to both Compton and Doriot (including MIT's **BRADLEY DEWEY** '40, and Ralph Flanders, who later became U.S. Senator for the state of Vermont). At the same time, several wealthy families were creating their own private venture capital firms (e.g., both the Whitneys and the Rockefellers in 1946), but ARD was the

AUTHOR'S NOTE

In attempting to sort out the credits for this undertaking, details provided by Doriot's biographer, Spencer Ante, help to indicate the key roles of Compton and MIT faculty and alumni. See Spencer Ante, *Creative Capital – Georges Doriot and the Birth of Venture Capital*, Harvard Business School Press, 2008.

first to raise money from nonfamily sources and to be professionally managed. Doriot temporarily became Chairman instead of President until he finished his government duties in November. The founding technical advisory board was all MIT: President Compton and Professors Edwin Gilliland '33 (later head of ChemE) and Jerome Hunsaker '12 (head of Aero). Ford became ARD's Treasurer (while continuing in his primary MIT role). MIT and three other universities (not including Harvard!) participated in the initial stock offering to raise ARD's capital base. The investors also included "the other MIT"—Massachusetts Investors Trust ☺. No other venture capital firm was started in Boston for the next 20 years!

ARD's investment pattern, as well as likely outcomes, was predicted by its first three ventures. The first investment was in Island Packers, a non-technology company that became a total loser. But the other two were MIT high-tech startups that performed reasonably, but not spectacularly: **HIGH VOLTAGE ENGINEERING**, co-founded by **DENIS ROBINSON** '31 and MIT Physics Professors Robert Van de Graaff and **JOHN TRUMP** '33, and **TRACERLAB**, formed by MIT alum **BILL BARBOUR** '33 with several more MIT alums as key employees. Dr. Compton served on both of their boards. A mode of operation evolved with MIT often providing space, heat, and light for numerous companies that came out of MIT, and ARD supplying the funding for salaries, capital investments, and additional operating expenses. For example, **IONICS**, based on new ion exchange desalination technology developed by Harvard and MIT scientists, was initially located in the basement of the MIT Chemical Engineering Building (#12), later moving its headquarters for several decades to just across the street from MIT.

EMPLOYEES and others frequently called Doriot "the General", referring to his war-time rank in the French army.

JOHN TRUMP was an uncle and summer employer of President Donald John Trump, who later described his working at MIT as his most exciting life experience!

ARD invested in a number of startups, but also went through a very dry period for several years. In 1954 Compton died, and shortly after in 1955 MIT sold its holdings in ARD. In 1957, ARD made a single investment of only $70,000 that produced most of its overall life-time profits: That investment was in **DIGITAL EQUIPMENT COMPANY (DEC)**, founded by **KEN OLSEN** and his MIT Lincoln Lab colleague **HARLAN ANDERSON**, with all of its initial products coming straight out of Lincoln Lab. Olsen had planned to call the company **DIGITAL COMPUTER COMPANY**, but Bill Congleton, one of the ARD key staff, advised Olsen that ARD would never invest in something so "dubious" as digital computers! Doriot was indeed very skeptical about making the investment. "According to industry lore, the General thought that DEC presented an opportunity for young Congleton to learn some lessons about the difficulties of picking winners. The early failure of a small investment would be instructive for his associate. Judging from the success of DEC, Congleton . . .

never had to learn the lesson!"[2] Incidentally, in Doriot's 1957 ARD annual report, he describes DEC as a company developing "digital building blocks", with no mention of the computer industry!

Another important part of the ARD portfolio was a later investment in **TERADYNE**, co-founded by MIT alumni **ALEX D'ARBELOFF** '49 and **NICK DEWOLF** '48. But most of ARD's investments were not very successful, and its overall portfo-lio returns, except for its star DEC, were okay but not impressive. Doriot and ARD went through year-long periods of no investments at all. Gradually, increasing numbers of key employees left ARD, most of them HBS MBAs, many to start venture capital firms primarily in Boston. Despite having invested heavily in technology-based companies, few of these VCs had personal technical or entrepreneurial experience, which colored the character of the Boston venture capital industry for several decades. Two ARD venture capital spinoffs that had MIT co-founders were **CHARLES RIVER VENTURES (CRV)**, with an entirely MIT technical advisory board and a stated intention of focusing on MIT startups, and **MORGAN-HOLLAND VENTURES** (**DAN HOLLAND** '58), a predecessor of Flagship Ventures (see more details in the Chapter 8 discussion of Noubar Afeyan).

Karl Compton had the original idea that became ARD and worked faithfully until his death on driving that notion forward while he was MIT President and then Chairman. But Compton's HBS partner and co-founder, Georges Doriot, was clearly ARD's builder and the continuing inspiration of his employees and his investors. Many of his portfolio CEOs, including Olsen and d'Arbeloff, gave unending kudos to him as a personal mentor and corporate counselor. General Doriot sold ARD to Textron in 1972, and it soon disappeared, but after estab-lishing its presence as a publicly-held, professionally-led firm that invested in early-stage primarily technical new companies. ARD is regarded as the father of modern venture capital.

SOME KEY EARLY MIT-ALUMNI U.S. VENTURE CAPITALISTS

The venture capital industry began to spread in the Boston area, then in New York, and gradually in the West Coast. Many of the early VCs were alumni of ARD, and even more from the Harvard Business School, a number of them having received earlier degrees from MIT. The California venture capitalists in particular frequently had deeper backgrounds in technology, and more actual experience with early-stage and technology-based organizations. That dramati-cally affected the differing character of the first decades of Boston vs. West Coast venture capital. Three key examples of MIT alumni VCs who molded the indus-try at its start are discussed below: David Morgenthaler, Thomas Perkins, and H. Dubose Montgomery.

David Morgenthaler and Morgenthaler Capital. While ARD was still in its infancy, **DAVID MORGENTHALER** '40, '41 was turning to personal venture investing from years of multiple leadership successes within the military, with large companies, and then with small firms that he took over and built into much larger ones! For most of his life he lived and worked in Cleveland, the heart of what is now called the "Rust Belt", but which had been the center of America's manufacturing industries. David was an exceptional student while growing up in the South. His high school English teacher recommended that with his analytical approach to everything, and his skills in math and science, David should go to an engineering school. His stepfather responded to that message with, "MIT is the best engineering school in the world, so you ought to apply there"—a wholly unknown place to this young boy.

David Morgenthaler

AUTHOR'S NOTE

Much of the content here derives from my listening to and enjoying the approximately four-hour YouTube video "Oral History of David Morgenthaler", carried out by the Computer History Museum when David was 92 years old. That information was supplemented by years of my personal conversations with David Morgenthaler, and by the telephone interview that fortunately was conducted by Michelle Choate just two months before David's death.

Morgenthaler started at MIT in 1936, with inadequate knowledge of calculus and physics, and he needed to adapt quickly and work hard to overcome his academic deficiencies. He learned and later preached to others the old saw, "'Tech' is for men to work, not boys to play"! But by his sophomore year, he was more relaxed, and carried out his co-op job efforts with General Electric while becoming very engaged in student activities. David eventually became captain of the swim team, president of his fraternity, president of the senior class, and a member of Osiris, MIT's secret society, in which he suddenly mingled with important MIT officers and alumni.

With his four years of MIT ROTC, David was called into active duty the day after the bombing of Pearl Harbor, and served in the Army Corps of Engineers with increasing responsibilities and rank until the very end of the war in Europe. Despite his double degree in mechanical engineering, he did essentially large-scale civil engineering in building airfields in North Africa, and then had command roles in Italy. His first civilian jobs upon return were in young firms that were engaged in various types of engineering applications. Then he became Vice President of Delavan Manufacturing, a Midwestern company specializing in jet engine nozzles, building it significantly. That caught the eye of J.H. Whitney and Co., which recruited Morgenthaler to become President and CEO of a Whitney investment, Foseco Inc., a Cleveland firm doing metallurgical chemicals, that David built dramatically over the next decade. By the end of his reign there, he was running the North American division of a British-headquartered firm with 57 companies worldwide, selling into 75 countries.

In 1968, David took his own money and started **MORGENTHALER & ASSOCIATES**, doing essentially angel investments in several companies, subsequently creating **MORGENTHALER CAPITAL**, a true venture capital firm based in Cleveland (not Boston or Palo Alto!). From his long and close ties to J.H. Whitney, he had learned much about equity investing and had developed his own perspectives on what made an attractive opportunity. David insisted that an appropriate investment situation required excellent, capable, and committed people, strong competitive technology, and an attractive market that could be captured and dominated. If one of those was missing, Morgenthaler said it was like a three-legged stool with one leg broken! His very first VC investment, in 1969, was in a time-sharing firm focused on the machine tool industry, Manufacturing Data Systems (MDS) of Ann Arbor, Michigan. Under David's very close managerial involvement, MDS went from his initial investment of 22 cents per share to a final sale price to Schlumberger of $64 per share, a model he adopted as his private goal to attempt to emulate in later investments.

I remember my first meeting with David. In 1971, he participated in the MIT Alumni Association Cleveland weekend entrepreneurship seminar on "How to Start Your Own Business" that I led. After that, David frequently visited MIT to learn more about what new things were happening there, and to meet entrepreneurial movers and shakers among the MIT faculty and within the Boston community, most from my mentions or introductions.

In 1989, when David's son Gary had completed about 20 years in entrepreneurial IT roles, Morgenthaler Capital opened its main office in Silicon Valley with Gary as a Managing Partner. David said: "I wanted to be at the crossroads of the world, where every opportunity passes you by", and California had become that in his view. Over time, the various Morgenthaler funds, now renamed as Morgenthaler Ventures, operated from Cleveland, Menlo Park, and Boston, investing over $3 billion in more than 300 companies.

But David Morgenthaler did far more for the VC industry than just provide an example of exceptional performance. While President and then Chairman of the National Venture Capital Association (NVCA) in the late 1970s, he was instrumental in persuading Congress to reduce the capital gains tax, and helped change federal regulations to allow pension funds to invest in private equity.

David and his wife Lindsay were devoted citizens of Cleveland and stalwart supporters of that community. Both were generous and active leaders and benefactors of Case Western University and the Cleveland Clinic, among others, and of Carnegie-Mellon, Lindsay's alma mater. At one early morning meeting with both of them at MIT, I asked Lindsay what she was going to do all day. She replied. "I'll just tag along with David and be bored!" With one lucky telephone call Lindsay ended up spending the rest of the day as a guest of the MIT Advisory Committee on the Arts, a much more fitting use of her time and talents!

And David was very important to MIT entrepreneurship. As described in Chapter 5, he provided the first prize money for the launch of the MIT $10K Business Plan Competition, and maintained that David and Lindsay Morgenthaler Prize Award for five years. Moreover, he credited Ken Morse, the first Managing Director of the MIT Entrepreneurship Center, with persuading him to be among the initial donors of endowed funding to the Center, making a gift of $1 million in the mid-1990s. David also provided major funding later for the MIT Sloan Leadership Center, and generous funds to Stanford's entrepreneurship program. My former MIT PhD student and co-author of our 2009 report on MIT entrepreneurship, Charles Eesley was a Morgenthaler Fellow in Entrepreneurship at Stanford, and recently received tenure there. David died in 2016 at age 96.

Thomas Perkins and Kleiner-Perkins.[3] Like many others who came to MIT, **THOMAS PERKINS** became interested in technology early in his life. In his 2007 autobiography *Valley Boy: The Education of Tom Perkins,* he wrote that as a youth he assembled television kits and had planned to be a TV repairman. He received his MIT S.B. in EE in 1953 and later, after working for Sperry Gyroscope, earned an MBA from Harvard Business School in 1957. Tom then moved to California, where he worked in the technology industry, accepting **BILL HEWLETT** '36 and Dave Packard's invitation in 1963 to become administrative head of their research department, the first MBA they had ever hired at **HEWLETT-PACKARD (HP)**.

Thomas Perkins

While working there, Perkins quickly found a great mentor who altered his career:

> "Dave Packard was the ultimate entrepreneur", he said. "I learned everything I know about venture capital from Dave." Packard even allowed him to start his own laser company while working full time at H-P. The result was **UNIVERSITY LABORATORIES (UL)**, which produced . . . helium-neon gas lasers based on his patented designs. Perkins guided UL through a merger with Spectra-Physics; then served on the Spectra-Physics Board as it became a leading laser company."[4]

Concurrently, Perkins moved swiftly up the ladder in HP, launched it into the minicomputer business, became the first general manager of its computer division, and propelled what became the base for HP's later primary growth.

> With the financial success of his own company [UL], Tom left HP in 1972 to become a venture capitalist, teaming up with fellow entrepreneur Eugene Kleiner. [Kleiner had been one of the so-called "Traitorous Eight" who left Shockley Semiconductor Laboratory to form Fairchild Semiconductor in 1957, along with seven more, including Bob Noyce and Gordon Moore, who later co-founded Intel.] The first **KLEINER-PERKINS** partnership, funded with $8 million, was at the time the largest venture capital company in the world. Kleiner and Perkins approached investing in a new way, taking a direct management role in the companies in their portfolio.[5]

That pioneering partnership combined the technical know-how in semiconductors and computers, as well as the managerial skills, of the two exceptional co-founders and provided a strong base not only for making insightful investments but for follow-through advice and counseling. This became the model for later Silicon Valley venture capitalists to attempt to follow, and is now emulated throughout the United States (including Boston) and worldwide. Later Frank Caufield and Brook Byers joined the firm, eventually becoming name partners of KPCB (Kleiner, Perkins, Caufield and Byers).

Over its 34 years to date, KPCB has invested in close to 500 companies, with nearly 200 that went public. These include such names as Amazon, AOL, Genentech, Google, and Netscape. Perkins served on the boards and often as Chairman of many of these companies. As previously indicated in Chapter 8, he was Chairman of Genentech from 1976 until 1990. "It was the most technically innovative company [I have] worked with and, since its products save lives, the most personally rewarding."[6]

Tom Perkins died on June 7, 2016, at age 84 after a prolonged illness. Because of his physical inability to attend the then-planned November MIT entrepreneurship celebration, we were in the process of arranging an interview when he died. But shortly before, in March 2016, he addressed the MIT Club of Northern California:

> "Go to MIT!" Perkins advised young people at the ... event. "I have used what I learned at MIT every day. MIT taught me to be comfortable and confident with technology, cope with complexity, and build on principles." In addition to giving advice to students, Perkins gave back to MIT, establishing the ... Perkins Professorship of Electrical Engineering.[7]

H. DuBose Montgomery and Menlo Ventures. Similar to David Morgenthaler, **HENRY DUBOSE MONTGOMERY** came to MIT from a small town of 5,000 in the Carolinas, where his father worked in a paper mill and his mother taught school. But he had longed for that MIT target from early childhood.

> I loved reading science fiction books, and as a kid I went to the little public library in my rural town and read every single Robert Heinlein and Isaac Asimov book that they had. In many of those books, the hero was typically the rocket scientist, and a lot of them had gone to this place called MIT. I didn't really know where MIT was. Somebody at one point said it's in Cambridge, and I thought "That's in England and a long way away!" I was 12 or 13 at that time. Later I discovered it was in Boston and was called the Massachusetts Institute of Technology. Even though I didn't think I had a prayer of getting in, I decided to apply anyway, and I got in ... remarkably.
>
> I had never been north of the Mason-Dixon line, never been to Boston, never seen the school ahead of time. I had grown up "swimming in this very small pond", doing very well with less than 100 people

AUTHOR'S NOTE

At the outset of a telephone interview, DuBose suggested that his recently completed oral biography should be the primary source for this section. See Jason Lopez, "Silicon Minds: DuBose Montgomery, from Asimov to Siri", October 29, 2016, accessed at venturewrite.tumblr.com on April 25, 2017. I took some minor editorial liberties in assembling DuBose's words!

> in my graduating class. Suddenly I'm at MIT with people who certainly had a lot more preparation in their education. But I ended up doing very well there, both academically as well as in extracurricular activities too! [Sounds just like Morgenthaler, and like how many more great MIT achievers???]
>
> I gravitated toward electrical engineering and computer science, because computer science at this time was really in its nascent development. I ended up getting a bachelor's and a master's in EECS and also getting a master's degree in management science from the Sloan School [all in 1972]. Against the advice of my mentors, I shifted from my PhD track at MIT and went to Harvard for an MBA.

H. DuBose Montgomery

Then came the unexpected crisis and consequences of the 1973 oil embargo. With oil prices tripling, heating costs in the Northeast skyrocketed, and DuBose and his new wife were in an apartment where the landlord turned the heat on for an hour in the morning and an hour in the evening!

> One morning I went out to find that my little Toyota that was parked on the street had been plowed in by the snow plows the night before, and my car was now encased in a solid block of ice! With my plastic hand-held scraper, it took about two hours to get my car out of the snow, and I resolved that I was never spending another winter in Boston! Literally, that weekend my wife and I went down to the Boston Public Library and checked out books on travel in the United States. We read them looking for a place that would have good weather, would never have snow, but would have some of the cultural aspects of Boston and some of the business and scientific opportunities too. We picked the San Francisco area, never having been there. And the rest, as they say, is history.

Soon after their relocation, DuBose started a company called **MENLO FINANCIAL** with some colleagues from Harvard and Stanford. Originally, they offered consulting services to smaller tech firms who couldn't afford the likes of McKinsey & Company, but they soon decided they'd rather invest in their client companies. DuBose remembers:

> This was 1974, in the depth of the worst recession since the Depression. We didn't use the term "venture capital" in any of our fundraising documents. It sounded way too risky for folks. But we went out talking

> about raising money to invest in small emerging growth companies. It took us two years to raise the money for a very small venture fund. We ended up having 81 meetings with an insurance company that we hoped would be our lead investor. In the end they agreed, probably because we had tired them out. So, we closed our first fund around Christmas of 1976. By then I was 27 years old, and I have been a venture capitalist ever since. Little did I know that I would be fortunate enough to experience wonderful investment successes through decades of funding new startups in technology and healthcare.

Since then, **MENLO VENTURES** has invested in over 400 companies, with 70 going public and over 100 mergers and acquisitions. It currently has over $5 billion under management.

One company that DuBose is most proud of is **GILEAD SCIENCES**. His story:

> Gilead was conceived of and incubated in Menlo Ventures's offices in 1987. I had a very bad cold [despite the wonderful California weather ☺], had gone to my doctor, and said, "Doc, can you give me something for it?" He responded, "If you had a bacterial infection, I'd give you an antibiotic. But you have a viral infection. There aren't any antivirals out there. Go home, eat some chicken soup, and feel better in 10 days." Once I did feel better, I came back into the office and asked, "Why aren't there any antivirals?" It turns out that a virus is very different from bacteria, so we did a lot of investigation on the research in this area. Menlo Ventures had an associate working at the firm, Michael Riordon, who had a medical degree, and together we started Gilead Sciences with Menlo Ventures as the founding venture investor. In search of a name, we realized that in the book of Genesis in the Bible you hear about getting balm from Gilead in ancient Palestine, the balm coming from the bark of a willow tree. It turns out that the sap of those trees is actually acetylsalicylic acid, which is aspirin! Today Gilead is the world's leading antiviral pharmaceutical company, probably saving over 50,000 lives a year of folks with HIV and other viral infections. It currently has a $50 billion market capitalization and we owned 100% of it at its beginning! [Gilead had a market cap on June 15, 2019 of $85 billion.]

Montgomery served as a member of the MIT Corporation and on two of its visiting committees, EECS and Sponsored Research. Montgomery imparts to all his favorite perspective: "Life is not a dress rehearsal—enjoy the journey!"

Other U.S. Venture Capital Founders from MIT. The U.S. VC pioneering stage was more or less over by the end of the '70s, but the industry's growth of firms and investment volume has continued in up-and-down spurts, corresponding somewhat with the economic growth of the country. In this section I cover, in sequence of founding, those MIT-alumni-founded VC organizations that I have been able to identify. Inevitably I have missed some or many!

Back in 1969, **L. ROBERT JOHNSON** '63 formed and led an early venture organization, **SPROUT GROUP**. But it in turn was a division of Donaldson, Lufkin & Jenrette, so this pioneering entity was more or less an "internal venture" of DLJ. In 1988, Johnson established **FOUNDERS CAPITAL PARTNERS** as an angel investors group, and relocated the firm to California in 1999. Inevitably, other MIT alumni played key roles, perhaps as founders, but certainly as partners of the several venture capital companies started during this early stage. Regrettably, however, they remain unidentified at this time.

Kevin Kinsella

The next MIT alumnus whom I identified who became a venture capital entrepreneur is **KEVIN KINSELLA** '67, who founded **AVALON VENTURES** in 1983. Kevin still runs the firm, with offices in Cambridge and La Jolla, which is focused heavily on bio-pharma startups. Avalon has made over 125 investments in early-stage companies, including in Vertex Pharmaceuticals in Boston. But his reputation is also based on his great success as an "old-fashioned" theatre angel investor, being the Tony Award–winning producer of "Jersey Boys" as well as of a number of major musical revivals.

Sacha Pfeifer, *Boston Globe* columnist, quotes Kevin:

> MIT has never given an honorary degree or athletic scholarship, so it's all about making it academically on your own. It's a very tough culture of competition, and you have to measure up every day among some of the brightest minds in science and tech. But there is no better place on the planet to do that. And once you get out, you're at the cutting-edge of things, you know how to grasp complicated concepts, and you build up a network of friends and associates who have gone through the same boot camp.[8]

Diana Frazier

DIANA FRAZIER '81 started out in BancBoston Ventures, eventually rising to be its President. In 1994, Diana founded **FLAG VENTURE PARTNERS** as an international venture capital and private equity "fund-of-funds", with offices in Boston; Stamford, Connecticut; and Hong Kong. Over its life, FLAG grew to total assets of $6.3 billion that it in turn invested in U.S. and global VCs and private equity firms. FLAG was sold to Aberdeen Capital in 2015.

FREDERICK WILSON '83 co-founded **FLATIRON PARTNERS** in 1996, and then in 2003 co-founded **UNION SQUARE VENTURES**, both in New York City. Flatiron focused on follow-on investments mostly in dot-com successes and failures, and generated extremely high performance for several years. But Wilson and his co-founder Jerry Colonna closed it down in 2001. Fred observed: "Flatiron had invested almost entirely in Internet deals. It made a fortune and then apparently lost it! But screwing up royally is good for you, if you learn from it." In 2003, he co-founded Union Square Ventures with the opposite investment orientation, primarily early-stage firms. Its "returns" performance has been remarkable, generating a billion dollar exit in each successive year. In 18 months, its first fund went from $110 million to $1.6 billion. Its 59 exits since 2003 include such well-known companies as Lending Club, MongoDB, Tumblr, Twilio, Twitter, and Zynga. Union Square has invested in 274 companies and has more than 75 companies in its portfolio (pitchbook.com, accessed on August 17, 2019). Fred has been cited regularly as one of the most successful venture investors in the world.

Fred Wilson

On April 13, 2017, Fred was the first Doriot Distinguished Lecturer on Entrepreneurship at the MIT Sloan School. The lectureship is sponsored by **MICHAEL KOERNER** '49, one of Doriot's former HBS students and a great Canadian finance entrepreneur. During his lecture Fred reminisced on his days at MIT. "MIT changed me and changed my life. I got a zero on my first test at MIT. But I then learned to study and to progress. And I met my wife!" He also remarked, "Early-stage risk-taking is the only legal way to get a 100X return on your money." When asked about his criteria for investing, Fred responded, "The best time to invest in something is when no one believes in it but you. And then invest only in those entrepreneurs who are (1) charismatic; (2) have technical expertise—not outsourcing the technical work to others!; and (3) have clear strong integrity."

BRADLEY FELD '87, '88 co-founded **MOBIUS VENTURE CAPITAL** in 1996 and **FOUNDRY GROUP** in 2007, both based in Boulder, Colorado. Having already received his bachelor's in management from MIT, Brad was a PhD student in the entrepreneurship program at MIT Sloan in the late 1980s. At the same time (1987), he founded a software firm, **FELD TECHNOLOGIES** (started when he was a student in Russ Olive's New Enterprises class). At the urging of his key MIT mentors, including me, Brad was pushed to decide between entrepreneuring and an academic future, and he left to devote himself full-time to being a software entrepreneur. He built and then sold Feld Technologies to AmeriData in 1993, becoming its CTO. He started **INTENSITY VENTURES** and made 40 seed investments in software and internet companies before co-founding what became Mobius (which was affiliated with SoftBank) in 1997. In 2007, he co-founded Foundry Group, focusing initially on early-stage technology investments, though it has more recently broadened its scope of interests. It currently manages over $1.5 billion, and is investing in other early-stage VC firms as well as technology

Brad Feld (and an old TRS-80)

companies. While doing all this, Brad also co-founded **TECHSTARS** in 2006. As discussed in Chapter 6, Techstars is a pioneering accelerator of and investor in young startups all over the world. In addition, Brad has managed to maintain his earlier academic interests in glorious fashion, having co-authored nine books on various aspects of entrepreneurship.

BRINGING AMERICAN VENTURE CAPITAL TO THE WORLD

Very often, international MIT alumni bring back to their home countries the entrepreneurial models they observe and perhaps have practiced in the United States, for example, Charles Zhang and Sohu.com in China. This is also true for the movement of U.S.-style venture capital to foreign countries. Beginning in the 1980s, prominent MIT grads attempted a number of new venture capital investment firms in developing countries. As might be expected, the earliest ones encountered significant difficulties.

Peter Brooke, the senior partner of Boston's Advent International, took the initiative of bringing U.S. venture capital to Asia. His first partnership was in 1984 with **YAICHI AYUKAWA** '52, '53, '57, creating **TECHNOVENTURES JAPAN**, the first venture capital firm in Japan. Jerome Wiesner, then President of MIT, had introduced Brooke and Ayukawa, correctly thinking that they might develop some type of useful relationship. Ayukawa was not very typical of Japanese scientists at that time. He had learned much, both from his family's significant industrial leadership background in Japan as well as from the very different environment he was exposed to for years at MIT. From its outset, TechnoVentures invested in technology-based startups, and Ayukawa, its President, worked to provide mentoring and direct involvement in those firms.

My memories of Yaichi begin with early discussions we had during his many visits to MIT. Soon after TechnoVentures Japan was off the ground, Yaichi invited **GORDON BATY** and me to visit him to help us raise funds for our Cambridge-based **ZERO STAGE CAPITAL**. He arranged for us to present to the Japanese Bankers Association. But Japanese financiers were far from believing that equity investments were appropriate in early-stage companies that lacked collateral assets that might back loans. So, we came away empty handed, but also sensing the difficulties that Yaichi was encountering. And Japanese societal attitudes toward risk-taking were not compatible with creating entrepreneurial companies. TechnoVentures Japan closed down after several years of trial and mostly failure. A few years later, Yaichi was selected as the first Japanese member of the MIT Corporation.

The year after he started his Japan venture, before any results were in, Peter Brooke continued his efforts to transform Asia toward American-style startup venture capital, again looking to MIT alumni for his partners. In 1985, Advent formed **TECHNOVENTURES HONG KONG**, with three MIT co-founders with strong credentials. First was **VICTOR FUNG**, double degrees in '66, grandson of the founder of Li & Fung, Hong Kong's largest trading company, which Victor later headed. Victor also later was Chairman of Prudential Asia, and currently runs Fung Holdings. **MARTIN TANG** '72 was the second co-founder, the third generation of his very philanthropic and successful business family to receive degrees from MIT, and later the first international President of the MIT Alumni Association. (Marty's son became the fourth generation of Tangs to get a degree from MIT!) Third was **KA-CHEONG (CHRISTOPHER) LEONG** '65, '70 who, before returning to Hong Kong, was a Senior Scientist for **AMERICAN SCIENCE & ENGINEERING** (founded by **MARTIN ANNIS** '51), the company that pioneered airport X-ray machines, among other innovations. Victor Fung described TechnoVentures as the first venture capital fund in Hong Kong (U.S. $22 million) to bring high tech projects to Hong Kong and China.[9]

Victor Fung

Martin Tang

Chris Leong

The partners followed the same technology focus and U.S.-style engagement as had been attempted in Japan, initially with similarly dismal outcomes. TechnoVentures Hong Kong even had a broader territorial field of play, with some early investments in Taiwan and in southern China. But the culture and attitudes encouraged few talented individuals to become entrepreneurs and even fewer individuals and institutions to want to participate in these kinds of investments. However, the team persisted and became even more ambitious. China activities began to increase, and they formed **TRANSPAC CAPITAL**, integrating TechnoVentures Hong Kong with DSB Bank and NatSteel of Singapore, becoming the first regional VC-Private Equity firm covering Greater China and ASEAN. Dr. Leong served as CEO for many years, investing over $900 million in more than 210 businesses.

In 1992, MIT Senior Executives Program alumnus '74 and Sloan School Senior Lecturer **THOMAS ("T") THOMAS** started India's first venture capital firm in Mumbai, **INDUS VENTURE CAPITAL**, while keeping close ties to a U.S. VC firm for guidance. Indus did acceptably well in its investment returns, but its primary portfolio was in "old-style companies", not in high-tech startups. T had a spectacular industry background, having risen to be Managing Director of Hindustan Lever, then becoming the first Indian member of the Lever Brothers main board in London, then later serving as Chairman of Glaxo India. But he still was not comfortable with technology startup entrepreneurs, and also at that time lacked a large set of investment opportunities to move aggressively in that direction.

Pat McGovern and International Data Group (IDG). Timing is often said to be a key to success for startup entrepreneurs. That seems also to be true for starting venture capital firms in a new geography. While the mid-'80s were not quite right for TechnoVentures, the tide was even then beginning to turn in China from the perspective of its government's policies as well as its people's readiness to jump out to seize new opportunities. **PATRICK MCGOVERN** '60 and his **IDG** operation in Beijing, China were among the earliest to take advantage of those shifts. But McGovern had long been an experienced entrepreneur and VC by then.

As an undergraduate, Pat became the editor of *The Tech* and served as a member of the MIT Activities Council, which I chaired, and where our long relationship first began that would grow to include many aspects of entrepreneurship. Soon after leaving MIT, McGovern started a consulting company that sold multi-company sponsorships of market studies of high-tech industries so as to keep each sponsor's cost low. At the outset, he stayed afloat personally by selling his old car for $5,000. Those market studies led to the creation of **INTERNATIONAL DATA CORPORATION (IDC)** as a market research firm, which then moved into publishing various computer-related journals, the largest of which was *Computerworld*. As he built his dual market research/publications firm, Pat began to reach out toward global markets for both. His biggest hits came in China, beginning in the early '90s when he established one after another of China's earliest foreign joint ventures between government agencies and each of his many technology-linked magazines. By that time, IDC had become the **INTERNATIONAL DATA GROUP (IDG)**.

Patrick McGovern

Pat started **IDG VENTURE CAPITAL** in 1996 to do venture capital investing in the United States. That fund quickly began its China entities. As mentioned in the discussion of Sohu.com in Chapter 9, the IDG Beijing VC fund made one of its first investments in the Series A round of Sohu. **IDG VC** successes in China rested in part on McGovern's experiences with his magazines, which produced his astute initiation of venture partnerships with China's major banks, in addition to key governmental organizations. IDG VC quickly spread its reach from Beijing via new VC funds across China, Vietnam, India, and Korea. These have been extremely successful. The IDG Venture Capital website indicates that the overall venture firm has $3.6 billion under management. The China venture firm alone is shown as having a portfolio of 500 companies with 120 successful exits.[10]

McGovern went from his humble start to the point that Ernst & Young named him "Entrepreneur of the Year". In Pat's view, "Ultimately, to be a successful entrepreneur, it's critical to marry vision with practicality. The key is to keep very close to your customers and tailor your innovation to fulfill their needs." During his life, Pat was very active in many aspects of MIT affairs. Early on he endowed the McGovern Awards for Outstanding Student Contributions to MIT Entrepreneurship. He had been a member of the MIT Corporation since 1989. And he and his wife established the McGovern Institute for Brain Research with the largest financial pledge that MIT has ever received.

Pat McGovern died in March 2014, leaving his IDG ownership to his Foundation. In 2017, the foundation sold IDG, its U.S. and foreign market research and publications, as well as its global venture funds, to a Chinese conglomerate of which IDG China is the primary element.

Sonny Wu and GSR Ventures. By 2005, China had developed a very active and competitive venture capital marketplace for its rapidly growing entrepreneurial community. While an MIT Sloan Fellow, **SONNY WU** '01 was already thinking seriously about becoming an entrepreneur. His master's thesis with me was on an optimal design for a hand-held device, like the iPhone would become. But Sonny was not there yet! After returning to China, with extensive technical and managerial experience there and in Canada, Sonny co-founded **GOLDEN SANDS RIVER FUND** (now **GSR VENTURES**) to invest in early-stage Chinese technology startups.

Sonny Wu

THE NAME is intended to communicate an image: The Golden Sands River starts as a small stream high in the mountains of China and eventually feeds into the mighty Yangtze!

Initial partnering with a prominent Silicon Valley VC, similar to the beginnings of the two TechnoVentures and Indus Ventures VC startups, provided the financial base for getting underway, while also giving Sonny and his co-founder initial mentoring in carrying out venture investing and assistance to its portfolio firms. By GSR's third fund, his Chinese firm was completely independent and its California partner had shifted into being one of its many Limited Partners. GSR now has $1.5 billion under management, with offices in Beijing, Palo Alto, and Singapore. Some recent investments have been in U.S. companies that have major manufacturing or marketing activities in China. More recently, Sonny has formed **GSR CAPITAL** in Hong Kong to carry out major acquisitions of firms and/or divisions of large corporations. In August 2017, Nissan Motors agreed to sell its lithium-ion battery business to GSR Capital for about $1 billion. Sonny has gone on to develop GSR Capital as a major mover-and-shaker in Asian energy areas, and has now created **GOLDEN SAND DIGITAL BANK** in Gibraltar.

In the same year (2005) that GSR was founded in China, two other MIT Sloan Fellows, **DR. ZI-LEI (MARK) QIU** and **GEORGE LI**, both MIT Sloan Fellows '98, co-founded **CHINA RENAISSANCE CAPITAL INVESTMENT** to make both later-stage and private-equity alternative investments throughout Greater China. With headquarters in Hong Kong, they have operated in Beijing and Shanghai as well, with Mark as CEO and George as a Managing Director of the funds. They have invested billions of dollars through their several funds. In recent years, they have broadened both the scope of their investment activities as well as the countries in which they invest, including the United States, Japan, and India.

In 2008, they established a charitable foundation, **CHONG REN FOUNDATION**, to promote education in China's less developed regions by financing school buildings, providing advanced IT equipment, and offering incentive schemes for outstanding teachers and students, and by financing other projects that promote the growth needs of youth in general.

NEW APPROACHES TO VENTURE INVESTING

Individuals and their friends and associates have long invested in early-stage companies, using their own invented approaches. And large corporations have done the same for years, investing in related startups or growing companies, or to foster attempted diversification, as indicated in both the Meditech and Applicon cases.[11]

But the continuing development of investment opportunities in funding early-stage and growing innovation-driven firms also stimulated more and more MIT alumni to create their own organizational ways of investing. In order of their founding date I present a variety of entrepreneurial approaches taken by a number of MIT grads since the '80s. No doubt I have not yet identified many others who would be appropriate for this book.

1981. **ZERO STAGE CAPITAL** became Boston's first "seed fund", providing $50,000–$100,000 as its initial investment in each selected startup, along with a required part-time advisor drawn from its General Partners or its Limited Partner investors. The co-founders were Paul Kelley of Harvard, **GORDON BATY**, **ARTHUR OBERMAYER**, and me, later joined by **JEROME GOLDSTEIN** (Baty—'61, '62, '67; Roberts—'57, '58, '60, '62; Obermayer—'56; and Goldstein—'64, '65, '67, '67). It took Zero Stage over two years to raise its Seed Fund I of $4.8 million, eventually attracting most of the Executive Committee of Salomon Brothers and senior officers of Bain & Co. (prior to their establishment of Bain Capital). Joe Lombard of Salomon Brothers became a General Partner in the firm. The company lasted over 30 years, and maintained numerous funds in Boston, Baltimore, and State College, Pennsylvania. Its peak fund was Seed Fund VII that raised $160 million in 2001. As indicated previously, one of its early investments was in PerSeptive Biosystems, founded by Noubar Afeyan in 1988.

1988. **RICHARD CHARPIE** '73, '75, '79 was founder and Managing Partner of **AMPERSAND CAPITAL**, which was organized to spin off projects and divisions from large materials companies, and later healthcare firms, into early-stage firms.

1998. Boston's first institutionalized angel investment group was **COMMONANGELS**, organized by the Massachusetts Software Council Executive Committee, then headed by **DAVID SOLOMONT** '80 along with **RICH CARPENTER** '64, '65, **PAUL EGERMAN** '71, and **ALAIN HANOVER** '70, '70. I was invited to lecture at its first meeting on how to invest in startups, and became the longest active member of CommonAngels. **JAMES GESHWILER** '00 started as its summer intern after its first year, and led the organization as its Managing Director for the rest of its active life (through 2016). For many years, upwards of 60 entrepreneurs and kindred folk, many from MIT, were actively engaged in early-stage investing with CommonAngels.

1998. At any point in time, **ALLAN WILL** Mgt. S.M. '81 is wearing so many hats that using any single profession to describe him would be a misnomer. But in 1998, he created **THE FOUNDRY** (and now serves as its Chairman) in Silicon Valley as an incubator of numerous medical device companies, co-founding 11 of them. Allan not only provided counsel to them, but he invested in many or all, and was CEO or Managing Director or Chairman of several. Since 1998, Will also was a Managing Director of Split Rock Partners and General Partner of St. Paul Venture Capital, both VC firms. He has generously donated to MIT's entrepreneurship program, and has lectured from time to time at the MIT Entrepreneurship Development Program, which he says is "a chance for me to reflect on the things that I have done and learned."[12] Incidentally, Allan holds over 30 issued patents.

Allan Will

2000. HUB ANGELS, INC. was co-founded by **CHARLES CAMERON** '79 and **DAVID VERRILL** '87 as a for-profit managed angel investment group. Its website indicates that there have been 90 members in Hub Angels funds I–VI, investing more than $40 million.

2000. As described more thoroughly in Chapter 8, **NOUBAR AFEYAN** co-founded and led **FLAGSHIP VENTURES** and its **FLAGSHIP VENTURELABS** into active and highly successful venture creation, going well beyond just venture investments into the full cycle of company development and eventual spinoff. It has recently changed its name to **FLAGSHIP PIONEERING**.

2000. DRAPER LABORATORY, a large non-profit technology development organization that was formerly the MIT Instrumentation Lab, created its own $25 million VC fund, **NAVIGATOR TECHNOLOGY VENTURES**, to invest in its spinoff companies as well as in startups that its staff and services could assist in growing. Navigator invested in 12 companies over its life, making its final follow-on investment in 2008, closing down shortly after. This "incubator"-style investing arm was a much later copy of the efforts of National Research Corporation (NRC, founded in 1940, and discussed in Chapter 1) to build companies based on its own research projects. Cabot Corporation renewed NRC's incubation efforts after it bought NRC out of Norton Corporation, the original purchaser of NRC. A small part of that "incubation" space at 70 Memorial Drive became the first offices of the MIT Entrepreneurship Center, and the entire building is now used by MIT for offices and classrooms.

2009. BABAK NIVI '97 co-created **ANGELLIST** to facilitate identification between entrepreneurs and angel investors, including data on who has already invested in what. AngelList also helps startup job posters and job seekers to find each other.

2011. **XIONGWEI "JOE" ZHOU** '08 organized and manages **BOSTON ANGEL CLUB**, an angels fund with membership drawn primarily from Greater Boston Chinese business people. The club heavily emphasizes technology companies founded by local Chinese students and researchers and/or that may potentially later link to China for marketing or manufacturing.

2012. **GREG BELOTE** '07, '08 and **MICHAEL NORMAN** '10 co-founded **WEFUNDER**, an early online crowdfunding service that connects startups with investors. WeFunder was instrumental in persuading Congress to change investment regulations to permit the crowdfunding of for-profit firms. It claims to be the largest by many measures of any platform for regulation crowdfunding. In the year ending in March 2019, it raised about $90 million for the firms that employed WeFunder as a source. Mike Norman left the firm in mid-2019.

QUANTITATIVE INVESTING AND TRADING

Major changes have occurred in finance since quantitative tools and techniques first began to assist investors and traders, then began to gradually replace those functions by automated decision-processes. This "sea-change" has escalated rapidly as the decision-making algorithms themselves have improved, along with the emergence of Artificial Intelligence and "machine learning". These changes have been facilitated by dramatic improvements in computer speed and capacity, and by the increasing availability of huge databases. MIT faculty and alums have contributed greatly to all aspects of these changes, and have helped to implement them by entrepreneurial actions. Many people began using simple computer monitoring, trend analysis, and forecasting models as early as the 1960s. A few more-visible MIT finance entrepreneur "quants", who created remarkably innovative firms with superb performance, are discussed below (again in order of founding date).

Helmut Weymar

1969. One early innovative MIT alumnus "quant" is **F. HELMUT WEYMAR** '58, '65. His successful financial entrepreneuring was based on sophisticated com-puter modeling and data acquisition techniques in commodity trading, and later also in trading other futures such as currency. Helmut learned computer mod-eling as a graduate research assistant in the MIT System Dynamics Group in the early 1960s. He ran an MIT project for Minute Maid Corporation to model the entire frozen orange juice industry in order to better understand the sources of supply, demand, and price fluctuations. On the side, Helmut and other System

Dynamics graduate students became intrigued by commodity market dynamics, and actually pooled their meager funds to engage in commodities speculation based on their own simple models, at a time when none of them could really afford the risks. Several of those "brilliant MIT grad students" remember converting our $375 per month research assistant stipends into $1,000 losses from combinations of potatoes, wheat, and soybeans futures!

Leaving MIT part-time to work in industry, Helmut began to seriously develop models of sugar and cocoa markets for James Welch Candy Company, while moving ahead in pursuit of a PhD in Economics. His distinguished committee was headed by commodities expert Paul Cootner (MIT faculty member from 1959 to 1970), and included mathematical economist and Nobel Prize winner in Economics (1970) Paul Samuelson (MIT faculty member from 1940 to 2009). Helmut's 1965 dissertation, *Dynamics of World Cocoa Markets*, integrated System Dynamics feedback model concepts with rigorous econometrics, and was published by MIT Press in 1968. Within a month of starting his work with Welch Candy, the company sold out to Nabisco, for which Helmut went to work full time as soon as his dissertation was completed. His commodity trading efforts contributed to such spectacular profits that Nabisco declared a one-time increased dividend for its shareholders.

In the very next year, 1969, Helmut launched and became CEO of **COMMODITIES CORPORATION (CC)** in Princeton, New Jersey, with Professors Cootner and Samuelson as founding investors and advisors, along with Nabisco itself. The successes of CC generated early attention, as noted in *Fortune*, which labeled them as "rich commodity scholars".[13] Helmut and Commodities Corporation continued their excellent performance up to CC's acquisition by Goldman Sachs in 1987 for a reputed $100 million price tag.[14] Among other kudos, CC was praised as generating around 20% annual returns on its funds for the previous decade, as well as having been the training ground for such Wall Street trading stars as Paul Tudor Jones and Bruce Kovner.

Gary Bergstrom

1977. GARY BERGSTROM got his PhD from MIT Sloan in 1968, a time that essentially preceded "modern finance". He absorbed lots of lessons on statistics, modeling, quantitative analysis, and information technology, as well as finance, during his doctoral program. Gary also remembers, "There was very little entrepreneurial environment at MIT at that time, but I did enroll in what was then the only entrepreneurship course at MIT, New Enterprises." Gary had previously worked for companies like IBM, AT&T, and other large firms, but the entrepreneurship course planted the idea that he could do more with his life than just working as a large company employee.

AUTHOR'S NOTE

Much of Gary Bergstrom's background information comes from an interview with Michelle Choate in September 2016, plus personal discussions as well as supplemental sources.

After a stint at a large investment company, Bergstrom decided to go out on his own, launching **ACADIAN FINANCIAL RESEARCH** in 1977. According to the company's website, Acadian designed, developed, and implemented the world's first international index-matching strategy, and later an active country selection strategy for State Street Bank and Trust.[15] In 1987, Gary co-founded and became CEO of **ACADIAN ASSET MANAGEMENT**, which began directly managing institutional assets. "Back at that time", said Gary,

> the industry had not much embraced in a practical way a lot of the new insights, advances, and developments that primarily came out of academic finance efforts. We used a lot of those perspectives from academic research and rigorous analytical modeling techniques and processes. Our company almost ran out of money, and had more than a few challenges, but we were able to persevere. One of my stories for new employees is how we maxed out my credit card at Staples and I had to share my desk with three other employees for a month until some revenue came in!

By 1992, Acadian evolved into a truly global all-cap equity manager, and in 2002 also moved into long/short strategies by applying its stock selection techniques to finding the lowest performing companies, as well as the best ones! While still based in Boston, Acadian now has world-wide offices and is owned by "Old Mutual", OM Asset Management plc. Bergstrom retired in 2011 to become a consultant to the firm. As of June 2017, Acadian managed over $86 billion on behalf of its 100 clients.

1982. **JAMES SIMONS** '75 is a world-class mathematician who founded and still chairs **RENAISSANCE TECHNOLOGIES**, one of the world's most successful hedge funds and one of the first to be based on sophisticated trading models. As an MIT freshman, Simons enrolled in a graduate math class. He earned his bachelor's at age 20, after studying for only three years. "I liked MIT. They just let me do what I wanted".[16] [Note the same comment in Chapter 9 by Bob Metcalfe, founder of 3Com.] Simons received his PhD at UC Berkeley at age 23. He then taught math at MIT and Harvard, and later at Stony Brook University, where he became department Chairman. In between, he worked on cracking codes for the National Security Agency! He has won numerous scientific prizes for theoretical contributions to mathematics.

James Simons

Simons vividly remembered playing poker with friends at MIT: "Mostly I lost, but eventually I became a pretty good poker player. Later I invested, along with my father, with those poker pals, Jimmy Mayer '58 and Edmundo Esquenazi '58, '59. Their business in Colombia, South America, vinyl floor tiles and later PVC piping, succeeded enough to finance my first fund" in 1978, which eventually became Renaissance Technologies.[17] Wikipedia adds: "For more than two decades, Simons' Renaissance Technologies' hedge funds, which trade in markets around the world, have employed mathematical models to analyze and execute trades, many automated ... analyzing as much data as can be gathered, then looking for non-random movements to make predictions."[18] "Working with the late algebraist James Ax, ... Simons created the Medallion Fund, ... ultimately run entirely for employees ... according to a 2014 Bloomberg report, 'returning more than 35% annualized over a 20-year span.'"[19] Jim described his several different tries at developing quantitative approaches for trading. All his early attempts seemed to work for a while and then fail. He declared a six-months break in trading to reassess his firm's techniques, causing some clients to abandon him (unfortunately for them!). During that break, Jim and one of his key people developed a whole new approach to trading that was much more short-term in nature. That is what they have stuck with since, of course subject to continuing analyses and improvement, but without any further dramatic change.[20] "Renaissance Technologies ... had roughly $65 billion worth of assets under management in 2015 [$110 billion as of June 30, 2019!], and the people working there have been called 'the best math-physics department in the world.'"[21]

Simons and his wife Marilyn have been extraordinarily generous philanthropists in many areas and in several countries. Their charitable foundation, started in 1994, now takes up most of Simons's time, and aside from the Howard Hughes Foundation is the largest private funder in the United States of basic science and math education. Simons is an MIT Corporation Life Member, and he and his wife have included MIT in their philanthropy. Their most recent gift has been the complete restoration and renovation of MIT Building 2, which all former undergrads certainly recall as the home of the Mathematics Department, now renamed as the Simons Building.

A very recent summary of his insights exclaims:

- "Don't give up easily. Stick to something. Be persistent."

His takeaway:

- "Companies rarely succeed in their first iteration. Be prepared to stay the course...."
- "Getting fired once can be a good experience. You just don't want to make a habit of it...."
- "Work with the smartest people you can. Hopefully smarter than you even."[22]

Arthur Samberg

1985. ARTHUR SAMBERG '62 built strongly on his aeronautical engineering background to move into the investment industry. Samberg went from MIT Aero to Stanford to Lockheed and then, with a Columbia MBA, into investment analysis for Kidder Peabody focused on aeronautics and defense electronics. Not long after that, Arthur joined the startup Weiss, Peck & Greer, where over the next 15 years he became a partner and then joined the management committee.

In 1985, he co-founded and became President of **DAWSON-SAMBERG CAPITAL MANAGEMENT**, starting there his first Pequot hedge fund in 1986. In 1999, he spun-off his funds into his separately founded **PEQUOT CAPITAL MANAGEMENT**, serving as CEO, President, and Chairman during the next decade. Its funds peaked at $15 billion in assets under management, at that time the largest hedge fund in the world, with a net return of 17.8%.

Art Samberg has been a major philanthropist for Columbia and MIT, and for many charitable institutions as well. His most recent gift to MIT has been the funding of the new Samberg Conference Center on the top two floors of the redone MIT Building 52, now named the Morris and Sophie Chang Building. Samberg is a Life Member of the MIT Corporation and a member of its Executive Committee. He also chaired the MIT Investment Management Company for five years.

1988. From the start of his several years at MIT, **BENNETT GOLUB** '78, '82, '84 began accruing deep knowledge of computers, along with finance and economics.[23] "But at MIT", said Ben, "I also learned that everything's possible, and that you can think big. The idea that you didn't know how to do something was a starting point!" After completing his doctorate in Applied Economics and Finance at MIT Sloan, he worked at First Boston Corporation, where he soon established its Financial Engineering Group. There Ben gained the experience of helping to structure over $25 billion of bonds, including many innovative collateralized mortgage obligations and asset-backed securities.

Ben Golub

That led to Ben becoming one of eight co-founders, and in his words the "house quant", of **BLACKSTONE FINANCIAL MANAGEMENT**, which provided institutional clients with asset management services from a risk management perspective. In 1992, it changed its name to **BLACKROCK FINANCIAL MANAGEMENT**, which became **BLACKROCK**, now the world's largest asset manager, with $6.4 trillion under management as of 2019! At the time of its founding, you really needed to be spending lots of money on big main-frame computers to deal in mortgage-backed securities. BlackRock gained competitive advantage by moving toward far less expensive minis, like Sun Microsystems. Ben describes the diverse skills of his co-founders:

> In BlackRock we fortunately had a variety of skill sets beyond technology and analytics. We had partners who understood how to manage people, and others who presented well and could persuade others of our ideas, and some who were wonderful in developing commercial relationships. In many ways I see having all of those talents together as a stroke of luck.

In 2000, Ben founded and became co-head of **BLACKROCK SOLUTIONS**, its risk-advisory business. He spent 20 years as a Managing Director at BlackRock, and Chief Risk Officer, rising to become its Vice Chairman. During his period there, he also authored many articles and books on financial analytics and risk management.

Ben's most recent service to MIT is on the North American Advisory Board of MIT Sloan. He recently funded the Bennett Golub Center for Finance and Policy at the MIT School of Management.

1998. Not every company founder plans in advance to take on that role. Some are thrust into leadership by circumstances, and then rise to the opportunity to help build significant organizations. This is the case for **GREGG E. BERMAN** '87, who became one of the founding members of **RISKMETRICS GROUP INC.**, unintentionally!

Although Gregg doesn't like being labeled a "quant", he became "quantitatively oriented" at a very early age. Several samples over time help to paint Gregg's picture clearly. "In my first year in junior high school, I announced . . . my intention of becoming a physicist and attending MIT. . . . I got a summer job in a computer store selling Commodore 64s, and started in the fall of 1983 as a freshman at MIT."[24] After several years, "while knee-deep in my experiment [for my PhD in physics at Princeton], I was fascinated about possibly moving to Wall Street." And with several more years in between, a cold call by a recruiter looking for possibly disaffected Princeton PhDs brought him to meetings at J. P. Morgan. "After a few days and a dozen or more intensive interviews, I joined RiskMetrics in September 1998 on the day the group spun out of JP Morgan" to become an independent corporate entity.

Berman continues: "It's been more than eight years, and I'm still at RiskMetrics. I've held a number of positions, ranging from product manager . . . to heading the market-risk business. And even to running the sales force." RiskMetrics went public in 2008, and then was purchased on March 1, 2010, for $1.55 billion. Gregg Berman became a successful entrepreneurial founder without ever intending to be ☺.

1999. ANDREW LO is among the most recent of the significant MIT-related founders of quantitatively-based investment firms. Lo, MIT Professor of Finance since 1988 and Director of the MIT Laboratory for Financial Engineering, has been the outspoken developer and advocate of the "Adaptive Market Hypothesis", which emphasizes that investment strategies need to allow for varying market dynamics and efficiency over time. To implement his theories, Andy founded and became Chief Scientific Officer of **ALPHASIMPLEX GROUP**, and now serves as its Chairman and Chief Investment Strategist as part of **NATIXIS**. The NATIXIS website argues: "Strategies are developed in a model-based quantitative framework with an emphasis on advanced risk management techniques and liquidity."[25] This concern for managing

Andrew Lo

risk reflects the same orientation as Ben Golub's position in BlackRock and Gregg Berman's efforts in RiskMetrics. The four AlphaSimplex funds have grown steadily, and totaled $6.3 billion as of December 31, 2016.

Lo has published extensively and with great recognition throughout his academic career, and has received numerous awards from finance-focused professional societies. In recent years, he has joined with Professor Antoinette Schoar in sponsoring the rapidly growing "FinTech" entrepreneurship activities in cooperation with the Martin Trust Center for MIT Entrepreneurship.

ELECTRONIC TRADING: BILL PORTER AND THE GREAT FINANCE REVOLUTION

Bill Porter

WILLIAM A. PORTER '67 was a high-school dropout who joined the Navy during WWII at age 16, only to get thrown out when they discovered his age. After the war he worked his way through a bachelor's and then master's education and became a hard-working physicist and engineer. Bill attributes his determination to his earlier demanding work as a young cowboy. "Hard, hard work. . . . When you're in the homesteading frame of mind, you just do things because they're right, and you have that self-confidence that just won't quit."[26]

Bill's technical career was impressive, and he grew fast in responsibilities. His 14 patents testify to the fact that his technical and innovative capabilities were first-rate. But he decided that he would benefit from more formal management education in a creative technology-intensive environment. So, Bill persuaded his boss to sponsor him to become an MIT Sloan Fellow in the one-year Executive Development master's program, earning his MBA in the Class of 1967. That time period was sufficient for Bill to become infected with the MIT zest for entrepreneurship.

Within a few months after graduating, Bill decided to start his own company, co-founding **COMMERCIAL ELECTRONICS (CEI)** with five others. They soon developed the first low-light night-vision electron microscopes, as well as the broadcast TV cameras still used universally today. After selling CEI, Bill did technical consulting on his own and then for Stanford Research Institute (SRI) until 1982.

While still at SRI, Bill had been doing increasing amounts of stock trading. He had purchased an Apple II computer to help him keep track of stock prices and activity, as well as to compute rudimentary formulas that he thought might help improve his trading results. He was contemplating the notion of starting an online brokerage house when at a cocktail party in 1979 he met Bernie Newcomb. The partially blind Newcomb was a superb computer programmer. Their party discussion led them to create together what became **TRADE-PLUS** in 1982. Bill saw its market as selling services to brokerage houses. He and Bernie, respectively, put in $10,000 and $5,000, splitting the company ownership pro rata at a price of $1 per share. In his autobiography, *I Did It My Way*, Bill points out that its value (when converted into E*Trade equivalents) 18 years later, at the peak of the dot-com boom, hit $42,300 per share![27]

As with most new pioneering companies, the first years were very difficult both technically and in fund raising. Bill sold off part of his ownership to stay afloat, and the company sold stock to anyone who would buy. The move to online trading was first achieved in mid-1983, but Trade-Plus was still in a vendor mode for brokerage firms. That was followed by ups and downs, increased competition, and several offers to buy the company, all of which were refused. Gradually the company enjoyed increasing success.

In 1992, **E*TRADE** (short for electronic trading) was formed with an important "pivot" to provide deeply discounted online trading for the individual, not the Trade-Plus role of servicing brokerage firms and stock exchanges. The U.S. Constitution's states' rights provisions created new hurdles to overcome, requiring E*Trade to gain individual licenses from every state in order to operate nationwide. (About 10 years later, Sohu.com encountered similar requirements for online trading in China, needing to be authorized for separate operation in each Chinese province. At Sohu we assumed at that time that this problem had to be unique to China!) The dramatic shift of product and market initiated a long period of growth and success for E*Trade (of course with bumps!), including a NASDAQ IPO, then later a shift to the New York Stock Exchange, as well as numerous M&A activities and shifts in management. But Bill Porter and E*Trade had revolutionized the financial markets with electronic online trading for everyone, worldwide. This dramatic change for the finance industry was accomplished with extensive electronic hardware, sophisticated software, and entrepreneurial innovation and perseverance. It is all documented and much more in Bill's 709-page autobiography.[28] In 1998, Ernst & Young presented him the "National Entrepreneur of the Year Award".

His autobiography also documents Bill's later co-founding with Marty Averbuch of the **INTERNATIONAL SECURITIES EXCHANGE (ISE)**, the first wholly electronic options exchange in the United States. Porter became its first Chairman on his 70th birthday in 1998. Bill had earlier conceived the idea for a "third market" for doing options trading, and with much study proposed that to the E*Trade board of directors. The board decided that it had too much on its plate already, especially with its then-impending IPO, to start a new business of that scope. With board permission, Porter and Averbuch visited all of the European exchanges in 1997 to observe their electronic options trading operations. The efforts to move ahead took three more years, and after encountering and dealing with every form of problem, ISE was approved by the SEC and began operations in March 2000. Its initial growth was dramatic, but September 11, 2001 was not far away, with the deaths and chaos that occurred then and continued beyond.

Eventually Bill Porter retired from all of his Wall Street-linked endeavors, and began to live a very different but still entrepreneurial life with his wife Joan in Hawaii, engaging in large-scale, long-term agricultural developments.

During Bill's active life as an electronics entrepreneur and then as a finance revolutionary, he was a very generous supporter of the institutions he viewed as instrumental to his personal growth and success. He donated major sums to his initial alma mater—Adams State College—to build its science and engineering capabilities and to provide scholarship funding for locals who could not afford college education.

But Bill's primary self-image was as an entrepreneur. He funded an MIT chair in entrepreneurship, and then he and his wife Joan contributed $25 million to kick off fundraising for the new headquarters building (now named after them) of the MIT Sloan School. At its groundbreaking in 1997, Porter testified to his underlying motivations: "[I am giving these funds] to leverage the Institute's technological capability through entrepreneurship for the betterment of the human condition." Bill loved MIT, and especially what he learned as a Sloan Fellow: "MIT is the leader in almost every field of science and technology, but it's one thing to come up with a brilliant technical widget and quite another to bring it to market. To me, MIT Sloan is the bridge to helping all these hot shot technical guys convert their widgets into meaningful inventions for the progress of mankind."

He actively supported the MIT entrepreneurship programs in many ways, giving a half-dozen speeches at MIT, the highlight being his inspiring keynote address to the nearly 1,000 MIT students at the then $50K Entrepreneurship Business Plan final awards. In a different form of expressing thanks to MIT, Bill rewarded two Deans of the MIT Sloan School, Lester Thurow and later Richard Schmalensee, by appointing them to the Boards of E*Trade and ISE, respectively.

William Porter died October 15, 2015, in Kauai, Hawaii, years after staging his multi-faceted revolution of the finance industry.

MIT FINTECH WILL PRODUCE A BOOM IN "MODERN FINANCE" ENTREPRENEURSHIP

MIT economics and finance faculty continue to advance the theory and practice of finance. Translating these ideas into startup firms will be accelerating, with academic leaders such as Professors Antoinette Schoar and Andrew Lo, as mentioned previously, heading the new FinTech activities at MIT, including its business plan prize competition. In December 2017, MIT Professor **ROBERT MERTON** '70, Nobel Prize winner as well as entrepreneur and angel investor, provided glimpses into the future of finance-based entrepreneurship in his final Sussman Award lecture on quantitative finance. Merton traversed various topics of finance, from Bitcoin to various forms of arbitrage, identifying in each area the potential for new companies being formed. The many students in the audience were taking copious notes, foretelling their later actions!

As MIT has now launched its new Artificial Intelligence Initiative, accompanied by its announcement of the Stephen A, Schwarzman College of Computing, it is a certainty that financial investing and trading will be one of the primary areas of attention, of course by management-oriented people but inevitably by lots of scientists and engineers as well. The future of quantitative finance and trading will inevitably be altered by a continuing rush of MIT-based entrepreneurial action.

REFERENCES AND NOTES

1. Spencer Ante, *Creative Capital — Georges Doriot and the Birth of Venture Capital*, Harvard Business School Press, 2008, p. 107.
2. William Bygrave & Jeffry Timmons, *Venture Capital at the Crossroads*, Harvard Business School Press, 1992.
3. Much of the background here comes from Maggie Bruzelius, "Tom Perkins '53", *Technology Review*, July–August 2006.
4. Bruzelius, *op. cit.*
5. *Ibid.*
6. *Ibid.*
7. *Ibid.*
8. Sacha Pfeifer, "Five Things You Should Know About Kevin Kinsella", *Boston Globe*, August 28, 2015.
9. Personal letter to me, April 1, 1986.
10. Accessed on April 27, 2017.
11. Our now outdated but widespread study of U.S. corporate venture capital: Edward Roberts, I. MacMillan, V. Livada & A. Wang, *Corporate Venture Capital (CVC): Seeking Innovation and Strategic Growth, National Institute of Standards & Technology Special Report GCR 08-916,* June 2008.
12. *MIT Management Alumni Magazine*, 2017.
13. Shawn Tully, "Princeton's Rich Commodity Scholars", *Fortune,* February 8, 1981.
14. Kenneth Gilpin, "Goldman Says It Will Buy Asset Adviser", *New York Times*, May 1, 1997.
15. Acadian, acadian-asset.com, accessed on May 1, 2017.
16. Amanda Schaffer, "The Polymath Philanthropist", *MIT News*, November/December 2016.
17. Interview by Michelle Choate, August 22, 2016.
18. "James Harris Simons", *Wikipedia*, https://en.wikipedia.org/wiki/James_Harris_Simons (last viewed March 29, 2018).
19. Sean Elder, "World's Smartest Billionaire", *UC Berkeley* California *Spring 2016 War Stories.*
20. Choate, *op. cit.*
21. Elder, *op. cit.*
22. From *Thinking Forward*, MIT Sloan School of Management, April 9, 2019.
23. Much of these details came from Golub's interview by Michelle Choate on October 5, 2016, as well as from supplemental sources.
24. Richard Lindsay & Barry Schachter eds., *How I Became a Quant: Insights from 25 of Wall Street's Elite*, John Wiley & Sons, 2009, Chapter 3.
25. Natixis Investment Managers, https://www.im.natixis.com/us/home (last viewed March 29, 2018).
26. "William A. Porter", *Wikipedia*, https://en.wikipedia.org/wiki/William_A._Porter (last viewed March 29, 2018).
27. William A. Porter, *I Did It My Way* [following the Frank Sinatra song title], privately published, 2013, p. 228.
28. *Ibid.* A more succinct overview of the phases of E*Trade's development is contained in "History of E*Trade Financial Corporation", fundinguniverse.com (last viewed May 5, 2017).

A Grand Hurrah!!

Part Two has evidenced many MIT alumni, frequently with MIT faculty in the lead, who have pioneered in four very different industries, founding and building great companies that have created jobs, generated taxes, produced important changes for society, and disseminated advances to our ways of life, in the United States and globally. Their MIT education and learning came from across the Institute. The evidence indicates what logically should have been expected: Chemistry and chemical engineering were critical backgrounds for those who created the biotechnology-related startups; electrical engineering dominated the Internet founders; mechanical engineering played a key role for many who pioneered CAD-CAM; and management education has been instrumental to most of the entrepreneurs in modern finance. Albeit, diversity of background education and experience is also observed throughout these four chapters, from MIT as well as from other universities and firms.

Most of those entrepreneurs have largely enjoyed meeting and overcoming many challenges to growth and success. Each of those four areas shows continuing promise for new firms being founded by MIT alumni entrepreneurs, and of course by many others. We extend our utmost congratulations to and deep appreciation for all of them. We also communicate our congratulations to the many other MIT-educated entrepreneurs in the same four industries whom we have inevitably not yet discovered as of this writing, as well as our apologies for those omissions.

The patterns of pioneering observed in Part Two can be displayed in many other fields, beginning with software and electronics, where the MIT entrepreneurial impact data show such large numbers of alumni founders.* MIT-based entrepreneurs are prolific in all fields, and in many countries, bringing the products and services derived from their education and their energy to benefit all, and we give deserved praise to all.

This tribute to all MIT entrepreneurs is indeed ***a grand hurrah!*** But let's pause for a brief retrospective on what they have taught us.

LESSONS LEARNED FROM A HALF-CENTURY OF MIT ENTREPRENEURS

These four chapters, and the many additional examples provided throughout the book so far (with more to follow in Chapter 12), convey some critical lessons

* Edward B. Roberts, Fiona Murray & J. Daniel Kim, *Entrepreneurship and Innovation at MIT: Continuing Global Growth and Impact*, MIT, December 2015.

to which aspiring and even current entrepreneurs might well pay attention. They not only match my personal learnings as a teacher and researcher of entrepreneuring, but I support these findings from my half-century of experiences in co-founding a dozen firms, being an active board member of more than three times that number, and being an angel investor in about 150 startups.

#1. BE SMART, ACT SMART. First, all of the entrepreneurs discussed in this volume were indeed quite well-educated and at the forefront of their technical fields. That is great. But the lesson from them is not just "It pays to be smart!" The lesson is that you must use your "smarts" to come up with innovative ideas that are ahead of the pack. Companies that merely replicate that which already exists have very low likelihood of survival, never mind success. If you start a "me-too" company, substantially undifferentiated from those already in the market, you had better be offering a cost-savings to customers of at least 25 to 50% to get their attention and to enable your startup firm to persuade many customers to switch from their existing suppliers to a novice firm.

Your innovative and attractive difference might indeed be technological, following the example of most of the startups we have presented, who provided meaningful advanced performance in their product offerings. But your innovation might be in dramatically improved service, or higher quality. Or you may be attacking the market through more convenient, faster, more reliable channels. This book has focused upon "innovative entrepreneurship". If you want merely to copy products or services, at least be sure to look for customers not yet being well-served, such as those in developing countries. Many of my students see wonderful products and services in the United States that are lacking in their native countries, just as Charles Zhang did with China and the Internet. That important change of market location is indeed itself a key innovation, with its own set of complex difficulties. But that pattern facilitates many of the firms that we "export" to the rest of the world.

#2. IT TAKES A LONG TIME. Second, with rare exceptions, building a new venture to sizable state and sustained profitability takes a very long time. Go back and review the time period of all of the firms we discussed in depth in the past four chapters. None was an "instant success". A founder must assume that a decade or more of persistence will be required before her or his company reaches a stage of significant size of employment, revenues, and, hopefully by then, meaningful and self-sustaining profitability.

#3. HAVE PATIENCE AND PERSISTENCE. That provides the basis for the third lesson: A company founder, and co-founding team members, must have the patience and fortitude to cope with this long time delay between initial vision and ultimate fulfillment. Reread the comments made by so many of the pioneering entrepreneurs in this book about how many years were needed to achieve their successes. But elapsed time is not the greatest of the issues to be overcome, as their stories clearly document. Hardly any company goes through its growth processes without encountering numerous obstacles, whether they are product misfits with the market, or co-founder misfits with each other, or economic slowdowns that lessen customer enthusiasm or ability to pay, or that constrain capital availability. These "scaling" obstacles frequently require "pivots" of strategy and tactics of the company, sometimes leading to or revealing incompatibility of the founding team's skill sets, needing key changes in the top management team, or at least leading to added delays of product/service growth and added costs to build the firm.

A stronger term than "persistence" is "resilience", which I define as being able to get up and continue after being knocked down. This applies to individuals as well as companies. Remember Tom Leighton's instantaneous reaction to the 9/11 killing of his key co-founder and CTO Danny Lewin. Consider Harry Lee's comments about how the Applicon co-founders reacted to their surprise new "second milestone". Business shocks are often wholly unsettling and need a coming-together of the founding team and their employees to achieve survival, before growth becomes a possibility.

 # 4. BEHAVIORAL KEYS TO FOUNDER SUCCESS. The ideas and plans of startup entrepreneurs contain great uncertainties. This is shown in the shift of Noubar Afeyan's own initiative after six months, in Applicon's refocus after one year, and Ray Stata's dramatic "betting of the company" (actually of his own ownership) to create dramatic change of direction. In deciding to invest in the earliest stages of so many companies, I have always sought the greater certainties of the entrepreneurs' personal attributes, rather than their specific ideas/plans—their drive to achieve, their openness to criticism, their adaptability to needed change, their trustworthiness, as well, of course, their personal brilliance. I see Lesson Number 4 as often resulting from attempted (and especially unsuccessful) scaling.

Original management attitudes and behavior of founder-leaders may have worked well when the number of employees was small and somewhat homogeneous, and when their objectives were somewhat simple and straightforward. But growth usually entails multiplicity of goals, heterogeneity of employees, and complexity of organization structure and required functions. The decisive founding CEO can perhaps get away with autocratic behavior among the few co-founders and early employees who often knew and related well to her or him in their previous employ. The most common founding team came primarily from the same organization, even the same project group.

But how does leadership style need to change as the firm gets to 50 or 100 employees and more? The many cases described in this volume do not in general get into the styles of management, albeit HubSpot (see Chapter 12) has just been named the Massachusetts company "for which it is best to work".

But one lesson from my research on entrepreneurial styles (using Kepner-Tregoe survey instruments). is that two characteristics of leaders are most strongly linked to company success. First is "high Need for Achievement" (n-Ach), i.e., strong drive to succeed, where success is measured in tangible terms such as number of employees, overall revenues, capital valuation. Clearly, if you have a strong drive to win, you have a higher likelihood of getting there.

The second key characteristic is more difficult to explain, and that is "moderate Need for Power". Need for Power (n-Pow) is reflected in the extent to which the leader "needs" to be in control. Someone with high need for power needs to be running everything—sometimes labelled "a control freak"! To be sure, that might make directions very clear, and eliminate any ambiguity of where you are trying to go and how you are proceeding to attempt to get there. But high Need for Power stifles the opportunities for subordinates to exercise any power at their own level of responsibility in the organization. At the opposite end of the power spectrum, low Need for Power generates uncertainty as to the next steps to take, and the ones after that! It is often labelled as representing "weak leadership". The power ideal is "moderate"—the leader exercises clear control over the primary goals and objectives of the firm (hopefully with collaboration in defining what those goals might be). But that "moderate n-Pow" leader does not try to run everything, passing down to subordinates their own opportunities to define sub-goals that are consistent with overall organizational targets, and encouraging (even rewarding) subordinates to determine how to achieve those sub-goals. That managerial style tends strongly to encourage many in the organization to be highly motivated by "their own piece of the decision-making action". It also shifts degrees of power down toward the levels where more complete and more accurate information may well exist that is needed to get those jobs done. These principles support the continuing search for openness about differences of viewpoints being encouraged, not suppressed nor merely tolerated. These attitudes support the development of organization-wide trust of its leaders and of each other. Today, this style of management is frequently referred to as "distributed leadership".

#5. TEAMS ARE CRITICAL. The fifth lesson for would-be entrepreneurs has been the base for our entrepreneurship education programs at MIT. That is, that teams of co-founders, not solo leaders, are far more likely to become successful. Note throughout the past four chapters (and reinforced in Chapter 12) that every one of the companies from MIT faculty and alumni that pioneered these industries was started by more than one founder. To be sure, one of the founders, likely the founding CEO or the one who remained in a key leadership role during the firm's time of greatest achievements, may have acquired the strongest personal reputation that is often identified with the firm. Who was Bill Gates' co-founder and partner for years? Who made Steve Jobs' ideas realistic and fulfilled? Or in this book, who were EG&G, or BB&N? Or Bob Metcalf's co-founder at 3COM? etc. In all of these cases, despite high repute often endowed upon a single CEO individual, the co-founding team provided complementary assets that enabled the company to grow and eventually achieve success. Not the least of those assets is the sharing of the variety of pains and suffering that accompany most efforts to grow a great firm!

Our earliest studies showed that companies formed by two individuals far out-performed solo founders. Those with three partners at the outset did even better on average, with the trend continuing for teams of four co-founders. I speak of success, NOT survival. Success is measured at least tangibly with employment, revenues, capital value, as well as perhaps intangibly with how much benefit to society it generated. Survival is merely how long did the firm stay alive, perhaps with just one or a few employees. Many solo entrepreneurs create life-style companies in which they work alone, or with a few employees, and they last forever. In that founder's eyes, that may well constitute "success", but hardly ever in significant tangible terms that impact the broader society. We call the latter long-time survivors "sustenance entrepreneurs", versus the growth-based entrepreneurs we have presented throughout this volume.

Furthermore, our research studies showed that most of the strongest founding teams had included multiple skillsets, not just one. The combination of technical and managerial backgrounds among the co-founders was highly desirable. Indeed, when a managerial member of the team had prior experience in marketing or sales, that combination with technology was the very best!

#6. MUTUAL TRUST. The final lesson to learn, in my experience and judgment, is that mutual trust is essential among co-founders, as well as between angel investors or venture capital groups and the leaders in whom they invest. Adhering to each other over long periods, surviving frequent crises that arise, sharing pain and joy as they are encountered, all demand openness and trust of each other. I say, "You had better have someone on whose shoulders you can cry! as you will most likely need that source of comforting." Many firms even come together at the outset by the initial discovery of such a trusting relationship. That causes the two (or more) partners to then work hard to find a common project on which they can stay together and seek mutual satisfaction. That is true in marriage, and in co-founding great enterprises.

(overleaf) top
WeCyclers, co-founded by Bilikiss Adebiyi-Abiola '13, uses low-cost cargo bicycles (called WeCycles) to provide convenient waste recycling services to households across Nigeria.

bottom right
Attendees of the MIT $100K Pitch Competition in October 2015.

bottom left
Students working at the Martin Trust Center for MIT Entrepreneurship.

Moving Forward

Perspectives from a Half-Century of MIT's Growth and Impact

The last section of the final chapter of my 1991 book is titled "The Future of Technological Entrepreneurship".[1] I saw brilliant growth worldwide happening in technological entrepreneurship, despite the fact that the economy was then in dismal condition. At MIT, signs of increasing student interest in entrepreneurship were abundant, but at my time of writing we still had only one subject focused on entrepreneurship, New Enterprises, and we did not yet have an MIT Entrepreneurship Center. My last words of that book were: "High-technology entrepreneurship remains a continuing and ever more important part of the American dream and reality, increasingly shared by aspiring young technologists all over the world."[2] I hope that my views of the future in Chapter 12 can turn out so accurately.

12

MIT Entrepreneurship and the Future

The future of MIT entrepreneurship is already here.
And it will change tomorrow!

This chapter examines several predictors of the continuing future growth and impact of MIT-based entrepreneurship, in the number and diversity of the founders, their purposes in starting a company, and their broadened fields of engagement. I will discuss more deeply "the MIT Engine", and what it tells us about MIT's missionary commitments to encourage and strengthen entrepreneurship, especially in those areas of global problem-solving that demand the most patient resources and nurturing. Finally, I will sum up what we have learned from the internal and external development of the "MIT entrepreneurial ecosystem" and its worldwide off-springs.

THE PATH OF MIT ENTREPRENEURIAL ACHIEVEMENT

Part Two presented histories of many MIT faculty and alumni who pioneered in starting and building great firms and wholly new industries. Most readers have no doubt perceived what is obvious: The nature and proliferation of MIT-based entrepreneurship, the identity of the founders, their purposes and places of starting, and perhaps even their success rates have changed dramatically over the past half-century.

In 1960, MIT had no system in place to either encourage or assist someone thinking about starting a company. History provided examples, culture provided the encouragement, and the traditions of learning at the forefront of knowledge—combined with the expectation that students and faculty would do things that matter with that knowledge—were what accounted for the earliest of MIT faculty and alumni entrepreneurs. For close to 60 years, MIT has created significant changes that support and encourage entrepreneurship. And since 1990, the students and faculty have experienced within MIT the gradually accelerating growth of all relevant resources linked to founding new companies. These include education of all sorts, experience-building opportunities, coaching, competitive inspirations, enhanced availability of space and equipment to aid the first stages of team, product, and company development, and even a modest availability of internal startup funding. These MIT resources have been matched by comparable explosive growth in Kendall Square, Boston, and the entire country. Increasingly, the world at large has seen the new initiatives that facilitate and accelerate entrepreneurship, as well as a major increase in startup and especially growth-stage venture funding. All that is reflected clearly in the new enterprises formed since 1990. (For the exponentially growing numbers, the rapidly declining ages of founders, and other details, please review the contents of Chapter 6 in Part One.) As we move close to the present, we see more obviously the evidence that today's new founders and new firms are outcomes of the comprehensive entrepreneurial ecosystem that has evolved at MIT.

The three sets of entrepreneurship examples that follow display how the changes in the MIT ecosystem have impacted the companies founded over the past several decades. They are: (1) an early giant firm, **QUALCOMM**; (2) two mid-growth enterprises that are more recent foundings, **HUBSPOT** and **PILLPACK**; and (3) the latest in breed of entrepreneuring, four very young firms built "On the Shoulders of Giants".

AUTHOR'S NOTE

The most frequent industry in which MIT entrepreneurship has occurred is software. Had I chosen either Electronics or Telecommunications as industries featured in Part Two, I certainly would have included both Linkabit and Qualcomm as significant pioneering firms!

ANOTHER GREAT PIONEERING FIRM

Irwin Jacobs

Qualcomm. Let's start by examining one more great MIT-borne success, started several decades ago, this time in the second-most frequent industry in which MIT entrepreneurship has occurred over the years—electronics.

But I cannot talk about **QUALCOMM** without first detailing **LINKABIT**, its predecessor in founders as well as in overall area of technological pioneering. Right after getting his doctorate at MIT, **IRWIN JACOBS** '57 , '59 joined the University of California, San Diego as an Assistant Professor. In 1968, he and two other Course 6 (EECS) double-degree holders—**ANDREW VITERBI** '57 and **LEONARD KLEINROCK** '59, '63, both friends on the UCLA faculty—started Linkabit Corporation. (Kleinrock left soon after the founding.)Linkabit did consulting and then government contracting, primarily in communications technologies. Jacobs relates:

Andrew Viterbi

> In 1971, I took a year's leave from UCSD to manage Linkabit. That provided an opportunity to show that the information theories that MIT's Claude Shannon '40 had created, and which we'd been teaching in class, could be very useful in the real world—a fact that many people viewed with skepticism. I retired from the university in 1972, and Linkabit grew rapidly. We developed the very first satellite-to-home TV for HBO, which then spread to the entire industry. We developed VSAT, "very small aperture terminals", which allowed business communications, first used by Walmart to connect all their stores and warehouses. Our company grew very rapidly. We sold it to **M/A-COM**, a Boston-area company, in August of 1980.[3]

During that time period, Viterbi developed a very significant patented algorithm, "the Viterbi decoding algorithm", that was important to Linkabit and to the communications industry. Linkabit employed large numbers of MIT alumni, many of whom later created their own companies. One report claimed that 76 companies are attributable to Linkabit alumni, contributing enormously to the cluster of communications companies in the San Diego area.

After staying on at M/A-COM for a few years, Jacobs and Viterbi co-founded Qualcomm (Quality Communications) in 1985, accompanied by several more of their former Linkabit employees. Jacobs describes its beginnings:

> We came up with the idea of applying CDMA (Code Division Multiple Access) to mobile communications, but we didn't have the resources initially. We set that idea aside until we developed a satellite terminal to put on trucks, to provide both two-way communications and also position location for the trucks.... We were then pushing CDMA for the mobile industry, but after long fighting the industry first "voted" in favor of our technical competitor, TDMA. Finally, we got to the demo stage in 1989 and won a lot of industry support, but it took until 1993 before our standard was approved. The first operation was in Hong Kong in 1995, and then we began to battle with Europe versus its favored GSM standard.
>
> The third generation of technology is all based on CDMA. What have been called the religious wars were over. At one point a professor

from Stanford said we were violating the laws of physics, so there was a lot of argument. Our history indicates that it was worth taking risks. But when you try to do something more innovative, there are always people who don't quite believe in it, or whose business would be harmed and therefore come out against it. You continually have to look at your technology, and make sure you're on a good path. Then if you believe so, continue on despite this competition and opposition.

The current stage of the continuing growth of Qualcomm, nearly 35 years after its founding, is that it had 2018 revenues of over $21 billion, and a market cap of over $88 billion.[4] For those unique firms that ever reach $1 billion in revenues, it usually takes 30 years. In Qualcomm's case, in over a bit more than 30 years it has achieved 20 times that amount!

Irwin Jacobs comments on his own life ambitions: "I assumed that I would remain in academia. Teaching is always very exciting. I rationalized going over to business by saying that would illustrate that the theories that we keep working on in academia can in fact be very useful in the real world. That was quite a shift for me. . . . Yet, it's quite clear that my MIT education, and also what I derived from having taught at MIT, provided knowledge and insights that served me enormously well in becoming an entrepreneur. My wife and I are delighted that we can now give back to MIT to help others attain those same benefits."

Again, as shown in Part Two, those who came through MIT and emerged as successful entrepreneurs had gained benefits that became instrumental for their companies. They surrounded themselves with many others from MIT, and they then "gave back" in appreciation. But these early companies achieved success without having formal entrepreneurial education, mentoring, team competitions, or much guidance in starting and building their companies. Their comparative advantages were limited to the superb technical education that MIT provided, and the lessons in fortitude and "can do" spirit that accompany an MIT education. Those benefits remain, but MIT has changed over the past 50 years in its ever-strengthening entrepreneurial environment, accompanied by multiple dimensions of entrepreneurial assistance.

MID-GROWTH COMPANIES

For every huge MIT alumnus success that exists, many more rapidly growing innovative companies are well on their way, with "mid-growth achievement" and promising futures ahead of them. And those firms are inevitably somewhat younger than the giants! When we examine those mid-growth firms formed by MIT alumni, we also find different facts about their bases. Let's consider **HUBSPOT** and **PILLPACK**, founded respectively 13 and 6 years ago, as two examples.

HubSpot. **BRIAN HALLIGAN** '05, HubSpot's founding CEO, explains:

> **HUBSPOT** was born in the halls of MIT while [founding CTO] **DHARMESH SHAH** '06 and I were classmates in the MIT Sloan Fellows Program. We had a lot of common interests and values. We both were interested in software, both excited about the opportunity to help small- and medium-sized businesses leverage the Internet. And we enjoyed working with each other on class projects. We used every opportunity in our classwork to make progress on what eventually became HubSpot. We took the New Enterprises class and wrote a business plan for LegalSpot (a "go to market" version for law firms of what eventually became HubSpot), and ended up concluding that was not such a great idea! We participated in the MIT $50K and made it to the semi-finals."[5]

Dharmesh Shah has a different starting point:

> I'd been the entrepreneur and CEO of my prior software company for 11 years, and sold it quite successfully. Given my undergrad in computer science, I'd always wanted to go back to do a computer science grad program. I'm a geek all the way through. But someone fortunately suggested that I might benefit more by getting a business degree that might round me out a little. I looked at the MIT Sloan Fellows program, which was moving into its first year merged with the MIT Management of Technology program. That combination appealed to me. (I think I was the last person to graduate with an S.M. from MIT in "Management

Brian Halligan and Dharmesh Shah, and a few HubSpot friends

of Technology".) After I sold my previous company, I had promised my wife that I wouldn't do startups anymore. I assumed that my most likely outcome after grad school was that I would do a PhD and go into teaching. It didn't turn out that way!

Dharmesh continues:

The idea for HubSpot came about while I was writing my master's thesis, with Ed Roberts as my thesis chair. I started a blog called "On Startups" to gather information from other software founders on how they thought Web 2.0 would affect software entrepreneurship. Brian Halligan had graduated and was working for a Boston venture firm to help build marketing programs for their investees. He and I got together once a week or so, chatted about what was going on, and thought further about starting a company together. The one thing we both observed was that my blog was growing its traffic much faster than the young companies Brian was helping.

Brian asked Dharmesh, "Why is your simple blog, written by a grad student, getting more traffic, more traction, and more attention than these websites built with professional marketers' budgets?" Dharmesh continues:

So, we dug into that. The underlying reason seemed to be that "On Startups" was using search engine optimization techniques that I had developed to pull people in to read the blog. That's how we had the idea together for HubSpot. What we wanted to create was not easy technically. There were lots of little parts of the problems to solve, and a platform for small businesses to build, to help them do what Brian uniquely labeled "Inbound Marketing" in the Internet world.

Brian provides their startup history:

HubSpot's "official" launch date was June 9, 2006. We provide all-in-one "inbound marketing" software that gives a business the tools it needs to create a website, get found in Google, convert web visitors into leads, and analyze the entire process. Our first office was a room at the Cambridge Innovation Center at One Broadway, conveniently located right opposite MIT Sloan. This let us stay plugged into the MIT ecosystem, which has proven very helpful for the company.

The company grew significantly since its founding. Our headquarters are still in Cambridge—a 10-minutes walk from MIT and from the Trust Center, where we both still hang out and help with teaching and mentoring. Our key initial team, and then many beyond them—our

> initial financing, many early customers—all came from MIT classmates, friends, and alums. We are part of the place and love being here.

HubSpot had its NASDAQ IPO in 2014. Its projected 2019 revenues are $650 million and its current market cap is $8 billion.[6]

PillPack. **PILLPACK** is an even younger firm, founded in 2013 by TJ Parker and **ELLIOT COHEN** '13 to create a new pharmacy that would alter the way people receive their medications. TJ, PillPack's CEO, is a second-generation pharmacist who had recently received his PharmD degree from Massachusetts College of Pharmacy and Health Sciences, while Elliot has degrees in computer science and neuroscience from Berkeley and an MBA from MIT Sloan. The two met while Elliot was working at the Trust Center as staff to Bill Aulet, prior to enrolling in Sloan in the E&I Track. Elliot, now PillPack's COO, tells the story:

> TJ was attracted to drop in at the Trust Center from what he had heard about the $100K. He volunteered to help and was welcomed with open arms. Together, we actively came up with the idea for MIT's first "Hacking Medicine" weekend. Bill Aulet enthusiastically hooked us up with **ZEN CHU**, an experienced medical entrepreneur and Senior Lecturer in the Trust Center, who was a great partner in generating the hackathon. Zen had won the Monosson Prize because of all of his efforts to nurture MIT entrepreneuring students. We moved ahead to implement Hacking Medicine, attracting mostly young people from all over the Greater Boston community, not just MIT. Really amazing senior people came too—including some of the world's leading biotech executives—and spoke, and participated as mentors. They never would have joined in if they had to fly across the country to do it, but they were all around us in Kendall Square.
>
> The hackathon went spectacularly well, and TJ and I started to dis-cuss seriously what kind of company we might start together.[7]

Now six years along, PillPack is still a private company, but today as a wholly-owned division of Amazon, so they won't release any financial information. But as early as August 2015, with PillPack barely two years old, the *New York Times* included PillPack on its list of "startup unicorns", young companies expected to hit $1 billion valuations.[8] Two years later, in 2017, the business press estimated PillPack's employee base as 500.[9] And the *Boston Business Journal* was projecting its then current annual revenues as $100 million:

> PillPack Inc., a medicine delivery startup that has raised more than $118 million to date, has unveiled new software and an at-home pill-dispensing device it hopes will lay a foundation for the next stage of

the company's growth.... The company's new software, PharmacyOS, makes it easier to track those prescriptions, pre-sort pills and communicate with patients.[10]

Finally, just one year later, in June 2018, and only five years after its founding, a contest between Walmart and Amazon ended with Amazon announcing its acquisition of PillPack for "a sum close to $1 billion", with TJ and Elliot continuing as the leaders of that new Amazon division. Press reports claimed that PillPack employed 800 people at the time of the acquisition, and had expected revenues for 2018 of over $200 million.

Elliot reflects on his continuing ties to MIT entrepreneurship:

> I come back any time Bill Aulet asks me. Our office is in Somerville [Massachusetts] so we're really close by. I usually talk at a New Enterprises class each semester, and then Bill often asks me to talk at some other class, or to come over to meet with students or visitors in the Trust Center. Sometimes that leads to a bit of mentorship outside of my visits. It continues to be really valuable for us, in part because it's fun to come back and feel like we're helping. But we've also recruited a number of people from MIT. So, every time we come, we end up meeting somebody new and often times helpful to PillPack. That's what you call positive reinforcement![11]

Elliot Cohen receiving an "Eddie" Award from Ed Roberts[12]

TJ and Elliot continue to run the PillPack division, now with goals to continue and to accelerate its growth, given the far greater resources available to them. But Elliot has also found the time to become a Senior Lecturer in Entrepreneurship at MIT Sloan, co-teaching the Scale-Up subject to our very enthusiastic students.

Numerous younger firms in their own mid-stages of growth are in all kinds of fields, and increasingly located around Cambridge. They have very close personal ties to MIT, and especially to the Trust Center, which has helped to nurture many of them. They have taken numerous entrepreneurship subjects at MIT, usually in Sloan or the Media Lab. Frequently, they competed in the $100K, were counseled by the Venture Mentoring Service, and have met, listened to, and frequently been helped by the leaders of the Deshpande Center, the TLO, the Legatum Center, and/or the MITII. They also usually participated in numerous MIT student activities. If the founders haven't yet made large fortunes with which they might show their appreciation, they inevitably "pay back" with their enthusiastic presence and support of the young entrepreneurs who are following close behind them.

ON THE SHOULDERS OF GIANTS

At our 2016 entrepreneurship celebration, Bill Aulet wanted to show our hundreds of attendees the increasingly diverse nature of MIT's youngest entrepreneurs. Of course, the bulk of the new company flow from MIT is still technology-based in some way, like HubSpot or PillPack. And the firms reflect the innovative ideas, and science and technology advances, that characterize MIT.

"On the Shoulders of Giants" panel: (left to right) Bill Aulet (chair), Shireen Yates, Chazz Sims, Ella Peinovich, and Bilikiss Adebiyi

But today's MIT startups (perhaps as many as 1,800 per year in the decade of the 2010s) increasingly combine explicit social consciousness and concerns about global problem-solving with their entrepreneurial intentions. This is not to diminish the wonderful examples of deliberately socially-conscious entrepreneurs of past years. As examples: **DAVID AUERBACH** '11 co-founded **SANERGY** with other MIT students to improve sanitation in Africa; **GAETAN BONHOMME** '08 co-founded **KURION** with other MIT students to pioneer nuclear waste cleanup; and **JAVIER LOZANO** '10 created **CLINICAS DEL AZUCAR** to provide diabetes clinics across Mexico. Incidentally, each of those three is a for-profit enterprise, as are the four firms featured in this section.

The founders of this current generation of MIT entrepreneurs come from all over the world, represent a wide diversity of races, and feature many more women than in past decades. And they are going to every place in the world to form and build their companies. To illustrate these trends, as well as the multiple paths that entrepreneurial aspirants now follow at MIT, Bill selected four former MIT students who had recently graduated from our MIT accelerator (originally named FSA, then GFSA, and now delta v, as described in Chapter 4). Their brief stories here help to better demonstrate what MIT entrepreneurship feels like today. We can best anticipate the future by focusing on today's reality, and observing carefully what if any meaningful trends seem associated with that reality.

REMINDER
d/dt (velocity) = acceleration, or more simply delta v = a.

The four selected entrepreneurs introduce themselves and then move to the founding, development, and current status of their companies.[13]

Shireen Taleghani Yates '13 and Nima Labs

Shireen Taleghani Yates

I grew up in the Bay Area, went to Penn undergrad, and was at Google for five years in sales and marketing. I wanted to go to Sloan to help people with food sensitivities, my own personal problem. I was interested in the entrepreneurship focus at Sloan, and enrolled in the E&I Track. But honestly, I never said, "I'm going to Sloan to start a company". I knew the space I wanted to be in, but being in the MIT environment, how could you not become an entrepreneur? The year I graduated I co-founded **6SENSORLABS** (now named **NIMA LABS**) with **SCOTT SUNDVOR** '12, to help concerned consumers know what's really in their foods, starting with gluten!

I took entrepreneurship classes from Professor Roberts, Bill Aulet, and others. Outside of Sloan, I got involved with the MIT $100K as a volunteer during my first year, just to see how the judges responded to pitches. The second year, once I had this nugget of an idea in mind, I got really involved in pitching. I met my co-founder and our lead scientific advisor at MIT, a PhD in chemical engineering and a mechanical engineer. I had some intense conversations with a person that I had started to get to know through the $100K, who ultimately has been my partner in crime for the last three years. We both made bets on each other. But we had the intense Global Founders' Skills Accelerator as a trial period as well, to test us working together as co-founders, and it was wonderful. And some of our first investments came from the MIT alumni network.

We're developing peace of mind at mealtime for the millions who suffer from dietary restrictions or food allergies. Our first product is Nima, a portable device that tests food for gluten, and we're launching into all other proteins; peanut is next. We have a team of 25 in San Francisco and a great set of investors fueling us. Foundry, Brad Feld's VC firm, led our series A round. We received the magazine "Best Invention of the Year" award, and recognized us as one of the top most important health innovations of 2016. So, we're doing wonderfully, and loving every minute of it!

AUTHOR'S NOTE

In our E&I Track entry course, I suggested in a class session on idea generation that each student might consider identifying a personal problem that could become the basis for starting a company. Shireen talked about dealing with gluten issues as her focus ☺.

Three years later, Shireen described her more recent progress, including a peanut sensor as Product #2. She now has a global customer base of over 10,000 and has shipped close to half a million food test capsules. Not only have she and Nima received great press on the Today show and in *USA Today*, but they have also received professional recognition in journals like the *Food Chemistry Journal* and the *Journal of Food Protection*. Nima Labs has received $3 million in grants from the National Institutes of Health and has raised over $20 million in venture capital, doing all this while Shireen also delivered two babies in the past three years! "With that said, I take no day for granted. The journey has been one of the most rewarding and demanding of my life, but we are still in a fragile state until we can be self-sustaining."[14]

Chazz Sims '13 and Wise Systems

Chazz Sims

I grew up in South Carolina and came to MIT as an undergrad in computer science. I didn't know what I wanted to do with my life. I did an internship at Goldman Sachs, doing some technology and some investment banking. I didn't really want to do that long term, so I went to Silicon Valley one summer and then seriously started to look into entrepreneurship. It was really important to me that I was supported by a great MIT entrepreneurial alum, **MITCH KAPOR** '81, who with a Sloan student had founded **LOTUS**, an amazing company. Mitch has been supporting diversity in entrepreneurship from the get-go.

Four years ago, during my senior year, my founding team came together in the Development Ventures classes growing at the MIT Media Lab to form **WISE SYSTEMS**, and started to develop a complex IT system that helps companies optimize their operations logistics. Two years after that, the GFSA experience really helped us go from research and a class project to "How do we make this into a real business?" The strong encouragement and guidance we received all along were critical. That plus the small cash resources that came from the Media Lab's support fund and the GFSA milestone payment gave us enough to keep going. All those other job opportunities, other things that seemed far more secure, tempted us. For us, the internal strength of our incredibly diverse team, plus the MIT resources, kept us going.

WHEN LOTUS 1-2-3 was released, it generated $100 million in revenues, the highest first-year sales of any company up to that date. As a "killer app" for the PC, it dramatically surpassed the earlier VisiCalc interactive spreadsheet developed by **SOFTWARE ARTS**, co-founded by **DAN BRICKLIN** '73 and **BOB FRANKSTON** '70. MIT pioneering entrepreneurs are everywhere!

My co-founder, **LAYLA SHAIKLEY** '13, is Iraqi, grew up in L.A., and did her master's at the MIT School of Architecture. My co-founder, **ALI KAMIL** '16, is from Pakistan, did his undergrad in computer science at Georgia Tech, and was in the MIT Systems Engineering Program. We also have Jemel Derbali, who studied at the Harvard Law School, but we still let him be a part of the team! And my background in the MIT computer science program helped provide the team additional strengths.

Wise Systems provides enterprise software to help make company logistics more efficient and their deliveries more predictable. We work with companies that are doing high volume deliveries, often in urban areas, from firms in the food and beverage industry, like Coca-Cola, or even the parcel or food home-delivery space. We look at all three phases of the delivery business: planning, execution (e.g., what happens on the day of delivery, traffic issues, a customer shows up late, a new order comes in), and then learning from all that data after the fact to improve the system over time. We have a team of ten people in Porter Square, Cambridge. Last year, we were in Techstars in Detroit, which was pretty exciting for us. It was mobility-focused and opened up a lot of doors for us. We got to work with some Global 500 companies, which really helped accelerate our business.

Before the end of 2017, Wise landed its first product-level launch with a major corporate client, Anheuser-Busch, both nationwide across the United States and in Canada, with Wise software servicing the real-time delivery and logistics needs of that massive organization. In 2018, four years after its founding, Wise received a $7 million investment from Google's AI fund, reinforcing Wise's more precise theme for its machine–learning-based software, "Autonomous Dispatch and Routing". It now has 30 people in the organization and 30 customers in active product use, with growing revenues now in excess of $1 million. Chazz is still driving the team forward as CEO, with his three other co-founders still in place!

Ella Peinovich '12 and Soko

Ella Peinovich

I grew up in Wisconsin, received a degree in architecture from the University of Wisconsin-Milwaukee, and spent 12 years between studying architecture and working in corporate architecture before coming to MIT for a master's in architecture. I quickly learned that design thinking and creative systems design were really what intrigued me most. I thought, "How do I take this into the world and use it for good?"

I had done Habitat for Humanity as an undergraduate and I was still looking to build upon those same values. Corporate architecture kind of sucks the soul out of you, and I came to MIT because I wanted to think about having a global stage and taking an interdisciplinary approach to things. A fellow student pointed me to the MIT Legatum Center, and I met the students who were working on starting **SANERGY**, a precast toilet solution for the slums in Kenya. I built the first toilet solution for them, but instantly fell in love with entrepreneurship. You could do good, build your company in a sustainable way to give it legs, and actually make some impact on the world. And you and your company can make money while you're doing it, so that your company can continue to perpetuate itself beyond you as an individual.

I didn't want to build toilets for the rest of my life, so I came back from Africa and decided to start my own business. Ultimately, I found my way to the Founders' Skills Accelerator (FSA) and launched what is now **SOKO**, a supply chain innovation that uses the mobile phone to connect independent artisan entrepreneurs from all over the world to us and our online customers, in an ethical and transparent "virtual factory".

We benefited from the incredible image that you get just from going to MIT. Being on the stage in Kresge Auditorium on Demo Day, and having the support of MIT essentially investing in you through a selective acceleration program like FSA, absolutely gave us the push that we needed. We were three female founders then, and we are still the same founding team. I met our Kenyan co-founder in Nairobi when I was building toilets in the slums. She was a computer science major, quite different from my background. Our third co-founder was another American woman, whom I also met in Nairobi, who does industrial design but was working with the Columbia Earth Institute. We shared strongly-held values, and we liked working with each other. My FSA connection to MIT allowed us to launch ourselves, even finding seed investors like Jean Hammond of LearnLaunch [see Chapter 6] and previously Golden Seeds [a VC focused upon supporting women entrepreneurs]. She believed in us before we were anything, and definitely invested in the team because we were a team.

At our Soko website we sell jewelry. But we're delivering that jewelry to our customers through a distributed supply chain model—a virtual factory created by our mobile-to-web resource planning system. We have 2,100 artisans in Kenya and Ethiopia (more to come) who are able to get purchase orders, get paid by mobile money, and have their inventory tracked all on their mobile phones. All that comes into a centralized, web-based platform, from which we fulfill orders to international clients. We sell to Nordstrom, Anthropologie, Fossil, Macy's, and to tens of thousands of individual customers in over 35 countries globally.

We're doubling every year. Only two years ago we launched our brand, and before that we had a developing platform. After five years, we became a "booming" business (from our perspectives ☺) with $2 million in revenue and a team of 75 people between the United States and Africa. We just secured another $1.5 million in a seed round.

In 2015, we moved our headquarters from Silicon Savannah to Silicon Valley, and we continue to grow globally, now at 2,500 artisan designer-developers.

Bill Aulet adds a side comment: "They're mission-driven, and they're not looking for handouts. They are working to make a sustainable business that's profitable, and that is empowering women in Africa as well as other places over time. It's really a very disciplined social entrepreneurial venture."

Bilikiss Adebiyi-Abiola '13 and WeCyclers

Bilikiss Adebiyi-Abiola

I'm from Lagos, Nigeria. I left when I was 16 to come to the U.S. to study. I got my bachelor's and master's degrees in computer science in Nashville, Tennessee. I got a job in Boston, worked for a few years, and started to transition from computer science because I was tired of writing code. I came to MIT to get an MBA and maybe a good job. I enrolled in the E&I Track, took an elective class called Development Ventures taught by Joost Bonsen, and it opened my eyes. I learned about people living in poverty in developing countries like my own, Nigeria, and one of the big issues that I learned about was waste management. It was then that I started getting sucked into entrepreneurship. With my co-founders we started **WECYCLERS**, using low-cost cargo bicycles we call WeCycles to provide convenient waste recycling services to households across Nigeria.

We got some help from the MIT Public Service Center. We got an MIT Ideas Global Challenge award and a Carroll Wilson Fellowship. Many MIT people helped us, especially Bill Aulet, who has been a great resource on a number of times when it's been quite rough. We'd come and knock on his door and run something by him. Venture Mentoring Service was also helpful for several years.

Wecyclers encourages people in low-income communities to give us their trash. We get them to sort out their plastics, metals, and all their recyclable waste. We have low-cost bicycles that go around to people's houses to collect their waste and take it to our neighborhood hubs, where we process it and sell to recyclers. Our bikers get points on their phones per kilogram delivered, which they can exchange for household items, electronics, and even cash. We have about 100 people working for us, and 11,000 people registered on our platform.

Since 2017, WeCyclers has grown to 17,000 subscribers and 200 employees in seven local communities of Lagos. In March 2019, out of 244 applicants,

WeCyclers was awarded the King Baudouin Foundation African Development Prize of 200,000 Euros. Its target for 2020 is to collect 5,000 tons of recyclables. WeCyclers is now moving heavily toward plastics collection and recycling, with an agreement underway with Serioplast, a large Italian supplier of plastics containers for the consumer market. Bilikiss has been joined by her MIT Sloan MBA alumna classmate, Olateju Abimbola '12, as CFO.

Bill Aulet

BILL AULET gives some perspective on these four young founders:

> It's important to see how they all mingled with many different touch points at MIT. Entrepreneurship is not an algorithm that takes you from here to a startup. You're doing something that has never exactly been done before. So, there's not just one path to entrepreneurship at MIT. Every one of these founders had multiple people, organizations, and activities that affected them throughout. The beauty of MIT is that it is a bottoms-up system. Every entrepreneur has had a different experience in our intermingled ecosystem.

These four founders reflect the dramatic differences in the experiences that MIT entrepreneurs have had over the past 50 years. In the first place, who gets to become an entrepreneur? What exposures have they had? What lessons have they learned while at MIT about starting and building a company? And what variety of motivations are driving them? Aulet points to two important aspects that help to forecast the future of MIT entrepreneurship. "Y Combinator [the pioneer of accelerators as pointed out in Chapter 6] said that 20% of its founding teams have females in their leadership. That was seen as a positive improvement from prior years at Y Combinator. So, I went back to our MIT GFSA data and looked up how many of our accelerator teams had females on a founding team. It was 90%." Bill's second point is about country of origin:

> I asked my advanced class how many were born outside of the United States. The number was 75%. One reason why I'm so proud to be at MIT is that this is a place of meritocracy. We don't care who are your mommy and daddy. We don't care what color you are. "Do you get the job done?" is the basic question. And at the end of the day, the most important part of the answer is the team. We can build teams that have a common vision, do something great like these people do, have complementary skills, and have shared values and trust in each other. These four founders illustrate that entrepreneurship at MIT has changed remarkably and continues to do so.

My research findings mentioned in Chapter 2 lay the framework for our focus on building teams, not just individuals. And data from the MIT Entrepreneurship and Innovation Track, which includes many MIT students with the strongest commitment to entrepreneurial careers, have numbers similar to Bill's — 60% of my E&I students were born abroad. Also, the percentage of women in E&I has been growing every year, now at 40+%. My strongly held personal opinion is that if we improve our visa rules to admit and hold on to these talented entrepreneurial aspirants, they will continue to contribute immensely to the United States. In any event, they'll no doubt be contributing to their home countries as well, which is not a bad outcome.

A final observation on the present state of MIT entrepreneurship is drawn from a recent *Forbes* publication: "Seventeen MIT Entrepreneurs Named to 2017 *Forbes* '30 Under 30' Lists", in many fields such as Healthcare, Consumer Technology, Enterprise Technology, Manufacturing and Industry, and others.[15] MIT students, alumni, and faculty entrepreneurs continue to excel in their fields, more than ever before. Clearly, we have built a viable, innovative program at MIT that contributes significantly to attracting the talented students and faculty who become the carriers of entrepreneurial behavior to benefit this country and the world. The future will be theirs.

THE MIT "ENGINE"

MIT President Rafael Reif

On October 26, 2016, MIT President **RAFAEL REIF** announced a new effort for accelerating breakthrough innovations in the toughest areas of science and technology. Called **"THE ENGINE"**, it represents a multifaceted change in MIT policies and programs and provides a critical focus on the future of MIT entrepreneurship. MIT highlights The Engine as: "designed to meet an underserved need. . . . Many breakthrough innovations cannot effectively leave the lab because companies pursuing capital- and time-intensive technologies have difficulty finding stable support and access to the resources they need."[16]

Working closely with MIT Executive Vice President and Treasurer **ISRAEL RUIZ** '01 and several academic leaders, President Reif pioneered: (1) the first time that MIT has identified as its mission an attack on global problems of all kinds via an emphasis on entrepreneurial approaches; (2) the first time that MIT has committed its own funds ($25 million) and recruited numerous other investors, building an initial fund that is now at $205 million, in order to focus on such entrepreneurial problem solving; and (3) the first time that MIT has initiated a new organizational entity, The Engine, and brought in an outside CEO and Managing Partner, **KATIE RAE**, and outside advisory and investment management leaders to take on such responsibilities.

As President Reif says:

> If we hope for serious solutions to the world's great challenges, we need to make sure the innovators working on those problems see a realistic pathway to the marketplace. . . . The Engine can provide that pathway by prioritizing breakthrough ideas over early profit, helping to shorten the time it takes these startups to become "VC-ready", providing comprehensive support in the meantime, and creating an enthusiastic community of inventors and supporters who share a focus on making a better world.

In many ways The Engine makes explicit a beginning answer to the need for "patient capital" that encourages and enables substantial developments that require years of nurturing and funding, not months. The announcement of The Engine was accompanied appropriately by recognition of the needs for nearby affordable space to nurture the invested startups and for shared access to MIT laboratories and equipment, as well as to those of collaborating local major corporations, now along with Harvard, to lessen the costliness of these long-term ventures. (MIT provided 26,000 square feet of space in Central Square, Cambridge, for the first group of Engine startups, in addition to MIT's $25 million initial investment.)

KATIE RAE has long and close ties to the MIT entrepreneurial ecosystem. She is a serial entrepreneur, headed Techstars Boston, which accelerated the growth and development of large numbers of MIT startups, and founded and directed her own venture capital fund. She has by now invested in 115 startup firms during her career. Among many other key roles she has played before joining The Engine, Katie has been guest speaker in numerous MIT entrepreneurship classes over the years, and was a Senior Lecturer in the Trust Center for MIT Entrepreneurship.

In September 2017, Katie Rae, The Engine's President and CEO, announced its first seven investments in what she calls "Tough Tech" startups: "We are so gratified by the quality and passion of the founders that have come to us. These entrepreneurs are on a mission, and with our help they are going to change the world for the better." An additional 12 firms have received Engine funding since then, from a very large number of investment prospects. In personal discussions in July 2019, Katie described five of those entities that have already received Series A and other quite large follow-on investments, as their progress and promise have become increasingly evident.

Katie talked about the growing network of similarly-oriented daring/patient investors who have become co-funders of The Engine companies. She states The Engine's goals as taking on the world's biggest problems, while creating and building real companies that will become economic engines for the New England region. Katie and her staff of 20 people are increasingly meeting with universities, government agencies, and prospective investors from around the world who want to better understand how they might follow similar entrepreneurial pathways toward long-term global problem-solving. The Engine is periodically issuing "Provocation" documents to identify key opportunities that other new firms might boldly address.

On August 27, 2019, Katie announced that The Engine would be expanding into an additional 200,000 square feet of nearby space in Cambridge. "The space will be specifically designed for companies at the convergence of technology disciplines across engineering and physical sciences, where access to diverse space and tools are essential for success."

I had earlier thought that it really didn't matter whether the MIT Engine succeeds in achieving its own immediate objectives. As MIT has always been a beacon of leadership to other institutions, so too I felt that MIT taking this initiative would inspire other universities, and governments around the world, to undertake similar efforts, different for each according to its own interests and circumstances. For example, during the past decade, Professor Andrew Lo of MIT Sloan has devoted extensive thought, research, and advocacy of global problem-solving via venture investments to eradicating cancer.[17] (Professor Lo is also Co-Director of the MIT FinTech Ventures program.) But in just three years since its beginnings, it is clear to me that the MIT Engine action is moving rapidly ahead to fulfilling its own objectives while perhaps even more importantly already accelerating comparable approaches by others.

I interpret all of this revolutionary movement from the perspective of the purpose of this chapter—to better see the future of MIT entrepreneurship. The MIT of today is so different from the MIT of 50+ years ago, as is evidenced by the many developments I've discussed. The President of MIT now goes far beyond extolling a *mens et manus* process as he applauds and supports the search for entrepreneurship outcomes. This is a dramatic extension of MIT's tradition and culture, and inevitably must continue beyond The Engine, however unique and significant it is by itself. In my opinion, MIT across the board must now acknowledge its institutional belief in entrepreneurship as an integral part of its internal mechanisms and its external role. MIT's underlying three broad goals of research, teaching, and public service now must explicitly be amplified to include innovation of all forms, and in particular the entrepreneurial movement of ideas to the marketplace. And other universities should strongly consider following this example!

MIT'S LEADERSHIP AND MIT ENTREPRENEURSHIP

Since 1980, the efforts to build a strong MIT entrepreneurship program have been blessed by four successive Institute Presidents who encouraged and supported the growth and developments indicated throughout this volume. I appreciate and thank each of them for their encouragement and help.

As previously identified, President **PAUL GRAY** advocated the creation of an MIT entrepreneurs honor society to reward those who had already achieved, and to encourage future MIT entrepreneurs. He was responsible for Event 128 and its follow-on in Silicon Valley that highlighted and praised so many successful MIT entrepreneurs. Gray engaged in public controversy to defend MIT's exclusive licensing of its startup entrepreneurs to give them competitive opportunities against much larger established firms. Following his term as MIT President, Professor Gray hosted the MIT Technology Breakfast that brought MIT faculty and their spinoff companies to the attention of large numbers of MIT alumni, who also enjoyed the camaraderie and idea exchange created in those sessions. His successor, President **CHARLES VEST**, wrote to all MIT alumni promoting the importance to the world of MIT entrepreneurs, and encouraging their participation in the first MIT survey of alumni entrepreneurship. He was closely engaged with the activities of the MIT Entrepreneurship Center, and was considered to be a key member of its so-called "Shareholders Group". Chuck (as he was fondly called across the Institute) backed the pilot efforts in Dubai to help bring MIT entrepreneurship to the Middle East and asked his Chancellor to represent him and MIT in that effort. President **SUSAN HOCKFIELD** moved our 2009 report of the alumni entrepreneurship survey to national and international attention, promoting the achievements of MIT alumni and urging the leaders of major corporations and other universities to move more ambitiously in the direction of MIT's E&I endeavors. During her term in office, President Hockfield sponsored

Four MIT Presidents who accelerated entrepreneurship growth (left to right): Charles Vest, Susan Hockfield, Rafael Reif, and Paul Gray

the Faculty Entrepreneurship Seminar Program to encourage and educate more MIT faculty in how to start new firms. She followed that effort by appointing two faculty committees to explore and report on all entrepreneurship activities across the campus, and to develop recommendations for further improvement of E&I, leading among other developments to the Undergraduate Minor in Entrepreneurship & Innovation.

President **RAFAEL REIF** has gone even further than his predecessors by initiating The Engine, and in making strong and unique moves in committing MIT funds, space, and broad support to nurturing and accelerating long-term-oriented entrepreneurs who focus on global problem solving. Prior to launching The Engine, President Reif decided to create the MIT Innovation Initiative (MITII) as a top-down organization to encourage broad collaboration across MIT in entrepreneurship and innovation research, education, and activities, and to expand reach into more global areas. President Reif's appointment of Co-Directors of MITII, and their concurrent appointments as Associate Deans for Innovation in the Schools of Engineering and Management, respectively, speak clearly for his strong support for advancing MIT's accomplishments in E&I. I quote from President Reif's remarks at the 2016 celebration of MIT entrepreneurship:

> Lester Thurow, Dean of the MIT Sloan School of Management, announced the MIT Entrepreneurship Center in 1990. In doing so, he started an entrepreneurship tornado that continues to blow at MIT. Innovation and entrepreneurship continue to unite us, bridging MIT schools, our faculty, students, staff, and alumni. They are the channels through which we impact the world. The energy of entrepreneurship rises through our campus classrooms, labs, and centers. It is central to who we are as an institution for 50 years of extraordinary service and achievement.

The efforts of these four MIT Presidents on behalf of entrepreneurship have certainly found responsive audiences and strongly supportive actions by the Deans of MIT's two largest schools since 1980, and in particular the most recent ones, **DAVID SCHMITTLEIN** of the MIT Sloan School of Management and **IAN WAITZ** and his current successor **ANANTHA CHANDRAKASAN** of the MIT School of Engineering.

THE CHALLENGES OF THE FUTURE

In continuing to move ahead on our goals for MIT and the world, the MIT entrepreneurship community faces three primary and related challenges in realizing the future we have projected: People, space, and money.

People

Everything accomplished over the past 50+ years has depended upon bold and highly capable people. They are of course the heart of the thousands upon thousands of companies formed by MITers. They are the initiators and implementers of our now large and still growing education and research program. They are the faculty and staff who have built the entirety of the MIT entrepreneurial ecosystem.

The key shortage is the academic faculty who carry out the research and the bulk of the teaching of the entrepreneurship curricula throughout MIT. They are also key informal mentors to their many students who approach them for quiet and trustworthy guidance. That shortage constrains more rapid movement into new areas of scholarship and classroom knowledge-sharing and values advocacy. Those faculty and the key staff members are also the sources of the new program ideas that have propelled MIT entrepreneurship so importantly during the past several decades, with even more innovative ideas wanted for the future.

Added faculty are especially needed in the MIT Sloan School of Management, which carries the bulk of the research and teaching load in entrepreneurship. But more faculty members are also needed in the School of Engineering and the Media Lab to aid their educational efforts that are dedicated to E&I.

Space

The 2011 addition of the Martin Trust Center for MIT Entrepreneurship has been a singular stimulus and enabler for growing MIT's entrepreneurship programs and our participating student population. It accommodates a far greater volume of daily traffic, provides homes for more student activities, facilitates individual and team working areas that accelerate their entrepreneurship developments. The added space has permitted the prototyping center to be created with appropriate "maker" equipment to help students move further along faster, and provides room for bringing in added skills resources such as the Boston University Law Clinic. And it has allowed an open office area to bring in more very capable staff support, including both full-time Entrepreneurs-in-Residence and more volunteer entrepreneurial and VC mentors. But in almost no time, that extra space has more than filled up. Bill Aulet's favorite related quote is from Yogi Berra[18]: "Nobody goes there anymore; it's too crowded!" The Trust Center for MIT Entrepreneurship in particular needs significantly more space to permit its future growth to satisfy the expanded demands. Some other parts of the "MIT entrepreneurship ecosystem" also have needs for increased space, but none plays host to anything like the number of students who use — and practically live in — the Trust Center.

Money

> **MIT ANNOUNCED** that its endowment generated a 13.5% investment return for the fiscal year ended on June 30, 2018. MIT typically distributes about 5% annually pro rata to the accounts of the "owners" of its endowed funds, retaining the balance as additions to the endowment accounts.

Dramatically increased funding could go a long way toward answering the challenges of people and space, but more funds are needed to underwrite existing and new programs as well. Targeted endowments for entrepreneurship faculty would certainly encourage and provide financial support for increasing departmental allocations of faculty slots. Endowments to support specific existing programs, such as delta v and the Practice Leaders Program, would assure their continuity and effective expansion. The naming of work spaces, conference rooms, office areas, and maker spaces would permit accumulation of endowed funds that produce income for discretionary use in covering the costs of people and programs. The Trust Center in particular is currently trying to raise its endowed funds to $50 million, which under today's MIT policies would provide annual cash flow to the Center of about $2.5 million, while adding approximately $4.5 million annually to the Center's endowment, enabling responsible further future growth. And more money would certainly go far in identifying and building out additional suitable space within MIT for entrepreneurship.

At the outset of this book, I indicated that this book is also a personal memoir. Please forgive me for communicating what I see as the challenges that need to be overcome to assure that the next 50 years dramatically surpass the past half-century.

CELEBRATING MIT ENTREPRENEURSHIP

This two-part volume traces the more than half-century history of building entrepreneurship at MIT to its present state of prolific formation of new firms, by increasing percentages of our students, faculty, and staff, with the global impact they have created. This closing section reviews the several different forms of achievements that we recognize here that took place during those 50+ years.

Recognize the Foundation Builders

By no means was MIT the first university entrepreneurship center. Entrepreneurship programs had existed all over the United States, as well as in a few other countries. All of those programs were led by present or former practitioners who shared with their students what they themselves had learned from their experiences. These leaders "spoke from the pulpit" as to what were essentially decrees of how to become a successful company founder.

When I started the MIT Entrepreneurship Center in 1990, it was the world's first one that aspired to bring rigorously defined knowledge to bear on the practice of entrepreneurship. In characteristic MIT style, the MIT Entrepreneurship Center was the first to attempt to question, challenge, and build a different kind of research base for entrepreneuring that might accompany, enhance, and sometimes challenge practitioner knowledge. From the outset, our goal was to give the student the opportunity to learn from two very different perspectives, but in an integrated fashion. Part One recognizes the exemplary role played by all our faculty, academic and practitioner, in moving the understandings of entrepreneurs and of new enterprises to a much higher level, with our dual-track program model now adopted by nearly every entrepreneurship program of leading institutions.

Thank the MIT Ecosystem Developers

Part One also documents all the creators and developers of the many organizational elements that together became the "MIT entrepreneurial ecosystem". The TLO, the Entrepreneurship Center and its associated educational programs, the Venture Mentoring Service, the Media Lab's curricula, the Deshpande Center, the Legatum Center, the Sandbox Fund, and many other entities were institutional creations that in most cases were pioneering examples to others of what might be done to accelerate entrepreneurship development. At MIT they separately played critical roles in aiding individuals and teams in moving forward more effectively in their startup efforts. Collectively, they became a powerhouse of complementary resources and alternative places to which students (as well as faculty, staff, and alumni) could go for help.

HONOR THE ENTREPRENEURS

I also intended to honor the entrepreneurs who have come out of MIT and what they have brought to the world. Part Two honored them by many examples and in several chapters, documenting multiple industries that MIT faculty and alumni started and built from scratch, founding and growing significant major corporations in the process. We honor all of these MIT entrepreneurs for their initiative and continuity that have brought such beneficial impact to us all.

Re-examination of the industries displayed in Part Two, Chapters 8 through 11, reveals the impact of the growing MIT entrepreneurial ecosystem on entrepreneurship that has come from MIT. Not only have the numbers of founders dramatically increased, but the more recent entrepreneurs have had so much more constructive education and guidance than their earlier predecessors. The "bookends" of those industries provide good examples of this change. In the biotech discussions, Bob Swanson did take the New Enterprises course, but Noubar Afeyan taught it and helped to create and teach iTeams with the overall approach that was also concurrently becoming critical to his amazing Flagship

VentureLabs. In the Internet history, Bob Metcalfe was pushed by an MIT Alumni Entrepreneurship seminar to start 3Com, but Frederic Kerrest experienced deep education in the Entrepreneurship & Innovation Track and great exposures in his leadership of the MIT $100K. In the CAD-CAM industry, all of the founders of Applicon and Computervision were perplexed by their lack of any exposure to the practical side of founding a new innovative firm, but Jon Hirschtick started his first CAD-CAM company while a student in New Enterprises.

We are in awe of what so many contributors to the MIT entrepreneurial ecosystem have achieved for so many years of MIT students via their variety of entrepreneurship-enhancing pathways. And, as this book also evidences, every one of these components not only aided our own MIT students and alumni, they provided help to other universities, regions throughout the United States and the world, and entire countries on what they might adopt or adapt for their own economic development.

Communicate How MIT Entrepreneurship Has Gone Beyond Its Own Boundaries

While MIT constantly strives to positively impact our local community, and the economy and well-being of the United States, MIT also always seeks to bring its base of advanced knowledge, and its students who have absorbed and gone beyond that knowledge base, to everyone wherever they may be. Our student body today reflects the fact that we have attracted the best of the rest of the world to our campus to absorb those benefits and share those goals. Chapters 6 and 7 of Part One focused on the impacts beyond MIT that MIT entrepreneurship has created. Within the United States initially, and now globally, our alumni have built unique organizations to accelerate entrepreneurial development. They have ventured into communities with little history of entrepreneurial developments and have sought to make a difference. From Techstars and MassChallenge to LearnLaunch, Greentown, and of course our own MIT delta v, these endeavors provide huge leverage for entrepreneurship development.

These wonderful activities followed the efforts of our alumni in spreading alumni seminars on how to start new firms across the country, and by the MIT Enterprise Forum to bring MIT nurturing of new companies to non-alumni as well as to other nations. They also followed the examples set by our students in trying to teach others via the MIT Global Startup Workshops how to stimulate innovative competitive contests that encourage young people toward entrepreneurship.

But once these earliest efforts were underway, each part of the ecosystem has undertaken its own programs of spreading the word and the insights of its functions to others, and in particular to other countries. The formal programs that have achieved this global impact include the likes of the Entrepreneurship Development Program (EDP), the Regional Entrepreneurship Acceleration

Program (REAP), the Venture Mentoring Service Outreach, and the large number of country E&I programs launched with significant effect by the Schools of Engineering and Management.

Observe the Trends that Forecast the Future

Finally, and throughout the book, I have noted the major changes that suggest what the future will bring to MIT entrepreneurship. Most visible is the continuing escalation of the numbers and percentages of MIT students who start new firms. That will inevitably be accelerated by the increasing number of students going to work for startups as "joiners", with high incidence of their own later firm founding. And the percentage of entrepreneurs who then repeat after their first experience (i.e., those we call "serial entrepreneurs") is also increasing decade by decade. This is further pushed by the continuing steady decline in the age of first firm formation. The earlier start at being an entrepreneur provides that much more time in life to begin later new firms. And although increasing numbers of students are starting companies while still at MIT, both in undergraduate and graduate school, very few decide to leave MIT before receiving their degrees. We strive hard in our entrepreneurship programs to provide committed entrepreneurial students with obvious value and benefits that motivate them to remain at MIT, learning and growing, rather than quitting early.

Beyond the magnitude numbers are the trends in who is becoming an entrepreneur. We have experienced continuing growth in the percent of our foreign-born students who become entrepreneurs. Something about being an immigrant, or perhaps even the child of immigrants, provides an extra drive that manifests itself in starting and trying to build a new company. Perhaps it stems from the guts needed to leave a setting in which you are comfortable with culture, language, habits, friends, and family, to go to the wholly new environs of the United States. Perhaps it arises from the need to overcome the uncertainties of being in a strange place and wanting to belong and to achieve. Our data do not provide answers to these hypotheses. But the trends data thus far on foreign-born entrepreneurs in the United States, including the data from MIT itself, are impressive.

And we observe with some degree of satisfaction the slow but steady growth within our MIT experiences of entrepreneurship by women and by African Americans and Hispanics, all of whom have been traditionally under-represented among our entrepreneurial population. The role models provided by the more visible current generation of these entrepreneurs should increase movements by those who follow in future years. Our segment earlier in this chapter, "On the Shoulders of Giants", is intended to illustrate these tendencies and hopefully to accelerate them. Along with these changes, and perhaps because of them, I also note an increasing social-consciousness among our students, as evidenced by what they want to do and where they want to do it. Most of them see that the best path for social impact is to create viable for-profit firms that earn their keep while they contribute in such areas as better healthcare, sanitation, and environmental improvement, along with creating jobs and wealth generation for themselves and others. They both "pay forward" as well as "pay back" the education they have received here and elsewhere, as well as their own desires to contribute to society.

Overall, I see great prospects to celebrate the achievements and impact of MIT entrepreneurship in 10, 20, and even 50 years hence!

EDWARD ROBERTS
MIT
Cambridge, Massachusetts
January 2020

REFERENCES AND NOTES

1. Edward B. Roberts, *Entrepreneurs in High Technology: Lessons from MIT and Beyond.* Oxford University Press, 1991.
2. *Op. cit.,* p. 357.
3. Edited from an interview with Irwin Jacobs by Michelle Choate on April 29, 2016, supplemented by various Internet sources.
4. Stock market data accessed on June 21, 2019.
5. Interviews by Michelle Choate with Brian Halligan on July 21, 2016 and Dharmesh Shah on July 26, 2016.
6. Stock market data accessed on August 15, 2019.
7. Interview by Michelle Choate on May 16, 2016.
8. "50 Companies that May Be the Next Start-Up Unicorns", *New York Times,* August 23, 2015.
9. MIT's Technology Review says that PillPack now has over 500 employees! Michael Blanding, "Modern Apothecary", *Technology Review,* July-August 2017.
10. Kelly J. O'Brien, *Boston Business Journal,* June 16, 2017, https://www.bizjournals.com/boston/news/2017/06/16/pillpack-unveils-new-products-eyes-100m-in-sales.html (last viewed March 30, 2018)
11. Choate, *op. cit.*
12. See the Entrepreneurship Awards part of the Donors section in Chapter 4.
13. For this entire section, "On the Shoulders of Giants", I edited the comments by Bill Aulet and the four young MIT entrepreneurs from the transcript of their session on November 12, 2016.
14. Personal communication, June 19, 2019.
15. Cited by Zach Church, January 4, 2017 in the *MIT Management Newsroom.*
16. Rob Matheson, "MIT Launches New Venture for World-Changing Entrepreneurs", MIT News Office, October 26, 2016.
17. Beth Healy, "MIT Professor Pitches Cancer Mega-Fund", *Boston Globe,* October 1, 2012.
18. How old do you have to be to remember Yogi Berra and his delightful speech?

Appendix

MIT ENTREPRENEURSHIP FACULTY

As indicated in Chapter 3, this Appendix identifies and provides some details on each of the academic entrepreneurship faculty from the MIT School of Management, followed by their colleagues from the School of Engineering. Then I introduce the practitioner faculty members who were critical contributors to the growth and development of the MIT entrepreneurship program.

MANAGEMENT FACULTY

The academic faculty members who have become the key players in our entrepreneurship efforts are presented here, usually in order of their entry to MIT, mentioning their primary research interest areas and the new entrepreneurship subjects and programs that they pioneered. I frequently identify with the academic faculty those practitioner Senior Lecturers who collaborated in bringing their external experiences into jointly-taught classrooms. Beginning with the current Sloan Management faculty, this first section ends with those who came into our efforts early but went on to longer careers in entrepreneurship at other institutions.

EDWARD ROBERTS '57: My pre-1990 research work and alumni activities leadership were presented early in this book. From 1990 up to the present, I have continued to lead and build the MIT entrepreneurship program, while evolving my teaching and research into new efforts that will be presented later. I started and taught for many years Corporate Entrepreneurship: Strategies for Technology Planning and New Business Development, our only offering for decades that bridged entrepreneurial processes with managing large corporations. At the E-Center's beginning I created an undergraduate seminar, Starting Your Own Business, but ended that soon due to heavy overload of working to build the MIT Entrepreneurship Center. With the creation of the MIT Entrepreneurship &

Innovation MBA Track, I helped create and teach our Innovation Teams (iTeams) subject, and then started and continue teaching the core E&I Track class, Introduction to Technological Entrepreneurship.

Tom Allen

TOM ALLEN '63 was on leave from a major aerospace company to do an advanced degree program at MIT when we started our NASA-funded research center. He immediately switched from the School of Engineering to MIT Sloan to become our first PhD student. Upon receipt of that degree, Tom joined our group as a faculty member. He pioneered the understanding of communication processes among engineers and scientists and the influences of organizational and spatial factors on technical productivity. Along with faculty from the Departments of Biology and Chemical Engineering, Tom co-taught the primary entrepreneurship subject of the **MIT BIOMEDICAL ENTERPRISE PROGRAM**. He also linked the Sloan School to the MIT Engineering School through his long academic leadership of the Leaders for Global Operations and the Systems Design & Management programs. With **RORY O'SHEA** (of University College Dublin, Ireland), a frequent visiting faculty member at MIT, Tom studied entrepreneurship programs at other universities and identified productive policies for developing them. He recently became MIT Professor Emeritus.

Eric Von Hippel

ERIC VON HIPPEL '68 came to MIT after having been the technical co-founder of a couple of companies (despite his undergraduate degree in Engineering coming from Harvard College ☺). Soon after arriving as a faculty member he discovered the importance of users as innovators, and subsequently pursued all aspects of that discovery, including user-based entrepreneurship.

Eric's books and continuing research and writings on "open innovation" emphasize open collaborative approaches to innovative outcomes, including company formation. When we were getting the entrepreneurship program underway, Eric quickly stepped up to join me in co-teaching New Enterprises. Later, he became Acting Director of the E-Center when I was on sabbatical.

JIM UTTERBACK '69 contributed heavily to the area of innovation strategy, visualizing the life cycles of new technologies from their birth and/or entrepreneurial implementation through to market growth, stabilization, and then decay. For years he introduced MIT undergraduates to entrepreneurship in his seminar, long preceding our **UNDERGRADUATE MINOR IN ENTREPRENEURSHIP AND INNOVATION**, now available to all MIT undergrads. Chapter 7 includes a description of Utterback's collaborative entrepreneurship studies in other countries. Jim became Professor Emeritus at MIT Sloan in July 2017.

Jim Utterback

Charlie Fine

CHARLES FINE moved from research and teaching of operations management in large firms into "operations for entrepreneurs" issues, especially when he began to lead MIT Sloan efforts focused upon other countries. In 2012, he became head of the new **TATA CENTER FOR TECHNOLOGY AND DESIGN**, focusing on technology and entrepreneurship for India and other emerging countries. Charlie is still on leave as President and Dean of the MIT Sloan endeavor in Malaysia, the **ASIA SCHOOL OF BUSINESS**, that in part emphasizes entrepreneurship and innovation. More on this is included in Chapter 7. **RAJESH NAIR** '14, a senior lecturer at MIT Sloan, assisted Charlie in India and has been the key developer and leader of the E&I Center in Malaysia.

MICHAEL CUSUMANO entered MIT as a business historian, fluent in Japanese, in an overlapping faculty position between the MIT Sloan Strategy and Technology Management groups. Michael's research interests quickly grew from his PhD work on auto factories to "software factories", both then areas of Japanese prominence, and soon broadened into all aspects of technological innovation and entrepreneurship. In 1997, he started a class called The Software Business (anticipating his 2004 book *The Business of Software*), which has been updated to Software and Internet Entrepreneurship, with heavy emphasis upon platform-based companies. Cusumano's experiences on the boards of young and growing companies, especially in software, have informed the research that underlies his many books on the strategies of successful founder-leaders and their firms. His recent book, *Strategy Rules: Timeless Lessons from Bill Gates, Andy Grove and Steve Jobs*, relates how different entrepreneurs form and implement the basis of their companies from thinking strategically about the same facts. Michael has long collaborated in his software classes with serial entrepreneur and Senior Lecturer **IMRAN SAYEED**. Michael has also been actively engaged in leading MIT Sloan programs in foreign universities, often built around our MIT entrepreneurship activities (see Chapter 7).

Michael Cusumano

Richard Locke

RICHARD LOCKE held joint appointments in the Sloan School and the Political Science department. But I cannot write about Richard without at the same time speaking about **SIMON JOHNSON** '89. The two maintained a unique faculty teaching partnership over many years. Rick's international interests led him to join Simon's Entrepreneurship Without Borders subject to meet overwhelming student demand for learning about the different issues faced when entrepreneuring outside of the United States. Entrepreneurs and executives in other countries could converse with Simon's and Rick's students via a telephone "squawk-box" in the classroom, bringing global entrepreneurship into day-to-day contact. I recall Charles Zhang, CEO of Sohu.com, being on the phone from Beijing with me, his Sohu co-founder, asking him delicate questions from the classroom to help the students learn what really was happening in building the Chinese Internet industry. (Charles Zhang and the Sohu story are more completely covered in Chapter 9, The Internet.) Professor Locke is now the Provost of Brown University.

Steve Eppinger

STEVE EPPINGER '83 used his MIT degrees in Mechanical Engineering as his knowledge base for leading the field of product design and development. Steve encounters many students and their teams inside and outside of his class who are in early planning stages for a possible company launch. He provides them with pragmatic insights on product development questions. The new ProtoWorks manufacturing "maker lab" in the Martin Trust Center, enables Steve to even help the students move up through prototyping their ideas. (Incidentally, Karl Ulrich '84, for many years Steve's close colleague and co-author, moved from MIT Sloan to the Wharton School of UPenn, where he now heads its entrepreneurship program.)

Scott Stern

SCOTT STERN was the first of the new entrepreneurship faculty to bring rigorous economic theories and methods to MIT entrepreneurship research and teaching. His prolific research has covered many fascinating areas, such as the determinants of entrepreneurial clusters and the drivers and consequences of entrepreneurial strategy. Scott's Entrepreneurial Strategy classes now apply strategic tools to mini-cases that he has created based on MIT spinoff firms, bringing both the theory and practice issues into one setting. Scott's critical role in our **REGIONAL ENTREPRENEURSHIP ACCELERATION PROGRAM (REAP)** is described in Chapter 7. Since my 2018 academic year sabbatical, Scott has acted as Faculty Director of the Trust Center.

SIMON JOHNSON's research focused on the impact of a country's culture and incentives on its entrepreneurial economic development. As described above, Johnson and Richard Locke built up the Entrepreneurship Without Borders subject, then co-founded **GLOBAL ENTREPRENEURSHIP LAB (G-LAB)** to enable students to go abroad in teams of four for a working three-week internship during January with a young firm, essentially anywhere in the world. This "internationalized" the Entrepreneurship Lab (E-Lab) team projects experience in the largest and perhaps most vibrant "action learning" endeavor at Sloan. They had great support throughout from **SHARI LOESSBERG** in particular, as well as from many other team mentors and certainly from the MIT Sloan Dean's office. Together they provided the foundation

Simon Johnson

for several similar single-country entrepreneurship subjects that have been developed for China, India, and Israel. Simon's most recent teaching is an experimental subject on building new companies based on the blockchain and Bitcoin concepts. And Simon's most recent book is the exciting *Jump-Starting America*, a visionary proposal of broad-based science and technology investments across the country to stimulate innovation, commercialization, and entrepreneurial growth.

FIONA MURRAY's strong interests in technological innovation were broadened by her very first teaching experience at MIT with Senior Lecturer **NOUBAR AFEYAN** '87, with whom she co-taught the Innovation Teams (iTeams) subject with mixed teams of engineering and management students working to commercialize outcomes from MIT faculty research. Fiona then did her own thing:

Fiona Murray

> The first new course I developed was called Strategic Decision Making in Life Sciences, focused on starting and building life science. This subject attracted both Sloan students and science-engineering majors, the kind of mix I had encountered and enjoyed in iTeams.[1]

Fiona encountered early challenges with convincing MIT science faculty members that her studies of technology innovation and entrepreneurship were also rigorous. As she puts it, "We study things that can't be put into a test tube."

Fiona's research interests have expanded into issues relating to patents and commercialization, as well as gender studies of life scientists and other would-be entrepreneurs. With Senior Lecturer **PHIL BUDDEN**, she is co-teaching Regional Entrepreneurship Acceleration Lab (REAL), discussed further in Chapter 7, as well as E&I subjects for our Executive Development degree programs. Fiona's significant MIT organizational responsibilities in innovation and entrepreneurship, as Associate Dean for Innovation in the Sloan School and by co-leading the MIT Innovation Initiative, are further described in Chapter 7.

Antoinette Schoar

ANTOINETTE SCHOAR brought her deep insights in Finance and Entrepreneurship from the University of Chicago to MIT. She created the subject Entrepreneurial Finance and Venture Capital, which she has taught since her arrival, along with carrying out her ambitious research studies of investment decision-making and management by angel investors, VCs, and private equity firms. Antoinette led our outreach to the global academic community through her long co-leadership of the National Bureau of

Economic Research (NBER) Working Group on Entrepreneurship. Antoinette now co-leads with Professor **ANDY LO** the new FinTech Entrepreneurship activities, while they also teach the FinTech Ventures core course.

Yasheng Huang

YASHENG HUANG researches entrepreneurial growth and economic development in China, and initiated the "ChinaLab" activity. ChinaLab uniquely integrates MIT Sloan students with International MBA students from four premier Chinese business schools in teams that work together with Chinese entrepreneurial firms. In a number of cases, MIT students have ended up partnering with Chinese student teammates in co-founding new enterprises!

Catherine Tucker

CATHERINE TUCKER is a faculty member in the Marketing Group who teaches marketing with a strong slant towards entrepreneurship. Her Pricing course has been invaluable for second-year MBA students, as well as for others across the Institute who are serious about launching a new venture. She has participated actively for the past decade in the Entrepreneurship Development Program as well as the MIT Entrepreneurship Bootcamp. She is also a great teacher—awarded the Jamieson Prize for Excellence in Teaching and also voted "Teacher of the Year" at MIT Sloan.

Pierre Azoulay

PIERRE AZOULAY '01 has recently added entrepreneurship to his large portfolio of innovation studies, with an increasing stream of research publications on who become entrepreneurs and who are more likely to succeed. Pierre co-teaches with **SCOTT STERN** the Strategy classes for both MBA and executive education students, and also is a member of the Trust Center Faculty Advisory Board.

Christian Catalini

CHRISTIAN CATALINI co-teaches E-Lab with Senior Lecturer **JIM DOUGHERTY.** Christian also gives seminars on new areas of entrepreneurial finance such as crowdfunding, Bitcoin, and blockchains, among today's hottest sources of both academic research and new company formation. In July 2017, Christian and Catherine Tucker were featured on the cover of *Science* magazine with their latest research on new perspectives on diffusion of innovation. His recent leave of absence from MIT was to aid Facebook in its efforts to create a new global "currency", Libra.

Jacob Cohen

JACOB COHEN's primary role is as Associate Dean for Programs at MIT Sloan. But in addition, he created and runs IsraelLab, a new "action learning" subject that follows the ChinaLab and IndiaLab models, but with longer January internships with startup Israeli high-tech firms.

CATHERINE TURCO is the newest MIT Sloan faculty member to join the entrepreneurship research and teaching faculty. Before joining the Sloan School, she worked as a technology investment banker and then in corporate venture capital for a software firm. Cat's latest book is *The Conversational Firm*, an in-depth analysis of the anonymous "TechCo Corporation" focused upon its internal organizational practices and strategy.

Catherine Turco

FORMER MANAGEMENT FACULTY

DOROTHY LEONARD (BARTON), an expert on diffusion of innovation, collaborated in our entrepreneurship research in Sweden, mentioned in Chapter 7. Following her formative years at MIT, Dorothy completed a long and successful academic career at the Harvard Business School.

MEL HORWITCH pioneered recognition of strategic efforts by large corporations to become more entrepreneurial through a variety of venture management approaches, anticipating our later teaching about corporate entrepreneurship managerial approaches. Mel has recently served as Dean and University Professor at the Central European University.

Scott Shane

SCOTT SHANE explored the uniqueness of MIT in his studies of MIT TLO, enabling his development of new theories and approaches to technological entrepreneurship. Scott has since built upon the lessons learned in his own prolific research and writings, and has developed and led major entrepreneurship programs at the University of Maryland and now at Case Western Reserve University.

Diane Burton

DIANE BURTON developed her research and teaching around the "human side of entrepreneurship", focusing specifically on issues arising among founder teams and the long-term impact of founder characteristics on enterprises. This was based on her extensive doctoral studies of entrepreneurial startups in Silicon Valley. Her very popular subject was Designing and Leading the Entrepreneurial Organization. Diane moved from MIT to Cornell University, where she continues to advance those interests.

Alexandra Kacperczyk

ALEXANDRA "OLENKA" KACPERCZYK examined the factors influencing whether one becomes an internal entrepreneur within a large organization or leaves it to start an independent new enterprise. Olenka also engaged in "social entrepreneurship" studies before leaving MIT to join the London Business School.

MATTHEW MARX '95 brought his decade of leadership in two high-tech startups to bear on his extensive analyses of the impact of employee non-compete agreements on individual engineers, early stage companies, and state-level economic development. He followed that with major studies of entrepreneurial strategy in his own technical field of speech recognition. Matt created and taught a deeply appreciated subject on the human side of entrepreneurial organizations. He recently joined the Strategy and Innovation faculty at Boston University.

Matt Marx

BENJAMIN ROIN moved briefly from a faculty position at the Harvard Law School to MIT Sloan to pursue his interests in the role played by intellectual property rights in innovation. He has co-taught Innovation Strategies as well as New Enterprises.

ENGINEERING FACULTY

Tony Sinskey

It is easy for me to identify all of the Sloan School faculty who are teaching entrepreneur-oriented subjects. But so many Engineering School departments are now beginning to engage in various aspects of entrepreneurship teaching that inevitably I must be omitting some Engineering faculty members, to whom I apologize, who are now aiding our across-the-Institute enhancement of entrepreneurship education.

ANTHONY SINSKEY '67 has long been a leading MIT faculty member in numerous areas of biology and biotechnology. His own serial entrepreneurial career greatly advanced his contributions to the **MIT-HST BIOMEDICAL ENTERPRISES PROGRAM**, in which he co-taught with Professors Allen, Cooney, and Gray, Senior Research Scientist **STAN FINKELSTEIN** '71, and others (discussed further in Chapter 5). He currently co-teaches Strategies in Drug Discovery and Development.

CHARLES COONEY '67 was an early leader in the area of biotechnology processing, engaging in forming major corporations in the life sciences (described in Chapter 8). He became the Founding Director of the **MIT DESHPANDE CENTER**, where he began his collaboration in MIT entrepreneurship education as well as in the many E&I programs carried out by MIT in other countries. (More on Charlie's multiple leadership roles is presented in Chapters 5 and 7.) His first entrepreneurship teaching began in 2005, when he collaborated with **KEN ZOLOT** '95 and me in the first several years of Innovation Teams.

Martha Gray

For years, **MARTHA GRAY** '81 headed the MIT-Harvard Health Sciences and Technology (HST) Program. She is an acknowledged leader in several areas of science, and has actively engaged in the Healthcare Ventures course. Senior Lecturer **ZEN CHU**, who had great success with creating our first **HEALTHCARE HACKATHON**, has worked closely with Gray. Previously, Martha was instrumental in designing and running the unfortunately short-lived MIT-Harvard HST Biomedical Enterprise Program, a double-degree Master's Program aimed at educating new leaders of biomedical commercialization, with emphasis upon entrepreneurship.

Alex Pentland

ALEXANDER "SANDY" PENTLAND, a long-time professor of the MIT Media Lab, has pioneered work in computational social sciences using big data. Sandy organized and runs the Media Lab Ventures Program, which includes several subjects that bring students into contact with faculty from different areas of research to stimulate their own ideas for new companies. His close collaborator has been Senior Lecturer **JOOST BONSEN** '90, who has led and/or taught in all the classes of the Media Lab program (discussed further in Chapter 5).

Joost Bonsen

The focus of **DOUGLAS HART**'s '85 current mechanical engineering research has been imaging systems, from which he has now founded several new companies. But when pushed to attend a session of the $50K Business Plan Competition prior to his first startup, **BRONTES SYSTEMS**, Doug emphatically said, "I came here to teach and do research, not to start companies!" His experiences in his first company wholly shifted his views to enthusiastic commitment to moving his ideas forward to the marketplace via new company formation. Doug became actively involved in the **MIT-SKOLKOVO** program with Russia in collaborating on the design, development, and implementation of its first E&I subjects. He then succeeded Charlie Cooney in taking responsibility for MIT's entire Skolkovo E&I program as well as for several other MIT School of Engineering E&I efforts in other countries (described further in Chapter 7). Doug teaches Engineering Systems Design and Engineering Systems Development, which he runs as a full-year sequence of entrepreneurial venturing efforts for his engineering students.

Doug Hart

EUGENE FITZGERALD was the first faculty member of the MIT School of Engineering to create a subject focused on entrepreneurship. His book, *Inside Real Innovation*, draws heavily from his prior experiences as a founder of two technology-based firms. Gene now co-teaches Venture Engineering with Scott Stern, the entry subject of the new MIT undergraduate

Eugene Fitzgerald

Martin Culpepper

minor in E&I. Gene also teaches Innovation and Commercialization of Materials Technology.

MARTIN CULPEPPER '97 has become the MIT "Maker Czar", bringing "maker spaces" of all sorts into reality across the Institute to move MIT students—especially those interested in entrepreneurial futures—more actively into *manus* activities. He has co-developed and is co-teaching the new Introduction to Making subject with **BILL AULET** '94, the Managing Director of the **MARTIN TRUST CENTER FOR MIT ENTREPRENEURSHIP**. Martin's core subject is Design and Manufacturing.

PRACTITIONER FACULTY

These critical contributors are featured below in alphabetical order (omitting those Practitioner Faculty who have been previously identified along with their academic co-teachers). Again, the continuing efforts by Bill Aulet to bring in new voices and new experiences suggest that I have inevitably omitted some of the newer practitioner faculty, for which I apologize.

NOUBAR AFEYAN moved on quickly from co-teaching New Enterprises into co-teaching the iTeams course that demands integrating both a practitioner and an academic. In building that course, Noubar was joined by Professor **FIONA MURRAY**, Senior Lecturer **LUIS PEREZ-BREVA** '07, and others. His serial entrepreneuring and major VC experiences permit Noubar to guide his students through all of the pre-formation stages of a new company, including coping with market identification, intellectual property protection, competitive analysis, team organization, and financing requirements. We soon followed the iTeams model, in which mixed teams of students work through the analysis and planning for potential commercialization of real faculty research projects, with similar venture courses in several fields, including Energy Ventures, Healthcare Ventures, and FinTech Ventures. Each subject was initiated by Senior Lecturers, sometimes with academic faculty as partners. (We even did a three-year stint with Linked Data Ventures in collaboration with MIT Professor Tim Berners-Lee, the inventor of the World Wide Web!) Noubar's primary role as co-founder and CEO of Flagship Ventures, now renamed Flagship Pioneering, is discussed in Chapter 8, in which he also discusses his own learning from teaching New Enterprises and iTeams.

John Akula

JOHN AKULA has been the vital teacher and coach of all entrepreneurial students who seek improved legal knowledge about founding and growing their enterprises. His Entrepreneurial Legal Tools and Frameworks and related classes explore the legal problems that arise at every stage of a company's life cycle, from birth to death. **JEFF MELDMAN** '65 has also taught for many years an entrepreneurship-related legal subject, Patents, Copyrights, and the Law of Intellectual Property.

HOWARD ANDERSON joined us in 1999 and served as a Senior Lecturer and then as the Bill Porter Distinguished Senior Lecturer for a decade of great contributions. He was a unique combination of a successful entrepreneur and venture capitalist and a marvelous human being. In 1970, Howard founded and built Yankee Group, leading it until its sale to Reuters in 2000. And he also co-founded Battery Ventures, for which he served as a General Partner from 1984 on. Not only did Howard frequently co-teach New Enterprises, but he also created the pioneering subjects Entrepreneurial Sales and Sales Management, Managing in Adversity, and Corporations at the Crossroads. Howard would often say something which at first might seem outrageous, but upon reflection was superb insight and advice. "I might exclaim, 'If you've got a terrific idea for a company in the middle of class, feel free to walk right out and go start it. Don't worry about that. And remember, you can always go get a job at Goldman Sachs or someplace like that as a backup.☺'"[2] Howard was awarded the Adolf Monosson Prize for Entrepreneurship Mentoring in recognition of his valued aid to so many.

Howard Anderson

PETER KURZINA '88 was a frequent and long-term collaborator with Howard, sharing many of the subjects and taking over some of them after Howard's departure from MIT.

Peter Kurzina

GEORGINA CAMPBELL FLATTER started in the Martin Trust Center for MIT Entrepreneurship and was soon promoted to Executive Director of the **LEGATUM CENTER**, which is discussed in Chapter 5. In this capacity, she led the teaching of Social Impact at Scale Through Innovation-Driven Entrepreneurship, until her move back home to the U.K.

ALEXANDER D'ARBELOFF '49 was co-founder and CEO of Teradyne, a major firm in semiconductor manufacturing, as well as an investor in and board member of numerous companies. He became Chair of the MIT Corporation and concurrently served as Professor of the Practice in MIT Sloan, with his first teaching being in innovation and entrepreneurship classes for graduate students in Mechanical Engineering. With gusto, Alex helped move E&I education into MIT's degreed executive programs in 2004, co-teaching MIT Sloan Fellows jointly with **MIKE CUSUMANO** and me (which was great fun for all of us).

Alex d'Arbeloff

Alex cared deeply about building entrepreneurship throughout MIT. He and I made the gifts to create offices in the initial small MIT Entrepreneurship

Center rooms. Alex was instrumental in persuading Desh Deshpande to fund the MIT Deshpande Center and further, to integrate the Deshpande activities with the MIT Entrepreneurship Center, as discussed in Chapter 5.

Trish Cotter

Jonathan Fleming

PATRICIA "TRISH" COTTER is now Senior Lecturer and Executive Director of the Trust Center. Following an impressive executive career in several early-stage companies, Trish joined the Trust Center as an Entrepreneur-in-Residence (EIR), providing in-depth counseling to students while increasingly assuming responsibility for guiding several Trust Center initiatives under the direction of Bill Aulet. Trish now co-teaches Building an Entrepreneurial Venture: Advanced Tools and Techniques with Bill and two other EIRs, **ELAINE CHEN** (also a Senior Lecturer) and **NICK MEYER** '08. This subject is part of the new series of "Skills Sets" launched to aid those who are actively developing a new enterprise. Trish also provides excellent leadership of delta v, the MIT Trust Center's accelerator, created and initially run by Bill Aulet, and was awarded the Monosson Prize for Entrepreneurship Mentoring in 2018.

In 2005, **JONATHAN FLEMING** took over teaching Strategic Decision-Making in the Biomedical Business, one of our earliest industry-focused entrepreneurship subjects. Jonathan's route into teaching at MIT shares many similarities with other successful entrepreneurs and venture capitalists who became part of our program.

> I first read Ed Roberts's work when I was a graduate student at Princeton. Then Ed and I served on the board of Inverness Medical and had a fabulous time together for several years, especially as the company ended up being acquired by Johnson & Johnson for $1.2 billion. I did on-and-off lecturing for three years in different MIT entrepreneurship subjects. Then I recruited my friend **ANDREY ZARUR** to co-teach with me the Biomedical Enterprises subject, with Andrey adding immense value to the students.[3]

Joe Hadzima

JOSEPH HADZIMA '73 has been a mainstay of MIT entrepreneurship since the earliest days of alumni-organized efforts. A lawyer by training and practice following his MIT undergraduate education, Joe created a series of inexpensive software packages to help a startup get going. He authored a series of mini-newsletters called "Nuts and Bolts of Business Plans" and transferred those into ongoing short courses during the MIT January Independent Activities Period (IAP).

BRIAN HALLIGAN '06 began partnering with his Sloan Fellows classmate **DHARMESH SHAH** '07 in class assignments during their shared MIT Sloan year. By the end of that year, Brian, a strong sales and marketing personality, had joined with Dharmesh, an already successful software entrepreneur, to figure out what company they would launch together. Brian comments:

> The result was HubSpot, a great success thus far, born at MIT, with its first office across the street, initial funding almost entirely out of MIT connections, and a large band of early employees from MIT! We started in June 2006, and our IPO was in October 2014. In 2016, we had about $300 million in revenues, and we [had] about 1,700 employees. [By 2018, it had $550 million in revenues and more than 2,600 employees.] It's easy to see that if we hadn't walked those hallways at MIT Sloan, there would be no HubSpot today. The least I can do to show how I feel is to be teaching classes at the Martin Trust Center and doing what I can to help today's "wanna-be" entrepreneurs to get going.[4]

Brian Halligan and Dharmesh Shah, the HubSpot co-founders

(HubSpot is discussed in greater depth in Chapter 12.) Brian has been teaching Scaling Entrepreneurial Ventures, another of our new Skill Sets subjects aimed at those who may already be underway with their startups.

Donna Levin

DONNA LEVIN '16 reflects the best of our criteria for recruiting Entrepreneurs-in-Residence. She had an extensive and successful career in multiple social entrepreneurial ventures, most significantly in her role as co-founder of Care.com. Donna also co-founded and was Vice President of Operations of Upromise, and has been actively engaged with other early-stage firms. During my sabbatical leave in the 2017–2018 academic year, Donna became Acting Director of the MIT Sloan Entrepreneurship & Innovation Track, taught Introduction to Technological Entrepreneurship, and handled the continuous demands for entrepreneurial counseling and life advice from the 120 E&I students. She now heads the Entrepreneurship Program at Worcester Polytechnic Institute.

Val Livada

VALENTIN LIVADA '70 has a long history of consulting and active involvement with startup firms in multiple areas of technology, and especially with all aspects of corporate venturing. As a Senior Lecturer,

Val taught Corporate Entrepreneurship for several years, and was instrumental in carrying out the national study of corporate venture capital activities.[5]

Shari Loessberg

SHARI LOESSBERG was identified earlier for her critical contributions over many years, up to the present, in implementing the Global Entrepreneurship Lab endeavor in close collaboration with Simon Johnson. But even earlier, she developed and still teaches Funding Strategies for Startups, previously titled Raising Early-Stage Capital. As one of our first subjects that was joint-listed in several departments of the Engineering School, Shari successfully attracted a mixed class of engineers and management students to help fulfill our educational objectives. Shari's personal career experiences in multiple countries that were at their own early stages of development make her uniquely able to address the financing issues and opportunities of those countries.

Luis Perez-Breva

LUIS PEREZ-BREVA has been the mainstay over many years in co-teaching the iTeams subject, so central to and popular in our entrepreneurship curriculum. His academic and practitioner co-teachers have changed many times during these years, but Luis has preserved iTeams's constancy in providing the students with an exceptional experience in taking real research ideas all the way through disciplined examination and development. Luis has built upon the lessons he has learned from co-teaching iTeams to become a key designer and teacher (along with Doug Hart and myself) of the early subjects created for the **MIT-SKOLKOVO INSTITUTE** collaboration. Luis also helped introduce these new subjects in Moscow in Skolkovo's early years. His insights are communicated in his recent exciting MIT Press book, *Innovating — A Doer's Manifesto.*

ANDREW WOLK brought us our first dedicated Social Entrepreneurship subject. To be sure, all entrepreneurship can be viewed as "social entrepreneurship" in that new firms provide new jobs and their growth creates meaningful economic benefits to their locales and their countries. But Andrew focused on those companies that were primarily oriented towards coping with social problems, frequently non-profit organizations. He brought his prior teaching experiences at Boston University and in the MIT Department of Urban Studies, along with his effective non-profit consulting experiences at his firm, Root Cause, to our students from across MIT. And Andrew communicated the need for clear metrics of performance, not just "hand-waving", as the needed barometers for planning and implementing social entrepreneurial causes. I strongly supported Andrew's efforts and later became Principal Investigator of a research project carried out with several dedicated students to strengthen the MIT Social Entrepreneurship ecosystem.

Andrew Wolk

In some classes, our students are fortunate to have a team teaching them who bring together a wide range of real-world experiences. Having multiple viewpoints expressed in the classroom is comparable to the benefits that accompany our combining an academic with a practitioner as co-teachers. For example, our Entrepreneurial Sales subject is co-taught by **LOUIS SHIPLEY** (CEO of BlackDuck Software until its sale in late 2017 to Synopsys), **KIRK ARNOLD** (CEO of Data Intensity), and **DENNIS HOFFMAN** (Senior Vice President of EMC, now Dell/EMC). Their multi-faceted diversity makes each class session a lively and content-filled experience for the students. This subject has grown to be full-capacity classes both semesters, often cited by alumni as among their most valuable courses during their time at MIT.

Lou Shipley

Kirk Arnold

All of the Trust Center practitioner Entrepreneurs-in-Residence (EIRs) also carry important teaching loads, some previously mentioned as collaborating with MIT Sloan academic faculty. Those additional EIR-faculty members include **ELAINE CHEN**, **KIT HICKEY**, **NICK MEYER** and **WILL SANCHEZ**.

REFERENCES AND NOTES

1. Interview by Michelle Choate on May 2, 2016.
2. Personal communication.
3. Interview by Michelle Choate on July 21, 2016.
4. Interview by Michelle Choate on July 28, 2016.
5. Edward Roberts, I. MacMillan, V. Livada & A. Wang, *Corporate Venture Capital (CVC): Seeking Innovation and Strategic Growth, National Institute of Standards & Technology Special Report GCR 08-916,* June 2008.

ACKNOWLEDGMENTS

MIT ENTREPRENEURSHIP

Even a modicum of thoughtfulness about our reasons for celebrating the growth and impact of MIT entrepreneurs leads us, and the world at large, to acknowledge and praise the many thousands of MIT entrepreneurs for what they have accomplished and contributed to the world! Since its founding in 1861, MIT's role in global advance has been amazing. And the achievements of all of its faculty, staff, and alumni—and of special note, those who pioneered in forming and building new industries and new enterprises—have been remarkable. Thank you to all MIT founders of new innovative enterprises. You and your firms have done so much to make the world a better place.

I express my deepest thanks to all of my MIT academic colleagues, identified and discussed primarily in Chapters 3, 4, and the Appendix, who cumulatively provided the research and education that have enlightened so many students, at MIT at all levels, and in so many other universities and countries. We have been together for many years, and I have proudly watched the growth, development, and successes of so many of you. Thank you for your years of colleagueship. ☺

Next, I thank my MIT associates, identified primarily in Chapter 5, who have built the several supporting organizations that provide counsel of all sorts and special, more targeted assistance to our aspiring entrepreneurs, here and abroad. Our Entrepreneurship Center together with all of these supporting organizations are identified by many as the "MIT Entrepreneurial Ecosystem", an amazing array of dedicated servers of young would-be founders from MIT. My MIT colleagues have also been successful internal "entrepreneurs", creating and building new and significant organizations inside of MIT.

I express gratitude to all the many donors, listed below, who made possible all of the entrepreneurship people and their programs through your generous financial support. In the Chapter 5 discussions of the various supporting organizations, I also identify and thank the principal donors to those endeavors. But far more individuals and organizations than I know of and have cited have contributed to annual campaigns and to various of our entrepreneurial program needs, all across the Institute, which have enabled important parts of our program to grow and develop.

All of these wonderful people are responsible for stimulating, assisting, and achieving the enormous growth, success, and impact of MIT entrepreneurship.

OUR CELEBRATION AND THIS BOOK

In 2016, we planned and implemented "Celebrating a Half-Century of MIT Entrepreneurship", a two-days event that was the culmination of 50+ years of my own efforts and the accomplishments of so many others as well. That celebration permitted the coming together of many key contributors to the growth and impact of MIT entrepreneurship. Much of this book's content arose from what we learned and celebrated at that event. And the words of many of the participants are remembered throughout this volume.

While planning that celebration, the initial idea for this volume was developed in meetings with Cathy Canney, the former Director of Communications for MIT Sloan, and Bill Aulet, the Managing Director of the Trust Center, now also Professor of the Practice. We thought about what ought to be done to generate a permanent record of the amazing half-century of MIT entrepreneurship, resulting in the idea for this two-part book.

Michelle Choate and her staff at Choate Creative carried out numerous interviews with entrepreneurial alumni, MIT entrepreneurship faculty, and organizational leaders. The information gained forms a major portion of this book.

And thanks also to all who agreed to be interviewed about your MIT and/or entrepreneurial activities. Those interviews and your own presentations at our celebration provide your own words of pleasure and entrepreneurial achievement during these past years.

Once the manuscript was well advanced, other critical contributors became instrumental in moving this project into and through the publication process, primarily Tom Daughhetee and his associates at The Froebe Group, who did the editing and photo assemblage, and who contributed enormously to the design of the book.

All of that effort was pulled together in the first edition of *Celebrating Entrepreneurship*, published in late 2018. That book was then privately distributed to all who had contributed to the growth and development of MIT entrepreneurship, as well as to all whose work and pioneering companies were described in the book. Their enthusiastic responses have led to this second edition, which updates many of the organizations and events presented in the earlier work, and focuses more on the people, primarily the entrepreneurs, who are responsible for MIT's enormous entrepreneurial impact upon the world. I thank Tom Daughhetee and his team at The Froebe Group for their continued critical help.

THE DONORS WHO MADE THE MIT ENTREPRENEURSHIP PROGRAM POSSIBLE

Anyone who runs a business knows that funds are essential to make things happen. A university's finances are more complex than most businesses, in that many developments at the university, such as new professorships, require an investment of capital to ensure that they will not be short-lived. So, universities seek to create "endowment funds" which are invested to generate income. The university then generally releases only some fraction of that income to underwrite its operating costs, such as the salaries and support expenses of faculty members. The remainder of the income earned is reinvested to increase the funds available from future income. At MIT, any new professorship or program must be backed by significant endowed funds to guarantee that it will have a long life.

Operational activities that are not regarded as "capital investments" also require funding support. Unlike in a business, few university programs generate the income required to enable them to be self-supporting. Annual or periodic campaigns are necessary to assure that a department or center can sustain its continuing and growing activities.

All company founders well understand that the fundraising task is arduous and continuous. I thank the Deans since 1990 and their Development Directors and staffs who have contributed so much to the extensive fundraising efforts for MIT Sloan entrepreneurship, as well as for those programs operated out of other parts of MIT.

In particular, I deeply appreciate those many donors who have contributed to our Trust Center endowment funds and to our annual fundraising campaigns. Together they have been the lifeblood of growing MIT entrepreneurship over the past half-century. Listed below, alphabetically in each category, are those who have funded entrepreneurship professorships, programs, and awards, whom we acknowledge and thank.

Inevitably, I am unintentionally omitting some important supporters over the years of our MIT entrepreneurship efforts. In particular, I knowingly have not attempted to list the hundreds of individuals and corporations that have contributed to our growth and development, for which I apologize.

ENDOWED PROFESSORSHIPS

MICHAEL KOERNER ('49), **RONALD KURTZ** ('54), **DAVID MCGRATH** ('59) *(gift of JoAnne McGrath)*, **BILL PORTER** ('67), **ALVIN SITEMAN** ('48).

ENDOWED CAREER DEVELOPMENT PROFESSORSHIPS

FRED KAYNE ('60), **RICHARD LEGHORN** ('39), **MAURICE STRONG**, **ZENON ZANNETOS** ('55).

ENDOWED FUNDS FOR CENTER PROJECTS AND UNRESTRICTED USE

GARY BERGSTROM ('68), **WENDELL COOK** ('68), **JEAN-JACQUES** ('93) and **VALERIA DEGROOF, DOUGLAS DRANE** ('85), **BRADLEY FELD** ('87), **JACK GOSS** and **ANNE GOSS FOUNDATION**, **JEAN HAMMOND** ('86) and **MICHAEL KRASNER** ('74), **CHARLES HARRIS** ('80), **ROBERT HUANG** ('79), **FREDERIC KERREST** ('09), **MICHAEL KOERNER** ('49), **RONALD KURTZ** ('54), **DAVID MORGENTHALER** ('40), **RICHARD MORSE** ('33), **RUSSELL** ('54) and **CYNTHIA OLIVE, EMERY OLCOTT** ('63), **BILL PORTER** ('67), **ROBERT POZEN, EDWARD ROBERTS** ('57), **EDWARD ROBERTS FRIENDS, RAY** ('57) and **MARIA STATA**, **ROBERT SWANSON** ('69) *(gift of Judith Swanson)*, **RAJ TAHIL** ('81), **PARVIS TAYEBATI, MARTIN** ('58) and **DINA TRUST, ALLAN WILL** ('81), **FRANCIS ZENIE** ('56).

Many donors have contributed significantly to fulfill the substantial annual cash needs of our accelerator program, from its initial FSA to GFSA to now delta v. Among those, all of whom we truly appreciate, are:

JOHN CUMMING ('84), **DIANE MACKIE** ('79), **PATRICK RIVELLI** ('91), **RICHARD WONG** ('91), **PAUL YANG** ('91).

I also thank the foundations and the many corporate and individual donors that have funded key programs and provided general support in our annual cam-paigns, among which are:

KAUFFMAN FOUNDATION, for its multiple grants to the Center, to our fac-ulty, and to many of our entrepreneurship PhD students; **CELIA LIPTON FARRIS** and **VICTOR W. FARRIS FOUNDATION**, for its multi-year support of the Practice Leaders Program; **WOLF GREENFIELD LLC**, for its generous and loyal support of the E-Center programs for many years; and so many individuals—primarily alumni, but also other good souls who believed that we were doing important things—who have helped us through their generosity to achieve our goals thus far.

ENDOWED FUNDS FOR ENTREPRENEURSHIP AWARDS

ROBERT GOLDBERG ('65) Fund to Support the Entrepreneurship Competition Grand Prize *(gift of Judith Goldberg)*; **PATRICK MCGOVERN JR.** ('60) Entrepreneurship Award to an individual student or team that has made a significant impact on entrepreneurship across the Institute; **ADOLF F. MONOSSON** ('48) Prize for Entrepreneurship Mentoring (gift of William ('56) and Ilene Grinker and the Monosson family) to recognize those who have made significant and ongoing efforts to nurture and mentor young entrepreneurs[1]; **DAVID** ('40) and **LINDSAY MORGENTHALER** Fellowships.

Finally. I owe deep debts of gratitude to a small group of entrepreneurial alumni whose generosity has made possible this book of memorabilia, celebration, and hopefully important lessons to be learned: **RAJAT BHARGAVA** ('94), **ERAN EGOZY** ('93), **SAMEER GANDHI** ('87), **WARREN KATZ** ('86), **ALEX RIGOPULOS** ('92), **MARK SIEGEL** ('86), **WILLIAM WARNER** ('80), and **WALTER WINSHALL** ('64). I thank you all for enabling this permanent record of all of our achievements. Above and beyond all others, my personal appreciation goes to **BRAD FELD** ('87), for his unique generosity and for recruiting all the other MIT alums who together are the "producers" of this volume. Brad, you are a shining gem.

ED ROBERTS
MIT
Cambridge, Massachusetts
January 2020

REFERENCES AND NOTES

1. Beginning in 2005, the Monosson Award winners were: Aaron Kleiner, Joseph Hadzima, MIT Venture Mentoring Service and its leadership, Edward Roberts, MIT Enterprise Forum, Howard Anderson, MIT Deshpande Center and its donors and leaders, Bill Aulet, Zen Chu, Jonathan Fleming, Elaine Chu, Shari Loessberg, and Trish Cotter.

PHOTO CREDITS

I would like to thank MIT Sloan School of Management and The Martin Trust Center for MIT Entrepreneurship for their permission to use many of the photographs and illustrations included in this book. As well, I would like to acknowledge the contributions from the following individuals and institutions:

Nancy Roberts, Aviva Maller; **MIT crest**, MIT Office of the President; **Richard Morse**, Morse Family Archives; Herb Wainer, Herb Wainer; C. Stark Draper in moon-rover mock-up, Draper Laboratory; **Martin Schrage**, Martin Schrage; **MIT Seminar for Young Alumni**, *How to Start & Operate a Small Business*, cover design by Susan E. Schur; **Lita Nelson**, Lita Nelsen; **Richard Locke**, Brown University, Office of the Provost; **Scott Shane**, Scott Shane; **Diane Burton**, Alice G. Patterson Photography; **Matt Marx**, Matt Marx; **Tony Sinskey**, MIT School of Engineering; **Martha Gray**, MIT School of Engineering; **Doug Hart**, MIT School of Engineering; **Eugene Fitzgerald**, MIT Department of Materials Science and Engineering; **Martin Culpepper**, MIT School of Engineering; **Brian Halligan and Dharmesh Shah**, HubSpot, Inc.; **Val Livada**, IPVision, Inc.; **Luis Perez-Breva**, TheEditorial.com; **Kirk Arnold**, David Arnold; **Lou Shipley**, Black Duck Software; **David Staelin**, MIT School of Engineering; **Alexander Dingee**, MIT School of Engineering; **Jaishree and Guraraj "Desh" Deshpande**, Jaishree and Guraraj "Desh" Deshpande; **Leon Sandler**, MIT School of Engineering; **Ian Waitz**, MIT School of Engineering; **Jinane Abounadi**, MIT School of Engineering; **Anantha Chandrakasan**, MIT School of Engineering; **Vladimir Bulović**, MIT School of Engineering; **Tim Rowe**, CIC, Inc.; **MIT Global Startup Workshop 2018 team**, MIT Global Startup Workshop; **Fudan-MIT ChinaLab project team**, MIT Global Startup Workshop; **charts of MIT-alumni-founded companies and alumni company founders**, Kimberly Mancino, MIT Office of Reference Publications; **Vincent Fulmer**, MIT Museum; **Verne Harnish**, Gazelles, Inc.; **Brad Feld**, Geek Wire; **John Harthorne**, MassChallenge; **Emily Reichert**, Greentown Labs; **Herbert Hollomon**, MIT Museum; **Shlomo Maital**,

Ofer Chen; **Robert Van de Graaff, electrostatic generator, and Karl Taylor Compton**; MIT Museum; **Jay Forrester, Whirlwind computer, and Bob Everett**, MIT Museum; Marc Meyer, Northeastern University; **Charles Koch**, Koch Industries; **Ray Stata**, Analog Devices; **A. Neil Pappalardo**, Lawrence Gallagher; **Robert Swanson and Herbert Boyer**, Genentech Archives; **Phillip Sharp**, Koch Institute for Integrative Cancer Research at MIT; **Kendall Square area in 1975**, Cambridge Redevelopment Authority; **Robert Langer**, Louis F. Bachrach; **Noubar Afeyan**, Flagship Ventures; **cluster of high-tech companies in Kendall Square**, MIT Investment Management Company (MITIMCo); **Lawrence Roberts**, Lawrence Roberts; **Edward Roberts and Charles Zhang**, Edward Roberts; **Daniel Lewin**, Akamai Technologies; **Thomas Leighton**, Akamai Technologies; **Frederic Kerrest**, Okta, Inc.; **Philippe Villers**, Philippe Villers; **Amnon Shashua**, Mobileye, an Intel Company; **Michael "Mick" Mountz**, Kiva Systems; **Karl Taylor Compton**, MIT Museum; **Georges F. Doriot**, HBS Archives Photograph Collection, Faculty and Staff, Baker Library, Harvard Business School (olvwork377916); **David Morgenthaler**, Morgenthaler Capital; **Thomas Perkins**, Tor Perkins; **H. Dubose Montgomery**, Menlo Ventures; **Diana Frazier**, Thasos Group; **Kevin Kinsella**, Avalon Ventures; **Brad Feld with a TRS-80**, Foundry Group; **Martin Tang**, Martin Tang; **Victor Fung**, Li & Fung; **Chris Leong**, Chris Leong; **Patrick McGovern**, McGovern Institute for Brain Research at MIT; **Sonny Wu**, GSR Capital Management; **Allan Will**, Studio Lovejoy; **Helmut Weymar**, Helmut Weymar; **Gary Bergstrom**, Acadian Asset Management; **James Simons**, Euclidean Capital; **Irwin Jacobs**, Qualcomm; **Andrew Viterbi**, Viterbi Group; **Brian Halligan, Dharmesh Shah, and friends**, Hubspot, Inc.; **MIT President Rafael Reif**, MIT Office of the President; **Katie Rae**, The Engine; **MIT Presidents Charles Vest, Susan Hockfield, Rafael Reif, and Paul Gray**, MIT Office of the President.

PEOPLE INDEX

MIT Faculty and Staff

Founders

Other Key Contributors

FIRM INDEX

SUBJECT INDEX

ABOUT THE AUTHOR

MIKHAIL GLABETS

EDWARD B. ROBERTS is the David Sarnoff Professor of Management of Technology at the MIT Sloan School of Management. His scholarship focuses on advanced technology management and entrepreneurship, and he founded and chairs the Martin Trust Center for MIT Entrepreneurship. His nine previous books include *Entrepreneurs in High-Technology*, the first research-based book on technology-based entrepreneurship. Roberts also cofounded numerous firms, including Medical Information Technology (Meditech), Sohu.com, and Zero-Stage Capital. He has been a board member of about 40 companies, and an angel investor in more than 150 high-tech startups, including Celo, HubSpot, Okta and Toast. In 2020, the Global Consortium of Entrepreneurship Centers awarded Professor Roberts its Legacy Award "for a lifetime of pioneering entrepreneurship".